C000246034

S IS FOR SAM

ALSO BY SARAH LeFANU

In the Chinks of the World Machine: Feminism and Science Fiction

Rose Macaulay

Dreaming of Rose: A Biographer's Journal

Radio Dramas

Thin Woman in a Morris Minor

Death Bredon

As editor

Colours of a New Day: Writing for South Africa
(with Stephen Hayward)

Sex, Drugs, Rock'n'Roll: Stories to End the Century

How Maxine Learned to Love her Legs and other Tales of Growing-Up

SARAH LeFANU

S is for Samora

A Lexical Biography of Samora Machel and the Mozambican Dream

HURST & COMPANY, LONDON

First published in the United Kingdom in 2012 by
C. Hurst & Co. (Publishers) Ltd.,
41 Great Russell Street, London, WC1B 3PL
© Sarah LeFanu 2012
All rights reserved.
Printed in India

The right of Sarah LeFanu to be identified as the author of this publication is asserted by her in accordance with the Copyright, Designs and Patents Act, 1988.

A Cataloguing-in-Publication data record for this book is available from the British Library.

ISBN: 978-184904-194-2 *paperback*

This book is printed using paper from registered sustainable and managed sources.

www.hurstpublishers.com

www.hurstblog.co.uk

For Chris

CONTENTS

ACKNOWLEDGEMENTS

S is for Samora: A Lexical Biography of Samora Machel and the Mozambican Dream was written with the support of a Wingate Scholarship, for which the author would like to gratefully thank the Scholarship Committee of the Harold Hyam Wingate Foundation.

The author would also like to gratefully acknowledge the Royal Literary Fund Fellowship Scheme.

My special thanks go to Paul Fauvet, who read the manuscript with scrupulous care, corrected many mistakes of fact and translation, and whose original reporting of the crash which killed Samora Machel I kept on coming back to. All errors are my own. Special thanks to my travelling companions, Christopher Collins and Monica McLean, both of whom read and commented on earlier versions of the book. I must also extend special thanks to my expert readers and critics in the Group of Three, Jenny Newman and Michèle Roberts, who read and commented on more of my early attempts to write about Mozambique than I care to remember, and who offered me steadfast critical support as the book changed shape. Two texts inspired the structure of this lexical biography: Michèle Roberts' meditative childhood memoir '*Une Glossaire*/A Glossary,' and *Moçambicanismos: Para um Léxico de Usos do Português Moçambicano*, edited by Armando Jorge Lopes, Salvador Júlio Sitoe and Paulino José Nhamuende. In their different ways both texts raise questions about memory, culture, politics and the drift of meanings within and between languages. I am grateful to Professor Catedrático Armando Jorge Lopes of the University of Eduardo Mondlane for his permission to quote from the Lexicon. I was helped with some of the translations by Gustavo Infante, but all translation decisions were finally my own. Thanks again to Gustavo Infante and also to João Cosmé for their help in polishing up my rusty spoken Portuguese.

My thanks to all those whose memories of Samora Machel I have drawn on, especially Isaias Funzamo, José Mateus Katupha, the late Valente Malangatana Ngwenya, Janet Rae Mondlane, Oscar Monteiro and Amélia de Souto.

Thanks for help in a variety of ways are also due to Julie Cliff, Alexander LeFanu Collins, HoneyBee Samora LeFanu Collins, Ismay LeFanu Collins, Moira Dick, Margaret Dickinson, Polly Gaster, David Hedges, Diana Hendry, Graça Machel, Jossefate Machel, Orlando Machel, Helder Martins, Barry Munslow, Jill Nicholls, Andy Richardson, Rino Scuccato, Jill Sheppard, Clare Simpson, Ingrid Sinclair, Marcello Vettorazzi, Richard Williams and James Wilson.

Finally I would like to thank Ted Honderich and the late Victor Suchar for their interest and encouragement during the early stages of this book.

Some names in this work have been changed.

ACRONYMS

AIM	*Agência de Informação de Moçambique* (Mozambique News Agency)
ANC	African National Congress
BOSS	Bureau of State Security
CFMAG	Committee for Freedom in Mozambique, Angola and Guinea-Bissau
CIA	Central Intelligence Agency
CIO	Central Intelligence Organisation
COMECON	Council for Mutual Economic Assistance
CONCP	*Conferência das Organizações Nacionalistas das Colónias Portuguesas* (Conference of the Nationalist Organisations of the Portuguese Colonies)
COREMO	*Comité Revolucionário de Moçambique* (Revolutionary Committee of Mozambique)
FPLM	*Forças Populares de Libertação de Moçambique* (People's Forces for the Liberation of Mozambique)
FRELIMO/Frelimo	*Frente de Libertação de Moçambique* (Mozambique Liberation Front) (see **Frelimo**)

GD	*Grupo Dinamizador* (Dynamizing Group/Dynamic Action Group)
IMF	International Monetary Fund
MAGIC	Mozambique, Angola and Guinea-Bissau Information Centre
MANU	Mozambique African National Union
MNR/RNM/Renamo	Mozambique National Resistance/ *Resistência Nacional de Moçambique*
MPLA	*Movimento Popular de Libertação de Angola* (People's Movement for the Liberation of Angola)
NESAM	*Núcleo dos Estudantes Africanos Secundários de Moçambique* (Nucleus of African Secondary Students of Mozambique)
OAU	Organisation of African Unity
OJM	*Organisação da Juventude Moçambicana* (Organisation of Mozambican Youth)
OMM	*Organisação da Mulher Moçambicana* (Organisation of Mozambican Women)
PAIGC	*Partido Africano para a Independência da Guiné e Cabo Verde* (African Party for the Independence of Guinea and Cape Verde
PIDE	*Polícia Internacional de Defesa do Estado* (International Police for the Defence of the State)
SAAF	South African Air Force
SADCC	Southern African Development Coordination Conference
SOAS	School of Oriental and African Studies

SWAPO	South West African People's Organisation
UDENAMO	*União Democrática Nacional de Moçambique* (National Democratic Union of Mozambique)
UN	United Nations
UNAMI	*União Nacional de Moçambique para a Independência* (National Union for Mozambican Independence)
VOR	Very high frequency omni-directional radio
WHO	World Health Organisation
ZANLA	Zimbabwean African National Liberation Army (armed wing of ZANU)
ZANU	Zimbabwe African National Union
ZANU-PF	Zimbabwe African National Union—Patriotic Front
ZAPU	Zimbabwe African People's Union

A

Aircraft

At twenty one minutes past nine (Mozambique time) on the night of 19 October 1986 a Tupolev 134, flying from Mbala in northern Zambia to Maputo, the capital of Mozambique, ploughed into a hillside at Mbuzini in South Africa's Transvaal province, close to the Mozambican border, killing President Samora Machel of Mozambique and thirty four other people on board.

It was not until ten minutes to seven the following morning that the South African authorities announced officially that a Mozambican plane flying from Zambia had crashed, an announcement they followed up with a flurry of stories: the plane had crashed in Natal province, not on the border but deep inside South Africa; it had crashed in a thunderstorm; the Soviet pilot had been drunk; the on-board navigational equipment was obsolete and had malfunctioned.

One story they did not report was that a man claiming to be a South African Air Force officer had rung the United Press International news agency in Johannesburg and told them that his own people had set up a decoy VOR beacon (the standard omnidirectional radio beacon used to guide planes into airports) inside South Africa in order to lure Flight Charlie Nine Charlie Alpha Alpha off course and into the hills of the border region.

By the time the Mozambican delegation, headed by the Minister of Security, Sérgio Vieira, arrived at Mbuzini, the South Africans had been busying themselves at the scene of the crash for over nine hours, rummaging through the wreckage and making off with all the documents they could find. A Russian crew member found alive had been taken to hospital in Johannesburg. The Mozambicans formally identified the bodies lying scattered and broken on the hillside. Sérgio Vieira called for a minute of silence. They wept as they stood with bowed heads.

The official Mozambican position has been for many years that the plane carrying the President was lured off course by the South Africans. But who knows? Who will ever know? All the papers in the South African archives relating to the events of that night disappeared during South Africa's period of transition from white minority to black majority rule.

During the long years of the armed struggle, Samora Machel championed the slow route to victory: small aims and small gains, a village at a time. But by 1986 he had become a man in a hurry. He needed to shake up the moribund leadership of the armed forces, to end the grinding, debilitating war with the anti-Frelimo group Renamo (see **Renamo**) that had by now lasted nearly as long as the liberation war itself, and to implement and make effective the economic changes that were part of the deal struck two years previously with the IMF (International Monetary Fund) and the World Bank. And he needed to do these things fast.

The Mbala meeting on 19 October with the Presidents of Angola, Zambia and Zaire had dragged on for longer than expected. Rather than waiting until the next morning to fly home Samora himself overrode his own Security Minister's Standing Instructions to those in charge of transport: the President was never to fly at night.

Why did Samora override those instructions? Who knew that he would be flying that night, and when did they know it? Versions of the story proliferate.

Versions proliferate, too, of the story of an earlier flight Samora had taken: the one he took in March 1963 to join the group of anti-colonial Mozambican rebels, recently unified under the name of Frelimo (*Frente de Libertação de Moçambique*—Mozambique Liberation Front), in Dar es Salaam in Tanzania.

Thirty-year-old Samora, who had fled Lourenço Marques with the infamous Portuguese security police on his tail (see **PIDE**), arrived in Francistown in Bechuanaland to find a chartered Douglas Dakota DC-3 about to take off for Dar es Salaam with twenty-six militants of the African National Congress aboard, heading into exile to escape imprisonment and torture in South Africa. The ANC had been banned by the South African government three years earlier, and the young lawyer Nelson Mandela and nine other defendants were about to be charged with sabotage in the Rivonia Trial. Joe Slovo, a Communist activist and one of the founding members of *Umkhonto weSizwe*, the armed wing of the ANC, was one of the passengers waiting to board. Twenty years later he described his first encounter with Samora Machel:

> A short while before our departing a thin, energetic young man asked if it was possible to get a seat on our plane as he wanted to join the FRELIMO forces. JB [J.B. Marks, the South African Communist leader] immediately took the decision that one of our cadres should be taken off the plane to make room for the FRELIMO recruit. The recruit who travelled with us (and he remembers it very well and tells the story today) is Comrade President Samora Machel.[1]

In another version of this story, Jacinto Veloso, in his memoir *Memórias em Voo Rasante*, gives us a commercial flight rather than a special ANC charter, and Joe Slovo as a passenger who gives up his own seat and thus personally facilitates Samora's journey to Frelimo and the eventual Presidency of an independent Mozambique[2]. While in both these versions the spotlight of history shines on a romantically solitary Samora, another version, written by his travelling companion Matias Mboa, reminds us that Samora was not alone when he walked across the tarmac to board the DC-3.[3] The different versions exemplify the ways that stories often grow around figures, unremarkable at the time, who later become heroes. 'We didn't realise what valuable cargo we were carrying,' said Joe Slovo after Samora's death, thinking back to that first, early plane journey.[4]

In the thrillers of Eric Ambler and Graham Greene the political players of pre-war and Cold War Europe traverse the continent to the rhythm of the wheels of steam trains, our British heroes one step ahead of the secret police waiting at the next station, or of the Gestapo goosestepping down the corridor towards their carriage. Under cover of steam and smoke they hurl themselves out of the train and roll out of sight before heading, in disguise if possible, for the nearest border and safety. In colonial and Cold War Africa it was planes rather than trains that criss-crossed the continent, stitching together narratives of hope, struggle, betrayal and death. The players were not so very different, and may in some cases have been the same.

When in 1960 the CIA (Central Intelligence Agency) wanted to get rid of the Congo's first nationalist leader Patrice Lumumba, they had him kidnapped, brutally beaten up and bundled onto a plane. His body was never found. It was whispered that when the killers had finished with him they opened the hatch and let his body plummet into the waters of the Gulf Stream.

The Secretary-General of the United Nations Dag Hammarskjöld was on board a Swedish-owned DC-6 Transair when it crashed mysteriously near the border of the Congo and Northern Rhodesia eight months later, in September 1961. He had been on his way to discuss a ceasefire with the Katanga rebel leader Moise Tshombe. Had the DC-6 been brought down by two smaller planes, as seen and heard by a number of local witnesses? Not according to the two inquiries set up by the Rhodesian Federation. It pleased them to find those witnesses unreliable and, in a couple of cases, deserving of imprisonment. They concluded that pilot error was to blame.

Counsel representing the Federal Government in the public inquiry into the crash that killed Hammarskjöld was a South African lawyer and ex-SAAF pilot called Cecil Margo. Over the course of the next twenty-five years he would represent the government of apartheid South Africa in no fewer than five public inquiries into air accidents, all of which were found to have been caused by pilot error. One of those was an inquiry into the crash at Mbuzini that killed President Samora Machel of Mozambique.[5]

Samora's journey as a revolutionary began in an American-built Douglas Dakota on an airstrip in the British Protectorate of Bechuanaland; it ended in a Soviet-built Tupolev on a hillside in apartheid South Africa (see **Mbuzini** and **Tupolev**).

AK47

The green, black, gold and red flag of Mozambique is the only national flag in the world to show an AK47. Crossed with a hoe above an open book, the Russian-made gun forms one side of the pyramid which represents the war of liberation and on which independence was built: armed struggle, tilling the land, reading and writing.

Aldeias Communais

Communal villages. Different, but not entirely different from the Portuguese *aldeamentos*, large villages or compounds near the main roads into which, in the north of the country, the colonial authorities herded the scattered rural populations in order to keep them away from—or to protect them from, depending on who you were listening to—the Frelimo guerrillas during the armed struggle. There and throughout the rest of the country the *aldeamentos* were relics of earlier colonial schemes for social and economic control, and dated back to the policy of compulsory cotton growing in the 1940s when each *aldeamento* was issued with a quota to fulfil. When, after Independence, these villages were transformed into communal villages, with the *ujamaa* villages of Tanzania as an inspiration and model, some of that historical taint still lingered.

The communal villages facilitated the bringing of health, education and other social services to the rural populations, but the grand economic idea which fuelled them—communal production for profit—never achieved the success so earnestly desired by policy-makers in the capital. For the villagers, as for any other people, the prime aim was to be able to feed themselves and their families. They failed to see the benefit of working in communal *machambas*—fields—at the expense of their own small ones, particularly when there was no infrastructure in place, no decent roads, no transport, nor, indeed, any markets to deal with any surplus that might be produced, and to turn it into profit.

How many communal villages were there? It's hard to say. How populous did a village have to be before it could be classified as communal? In the immediate post-independence years the northern province of Cabo Delgado boasted the greatest number: some of them former *aldeamentos*, some of them villages set up by refugees returning from Tanzania across the Rovuma, others the legacy of life in the liberated zones during the armed struggle.

But in the early 1980s, as the war with Renamo spread across the country, the role of the communal villages reverted to that of the old *aldeamentos*: they were a means of separating and protecting villagers from the ravages of the *bandidos armados*—armed bandits—of Renamo, whose principal targets were the rural poor. The very idea of communal production for profit became a faint dream, one of the many ideals crushed in the exigencies of surviving the war of destabilisation waged by apartheid South Africa against the Mozambican people (see **Renamo**).

Alfabetização/Literacy

From the Rovuma river in the north to the capital city Maputo in the south Mozambique stretches over 3,000 kilometres and holds within its long and slender shape more than forty separate languages. If a Makonde teenager in the north, with his teeth filed to needle-sharp points, could read the same newspaper or magazine as a middle-aged Nyaka fishseller in *capulana* and headscarf at her stall in the central market of the capital in the south, then the polyglottal peoples of what Portugal used to call one of its 'overseas provinces' could begin to share a common identity. That was the Frelimo line, worked out amongst the multi-tongued exiles in Tanzania and later implemented in the new Mozambique. Portuguese, the language of the colonisers, was adopted as Mozambique's first language.

In the first years after Independence, Year Nine students, 14-, 15- and 16-year olds, were sent out into the countryside from their schools in the cities to teach literacy to the villagers and peasants. Literacy rose from a pre-independence rate of 5 per cent to 30 per cent ten years later. And then it fell. The revolutionary trinity of book, hoe and gun was chewed up and swallowed by the ravening war with Renamo, and spat out as the singularity of the gun.

In 1978, three years after Independence, I went to Mozambique (see ***Cooperante***) and lived there for two years. Up in the northern province of Niassa I struggled alongside my colleagues and students in the Escola Ngungunhana to become literate in the language of the revolution. We tried hard but we didn't always get it right.

* * *

Revolutionary dialogue:

'Is everyone who lives in a socialist country a socialist?' asks Comrade Alberto. 'And is everyone who lives in a capitalist country a capitalist?' It's Saturday afternoon and we're approaching the end of a long day of political study.

The girls look at each other. They want to give the right answer, but what is it? Alberto's one of the few *dirigentes*—leaders—to make an effort to encourage the girls to speak.

Luisa puts up her hand, as if she's still a schoolgirl rather than a teacher. 'Yes?' she answers, her eyebrows arched in question.

Alberto smiles kindly.

'But what about comrade Sarah? She comes from a capitalist country but obviously she is not a capitalist.'

Luisa looks at me in distress. The other girls giggle.

'Perhaps that's enough for today,' says Alberto. He was something-or-other in the armed struggle, which gives him the confidence and the authority to bend the rules about obligatory all-day political study. With the headmaster or the deputy in charge, both of them southerners in their early twenties and nervous about their positions, all-day study means all-day study and not a minute less.

* * *

The ABC of the revolution: while Western *cooperantes* squabbled over ideological differences and bandied words and phrases from their Marxist-Leninist lexicons, for Mozambicans it became important not to say the wrong thing. A one-party state exists as a binary system: if you're not for the Party, then you're against it. In a one-party state there are right words and wrong words. In *Moçambicanismos*, a dictionary of Mozambican Portuguese usage published in 2000 (see ***Moçambicanismos***), some of the words in common use in post-independence Mozambique are annotated with the phrase *'o termo caiu em desuso'* (the term has fallen out of use). Within one generation those words have lost not just their power but their meaning: *abaixo*—down with; *camarada*—comrade; *a linha política do Partido*—the political line of the Party. In the 1970s if you spoke enough wrong words for long enough you were sent for re-education (see ***Reeducação***): to learn the right words. As I watched self-regarding Mozambican *estruturas* (see ***Estruturas***) or pompous Western *cooperantes* mouth the words '*viva Frelimo!*' I understood the meaning of the phrase 'lip service.'

Yet when Samora hailed the Mozambican people from the Rovuma to the Maputo, the northernmost and southernmost rivers of a rivery country, he gave them a vision of themselves united despite differences of tribe, culture and language. In his words: 'We killed the tribe to give birth to the nation.'[6] He gave them a vision of *moçambicanidade*—Mozambicanness.

Later, after 1992, when the Renamo leader Afonso Dhlakama had been bought off with whisky and palaces and when political pathologists rushed to dissect the corpse of the Mozambican revolution, one of the counts on which Samora was found guilty was that of denying difference by promulgating that shared Mozambicanness.

Antepassados

Ancestors. Samora's grandfather, Moisés Malengane Machel, and his great uncle fought under the Tsonga general Maguiguane Khosa in the army of the Gaza Emperor Ngungunhana in the 1880s and 90s, when the Portuguese were trying to extend their control inland from their narrow hold on the coastline (see **Ngungunhana**). Although Ngungunhana was captured in 1895 and sent into exile on the island of Terceira in the Azores (see **Azores**), where he died, the war continued bloodily for another two years before Maguiguane Khosa's final defeat in the face of the hugely superior firepower of the Portuguese army. Of all the heroes of the resistance, it was with Maguiguane that Samora most closely identified, and whose military campaigns he knew in detail.[7]

Samora drank in a history of resistance of one kind from his father's side of the family; from his mother flowed stories of much earlier examples of resistance. His brother Orlando remembers how their mother, Gugiye Thema Dzimba, used to quote the Bible: '[She] used to say that just as Moses freed the people of Israel, so we must go to war to free Mozambique, for nobody else was going to do it for us.'[8] According to Orlando, Samora, named like his brothers not just after their father and grandfather but also after the Moses who led his people to freedom, set out to do precisely that.

Antigamente

Back in the day; in days gone by; formerly. More precisely, in the days of Portuguese colonialism; before Independence. Throughout *o tempo de Samora*, the time of Samora—from the end of the armed struggle in 1974 until his sudden shocking death twelve years later—everyone used *antigamente* to mean the bad old days when life was shaped and circumscribed by the organs of the Portuguese state: the army, the secret police, the not-so-secret police, and the whole colonialist administrative structure, with full backing from the Catholic Church, which was recognised by Salazar in the Colonial Act of 1930 as 'an instrument of civilisation and national influence.'[9]

Antigamente carried a full freight of specific historical meaning. *Antigamente* was a place of harshness, or even horror. And the privileged few who might reasonably have harboured nostalgia for it had mainly left the country.

In times of rapid social and political change, 'formerly' is rarely a neutral term. A new generation has shifted *antigamente* forward in time, so that it now refers to *o tempo de Samora*. Uttered with a sigh and a shake of the head, *antigamente* looks back to the hopes of Independence Day, before the dream was broken.

Assimilado

Literally, assimilated. Black Mozambicans who were given honorary white status by the colonial authorities and classified alongside Europeans, Asians and those of mixed race as *não-indígena* rather than *indígena* or 'native.' In this way Salazar's fascist Portuguese state was able to claim that it was not founded on a racial divide: look, we treat black citizens, *assimilados*, as if they were white or brown. In a similar fashion Portugal denied that it was a colonial power, naming the vast areas of land it ruled in Africa not as colonies but as 'overseas provinces' of a Mother Country.

Assimilados were nominally granted the same rights and privileges as the whites and Asians. They were subject to Portuguese law, exempt from 'native' taxes and the labour legislation that controlled black male employment, and had access to secondary and higher education, whereas education for 'natives,' if they had access to any at all, was, in the words of Eduardo Mondlane, 'designed to produce not citizens, but servants of Portugal,' and came to an end after four grades of primary school.[10]

By 1950 about 4,500 people had achieved *assimilado* status out of a black population of over five million: fewer than 0.1 per cent. Soon afterwards the status of *assimilado* began to be phased out, at the very time that Samora Machel applied for it so as to be able to gain a nursing qualification higher than the basic level above which 'natives' could not rise (see **Hospital**). Both Josina Muthemba, Samora's first wife, and Graça Simbine, his second, came from *assimilado* families. Josina was a pupil at the Commercial School in the capital ('about fifty Africans to several hundred Portuguese,' she said[11]) before fleeing the country in her final year to join the liberation movement in Tanzania. Some years later Graça graduated from university in Portugal before joining Frelimo.

Azores

A Portuguese archipelago of nine volcanic islands in the middle of the North Atlantic, about 1,500 km west of Lisbon, and 4,000 km east of the USA. *Os Açores* in Portuguese, named perhaps for a bird of prey erroneously identified, so the story goes, as a goshawk, or named possibly for a dialect variation of *azul*—blue. Blue? Hardly the colour of the North Atlantic, but maybe the islands themselves appear blue as you approach them over the cold grey waves.

'At Flores in the Azores Sir Richard Grenville lay,
And a pinnace, like a fluttered bird, came flying from far away;'

Tennyson's fluttered bird, goshawk or not, is so wonderfully precise: fluttered by distance and the wind, flying to Flores. The pinnace heralds the enemy, the Spanish fleet, or 'the dogs of Seville, the children of the devil,' as Sir Richard calls them.

Three hundred years after Sir Richard Grenville, the Emperor Ngungunhana, also known as the Lion of Gaza, lay at Terceira in the Azores, where he had been exiled by the Portuguese in 1895 (see **Ngungunhana**).

At the end of the Second World War the United States Air Force began operating from the Azores out of an air base called Lajes Field. By 1960, when Dr Eduardo Mondlane (see **Mondlane**) was making representations to the Kennedy administration about independence for Mozambique, Lajes Field had become the centre for anti-Soviet submarine operations in the North Atlantic. The Kennedy administration on the whole liked Dr Mondlane and was minded to support him (under US guidance of course); but needs must and their toehold on those nine bare rocky islands in the middle of the vast grey North Atlantic trumped the aspirations, however reasonable, of six million or so Mozambicans.[12]

B

Baobab

This is the very spot 'where his umbilical cord fell to the earth,' Samora Machel's widow Graça (now Mandela) tells me. She points at a spindly baobab sapling that grows on the site of the hut where Samora Moisés Machel was born on 29 September 1933. Two or three metres from the young baobab stands a low leafy evergreen (see **Malangatana** and **Mbuzini**). This is the tree in whose shade Samora's mother, Gugiye Thema Dzimba, used to pound the maize and shell the beans for the evening meal of *chima* (see **Chima**) and *matapa* (see **Matapa**) and vegetable stew.

The hut stood on the edge of the village of Xilembene (pronounced 'shill-em-bay-nee') in the broad flat plain of the Limpopo valley in Gaza Province. The Limpopo valley was the breadbasket of Mozambique, rich in crops and cattle, and the whole of Gaza Province was rich in labour for the South African gold mines only 100 km to the west.

Samora was the third of five surviving boys born to Gugiye Thema and Mandhande Moisés Machel.[1] He was given the name of an earlier baby boy who'd died in infancy, who himself was named after one of Thema's relatives, a Makonde who had fought in the Portuguese army and adopted the Portuguese name Samora as his own. The boys' only sister, Paulina, died in childhood. Graça Machel thinks she was thirteen, but the historian Gerhard Liesegang says she died aged six, in 1941. The latter seems more likely, as she was born after Samora, and, had she lived until 1948 or 1949, would surely have featured more prominently in family stories. Years later, when she came to Xilembene as Samora's wife, Graça would be welcomed by the old man as his 'first daughter.'[2] This too suggests Paulina died as a small child rather than as a young woman.

Samora's father, Mandhande, had been one of the thousands 'sold,' as Samora put it, to the South African mines. For every mineworker who came from Mozambique the South Africans paid a proportion of his wages directly to the Portuguese authorities in gold. The resale of the gold at international rates of exchange provided a lucrative income for the colonial administration. Although the miners were well paid by Mozambican standards and returned home with money in their pockets, often their health was permanently ruined. Isaias, Samora's eldest brother, was one of the many who never returned at all. A small insurance payment for his death was offered to the family, on humiliating terms. 'When [my brother] died in the South African mines,' said Samora, 'my father received a note from the administration to say that he should go and collect £40 indemnity. But they said that they couldn't hand over the whole amount all at once. He could only have £10 and the remaining £30 would stay in the cash box at the administration and he should go and request small amounts as and when he needed them.'[3]

Yet Mandhande himself returned from South Africa to Gaza in the mid-1920s with enough money to invest in land, cattle and ploughs, and Samora was born into a relatively prosperous family. Mandhande also brought back membership of the Compound Mission, a Methodist church which later became the Free Methodist Mission, and which would suffer, like all the Protestant churches did, under the Colonial Act of 1930 (see ***Antigamente***). A number of people who knew Samora stress the importance of Protestant social practice in his own later practice as leader of Frelimo: that is, the involvement of the whole congregation in lengthy meetings in which the deep causes of problems are studied and discussed (see ***Pensamento Unico***). His experience of an increasingly powerful Catholic Church's persecution of Protestant believers was also formative. 'These old Protestants were always persecuted. They took part in the war of resistance against the colonial occupation of our country. When they became Protestants, it was a form of resistance. It was they who inspired us, these elders from here,' said Samora, on a visit to his family home after Independence. He went on: 'No book by Marx ever arrived here, nor any other book that spoke against colonialism. Our books were these elders. It was they who taught us what colonialism is, the evils of colonialism and what the colonialists did when they came here. They were our source of inspiration.'[4] To the question, when did you first read Marx?, Samora replied: 'I read Marx in the soil of my own land.'[5]

One of Samora's duties as a little boy was to herd his parents' cows from one pasture to another along the banks of the Limpopo river, characterised by Rudyard Kipling as 'the great, grey-green, greasy' Limpopo 'all set about with fever trees' and known to generations of English children brought up on the *Just So Stories* as home to dangerously cunning crocodiles. Iain Christie, in his 1986 biography of Samora Machel, tells a story of the seven- or eight-year-old Samora letting one of the herd's calves wander too close to the bank of the river. A lurking crocodile sank its teeth into the calf's leg and began to drag it into deeper water. The boy jumped into the river beside the calf, shouting, screaming, and hitting the crocodile's snout with his stick. The crocodile, whether in fear, or surprise, or perhaps greedily hoping for two meals, opened its mouth. Samora scrambled out of the river and pulled the calf out by its tail, and the crocodile drifted off downstream. As Christie says, any clever little boy looking after his family's cattle would have done the same. The story illustrates not bravado, but shrewdness and good judgment. Samora, suggests Christie, 'went on to spend most of his life fighting crocodiles of a different species, sometimes getting the better of the beast and sometimes getting badly mauled.'[6]

Versions of this story published after Samora's death have him actually killing the crocodile, in a manner unspecified, and also killing a huge mamba by grabbing the end of its tail and whirling it through the air to smash its head against the ground. In 2008 I read an account of these feats of strength and bravery under the title 'A Hero Even in his Infancy.' The article, written to commemorate what would have been Samora's seventy-fifth birthday, concludes: 'These deeds made Samora a bit of a local hero, without anyone imagining that actually they were the harbingers of the journey that would take him all the way to the *Ponta Vermelha* [the Presidential Palace].'[7]

Hero or not, Samora was still a child when he first came across what Iain Christie calls the 'crocodiles of a different species': Portuguese farmers always on the alert to snap up any wandering cow or calf. 'African cows weren't registered and couldn't carry a brand,' Samora told historian John Saul. 'This enabled the European farmers to steal African cattle. At times cattle belonging to 'natives' got mixed up with the European-owned cattle and, when this happened, the Europeans immediately branded them—likewise with sheep and goats—and thus these animals automatically belonged to those Europeans.'[8]

All the local farmers grew crops for sale as well as keeping cattle, but here too regulations favoured the Europeans over the black farmers, who, unlike the Europeans, were obliged to sell their produce at prices fixed by the colonial administration.

'For example, we would produce and sell one kilo of beans at three and a half escudos while the European farmers produced and sold at five escudos a kilo,' Samora explained. 'And the day after we had sold our crops we would have to buy these very same products at six escudos—double the price we ourselves received. If on occasion, by special agreement, we managed to sell direct to a caterer or trader (for example, at four escudos a kilo) we were compelled to receive payment half in cash and half in goods ... Moreover we couldn't become traders. 'Natives' couldn't enter into any form of commerce. They could only be producers for European traders.'[9]

However, despite the universal racial discrimination practised by the colonial authorities, the land worked by the African farmers in the Limpopo Valley was able to support extended family networks in modest comfort. It may well have been his own experience of such a stable and functioning, modestly prosperous rural economy that gave Samora such cause for unease during the political battles over agricultural policy in Frelimo's Marxist-Leninist years, when economic support for the family-based farm or *machamba* was sacrificed to the demands of the state farms (see ***Machamba Estatal***).

When he was eight Samora started at Uamexinga primary school in the village of Souguene, eight kilometres from home. (Uamexinga, daughter of a Xilembene chief, had herself ruled the district after her father's death at the turn of the century.) It was 1941, and the Catholic Church was by then responsible for almost all 'native education' in the country.

At the primary school, a basic one-room structure with a raised cement floor and waist-high external walls, an education was offered up to grade three, but each grade was subdivided, and with the emphasis on religious indoctrination as much as on reading and writing, it often took five or six years to achieve a grade three qualification. Samora was a quick learner and was already on his grade two when, only two years after he had started, he was expelled. Gerhard Liesegang suggests he was expelled for the simple reason that his parents were Protestants, for Portugal had just signed a deal with the Vatican that massively increased Catholic control over education in the colonies.[10]

For the next three years Samora went back to herding cows, harvesting the maize and cotton, and driving the oxcart to gather firewood. But in 1946, Mandhande somehow managed to re-enrol his son in Uamexinga in order to complete his third grade.

Africans needed a grade four qualification in order to find employment as anything other than a manual labourer or house servant, and in order to achieve this, Samora, at fifteen, moved thirty kilometers away to the small town of Macia and the São Paolo de Massano Mission School. To call the teaching unexceptional would be an understatement. The teachers were Franciscan nuns, most of whom were simple catechists with only rudimentary, if any, qualifications. Already Samora was ambitious. He recognised the meagreness of the education offered and its ideological thrust, saying later that 'the main concern of the Mission was to indoctrinate, to make us Roman Catholics.'[11] But it was the only education available and he grasped it.

Samora's analysis of the economics of the mission school reveals a system geared to profit rather than a system based on Christian charity:

> Our parents had to supply ten bags of maize and five bags of beans of each type. Over and above this we had to grow rice in the mission ... and we also grew potatoes and bananas. In other words we produced and we paid to produce, because every year our parents had to pay our board at the mission. We slept on mats and the covers were brought by our fathers. We got absolutely nothing from the mission apart from the teacher. We ate stiff maize porridge with a mash made of groundnuts, water and salt. And if some pupils didn't leave with destroyed livers or tuberculosis it was only because of the strength of human resistance. And the maize was carefully measured out with a special piece of wood that indicated how many grammes. I don't know how much it was but they certainly knew.[12]

His parents made the necessary sacrifices to keep him in school until he got his fourth grade. Then Samora too was obliged to make a further sacrifice. The school authorities decided that Samora couldn't take the exams unless he was baptised as a Catholic. Samora described the scene to historian Fernando Ganhão in 1983: 'When there were just fifteen days to go before the fourth grade exam, they told me: either you are baptized, or you leave the mission. ...It was blackmail. I agreed, and I was baptized and christened. They gave me a lot of gifts. Bags with a picture of St Francis Xavier and suchlike. They were pleased because they had won, they had converted a Protestant.' Ganhão suggests that Samora experienced this incident as a 'violent form of alienation,' one of two such incidents—*duas formas tão violentas de alienação*—around this time, through which his spirit of rebellion was forged and formed.[13] But I would offer a different interpretation. If, later on, Samora's leadership first of Frelimo and then of Mozambique can be seen in terms of a balancing act between principles and pragmatism, then here, at the age of seventeen, we see him making a pragmatic decision. He became a Catholic, and sat the exams. He was one of only three, or possibly four, pupils to pass.

Now Samora wanted to go on, as all white children in Mozambique would already have gone on, to secondary school. He was clever and curious, and he understood the value of knowledge and of intellectual endeavour. But the colonial powers had no interest in educating Africans beyond fourth grade, unless they had honorary European status (see ***Assimilado***). The only further education available to him, Samora was told, was in a seminary. It was the priesthood or nothing.

This time there was no decision to take. He wouldn't, and couldn't, become a Catholic priest. He left the Mission and went south to the capital Lourenço Marques (now Maputo) where, he'd heard, a more liberal attitude prevailed and where he might, somehow, wangle his way into one of the city's schools. Later he blamed the failure of this plan on 'the padres' again, although it is not clear how they were involved.[14] Instead, armed with the necessary grade four qualification, he applied for and was accepted onto a training course for the most prestigious profession available to an African in Mozambique: nursing. While waiting for the course to begin he returned to his home province and worked for six months as an auxiliary or apprentice nurse at the hospital in Xai-Xai, the provincial capital. It was 1950.

That same year much of the Machel land was expropriated as part of the Limpopo Colonato, and many new properties built for newly-arriving immigrants from Portugal, tempted by free passage and the promise of irrigated settlements close to rivers, with loans and grants to help them settle in. An administration post, a prison and a block of police living quarters were erected within spitting distance of the family home. Ten years later, with one son in the notorious PIDE prison in Machava, and another directing the armed struggle in the far north of the country, Mandhande and his wife were moved to a small prefabricated house nearby where they were kept under close surveillance by the Portuguese authorities who had taken over the land where the Machel boys had once run barefoot after their father's cows.

The baobab sapling that grows from the very piece of earth on which Gugiye Thema Machel gave birth to the future leader of the revolution and first President of Mozambique was planted on the tenth anniversary of his death, 19 October 1996, by Mozambique's second President, Joaquim Chissano. 'I'm a bit worried that as it grows it's going to jeopardise this other tree, the tree that shaded my mother-in-law as she pounded the maize,' says Graça Machel, and then, with a quiet laugh, 'well, I guess none of us will be around to see that happen.'

The sapling is slender enough for you to put your hands round. I've been told that baobab trunks grow a metre in diameter every hundred years, and I've stood at the foot of what people claim is Mozambique's oldest baobab, two thousand years old, on the shore of Lake Niassa. When this baobab achieves the vast dimensions of that one, there will be no other sign left of Samora in Xilembene. I think that if any trees were sentient then surely it would be the baobabs, the elephants of the tree world, silent guardians of the land, home to the spirits of all who have lived there.

Behind the Lines

In September 1970 a twenty-seven-year-old English filmmaker called Margaret Dickinson met a small brigade of Frelimo guerrillas on the north, Tanzanian bank of the Rovuma river and with them waded across the river into the liberated zone of eastern Niassa. She had flown south from Dar es Salaam in a small plane with her cameraman, John Fletcher, and their equipment—two hefty cameras, an Arriflex and a wind-up Bolex, and a Nagra sound recorder.

The film they made, *Behind the Lines*, had achieved almost mythical status by the time I became involved with the Frelimo support committee in the UK (see **CFMAG**) in the mid-seventies. But I never saw the film, and when, years later, I began to research that period, I couldn't find anybody else who'd seen it. Margaret's name was familiar to me as the director, but again, I'd never met her. I was keen to see the film, but how to track down Margaret, and would she still have a copy? I asked Jill Sheppard, who had been involved with CFMAG earlier than I had, and who for some years ran MAGIC (Mozambique, Angola and Guinea-Bissau Information Centre), the organisation into which CFMAG morphed at Independence. When I told her I was trying to track down *Behind the Lines*, I was amazed to hear that she, too, had never seen it. Who on earth had seen this film? But Jill dug out an old phone number and a postal address. Every time I rang the number I was deafened by the high-pitched shriek of a fax, and the letter I posted elicited no response. An internet search produced nothing. I had almost given up when, a couple of weeks later, I received a letter from Margaret with apologies for having mislaid my letter, and giving me a different phone number and an email address. Yes, she had copies of both versions of *Behind the Lines* (both? I'd no idea there were two) but they were poor quality VHS and I'd have to come to her house to view them.

In answer to the questions I'd asked in my letter: yes, she'd known Samora at the time she was making the film, although not very well, and for a time, while she was living in Dar, she'd been very close to his first wife (see **Josina**). Jill and I would be welcome to come one morning the following week.

Margaret is small and delicate-looking, not what you'd expect of a frontline (as she turned out to be, rather than behind the lines) filmmaker. Her hesitant manner of speech belies a tough resolve. She told me that her original plan for the film had been to settle for a few weeks in one of the villages where guerrillas and local peasants lived side by side, and to record their daily interactions. By 1970 life in the liberated zones was already being theorised by Samora and the other Frelimo leaders as the model for an independent Mozambique based on the principles of social justice, self-sufficiency, universal literacy, and a citizenry that would transcend differences of tribe and culture. People on the Left in the West were interested in such experiments in living—indeed, the social democratic governments of the Scandinavian countries already supported Frelimo's work in health and education—and Margaret's film would provide documentary evidence of what was being achieved.

But in the spring of 1970, the newly appointed Portuguese military commander General Kaulza de Arriaga launched the Gordian Knot offensive, a massive military onslaught which, Portugal hoped, would totally eliminate Frelimo from the northern provinces of Niassa and Cabo Delgado (see ***Nó Gordio***). Because of the increased presence of Portuguese troops, Margaret and her cameraman were only allowed to stay two weeks in Niassa, and during that time were obliged to be almost constantly on the move.

'So what was it like?,' I asked. She told me:

The thing was, that when we came down from Dar to southern Tanzania in a low-flying plane I looked out and realized I had a clear bird's eye view of everything on the ground: I could see every tethered goat outside every village hut. So when the Portuguese planes came roaring overhead that was what I thought of. There was hardly any cover in that bit of Niassa. I was really surprised because I'd expected it to be thickly wooded, but no, the trees were sparse and as it was the end of winter, the cold dry season, lots of them had lost their leaves. When we heard the planes coming up from the south we had to run for the nearest tree and press ourselves against the trunk and stay absolutely motionless until they'd passed over us. I'd be trembling from head to foot, convinced that we were in plain sight and that we were about to be bombed to smithereens.

And it was exhausting as well. We were always on the move, and I felt really guilty because the soldiers carried all our equipment for us. I felt awful about it, but it was about all I could do to stagger the twenty miles or so from one camp to the next without carrying anything except my own rucksack.

I told her that when Iain Christie was marching with Samora Machel in the liberated zones he said the soldiers told him they were very grateful for his presence: so that Christie could keep up, Samora limited the duration of each day's march and allowed the soldiers to slow their pace.[15] 'I tell you, it didn't feel very slow to me,' Margaret replied. 'So, do you want to watch my version first, the long version?' 'Yes, please.' She took a videotape out of a battered cardboard sleeve and slid it into the player. 'I'll be next door in the study,' she said, and left the room.

The film mixes interviews with footage of temporary Frelimo bases and of village life. The bases consist of a handful of neat square houses made of light wood or grass, built in an afternoon and able to be abandoned at a moment's notice. In one of them we look through a window and see a young man in army fatigues sitting at a table. The papers he's studying shift in the breeze. In the clearing outside another young man stirs the stew that's simmering in a cooking pot over a smouldering fire.

The brigade commander's name is Alberto Joaquim. He tells us about how the armed struggle was launched in Cabo Delgado province six years previously, by twenty-two guerrillas. He talks of it as if he had been present. Now, he tells us (that is, 1970), there are 10,000 Frelimo soldiers. His deputy, Pedro Juma, appears to be barely out of his teens but says that he too has been with Frelimo since the beginning of the armed struggle. As he talks he swats a persistent fly from the back of his neck.

They talk about how important it is for the guerrillas to be self-sufficient in food, but how the *machambas* need to be two or three hours distant from the bases for fear of discovery from the air. It's hard to hide cultivated ground. Local people help them with the clearing and the planting, and in return the guerrillas teach them about crop rotation and how to increase their yields. We see a long line of soldiers and peasants returning from the fields; all the women are carrying babies snugly tied to their backs (see ***Capulanas***). They ford a river and as they climb up the bank towards the camera, each woman breaks in turn from the single file and dances forwards, twirls theatrically, and falls back into line with a giggle and a smile.

Margaret interviews three of the women in the brigade: Monica and Maria, who are both from Niassa, and Mary who comes from Cabo Delgado and attended the Frelimo school in Tanzania, where she learned English and got two 'O' levels. They plait each other's hair as they talk about their work with war orphans and the literacy campaigns they run. The camera then moves into a clearing in the centre of a village, and we see a guerrilla pointing at the letters of the alphabet chalked on a board nailed to a tree. They're teaching the Portuguese language as well as reading and writing. A mixed group of adults and children sit on the ground, shouting out the letters. Off to one side, an older woman takes a deep drag of a hand-rolled cigarette. She looks as if she still needs convincing of the value of such learning. Above the doorway into one of the huts are chalked the words *posto de saúde*—health post. Inside we watch in close-up something nasty being carefully tweezered from a big toe. 'Civilians with guns,' is how the guerrillas describe themselves.

In a sequence towards the end of the film we're shown a series of posters and leaflets that were dropped from the air by the Portuguese in an attempt to win hearts and minds. One in Arabic is aimed at the Muslim population of Niassa, another shows a white hand clasping a black hand, and on some you can read the name Lazaro N'kavandame, an ex-Frelimo man who joined the Portuguese (see **Frelimo**). These shots are alternated with photographs that provide a rather different picture of relations between Portuguese soldiers and the civilians living in the liberated zones. One of them shows three or four white Portuguese soldiers with a naked black prisoner spread-eagled between them. In the next picture the prisoner has been beheaded, and one of the soldiers holds his decapitated head aloft by the ears, while the others grin and caper on either side.

We watch a pageant in the cathedral square in Lisbon. Riders in uniforms of gold and red hold huge standards aloft as they wheel their white stallions in tight formation, and Prime Minister Caetano intones: 'We are nothing without our empire.' Behind the lines in eastern Niassa we see figures snaking across a village clearing: children in ragged shorts and dusty dresses, women with babies on their backs, men and women in army caps and camouflage gear. The villagers are teaching their Frelimo guests their own songs and dances. There's Alberto Joaquim in the middle of the line, and then it struck me: could he be Alberto Joaquim Chipande, the man who fired the very first shot of the armed struggle, as related in Eduardo Mondlane's *The Struggle for Mozambique*?

When the film ended Margaret came back into the room and asked if we'd like to see the other version. This other version was made because the distributors, Contemporary Films, were not confident that they would be able to sell the original film to television; they asked Lindsay Anderson to view it and advise. He suggested recutting it as a half-hour, snappier version. 'And was it shown on television?' I asked. 'We sold it to six or seven small countries, like Denmark and Romania. We couldn't sell it here, nor in any of the NATO countries, because of course I hadn't included any balancing interviews with Portuguese fascists.'

I asked about the commander called Alberto Joaquim. Yes, said Margaret, that was Chipande. Five years after she filmed him behind the lines in Niassa, he was the man who raised the flag of the People's Republic of Mozambique in Machava Stadium in the south of the country, on 25 June 1975, at the very moment of Independence.

Soon after Jill and I had finally seen *Behind the Lines*, Margaret had her VHS tape digitised; it was showcased in 2010 at Dockanema, the International Festival of Documentary Films held annually in Maputo.

Bússola/Lodestone

Raimundo Domingos Pachinuapa, in his memoir of the Second Congress (see **Matchedje**), writes:

'*II Congresso que foi e sempre será a bússola do povo moçambicano na construção deste vasto território onde vivem vários grupos com hábitos e costumes diferentes formando, assim, um rico mozaíco. O II Congresso foi inspirador do processo de construção da nação moçambicana.*'

'The Second Congress was and always will be the lodestone for the people of Mozambique in their building of our sprawling nation, wherein live so many groups with different customs and cultures which make up such a rich mosaic. The Second Congress was the inspiration for the making of the Mozambican nation.'[16]

C

Cajulima

Also known as *cajuada*. A strong drink distilled from the fermented juice of cashew apples. Illegal. Counter-revolutionary.

October 1978: There's been no alcohol available in the northern province of Niassa for some weeks now. Rumours of consignments of beer arriving on the twice-weekly train from Nampula turn out to be ... rumours. Christopher and I (see ***Cooperantes***) would dearly like a drink, especially now that the rainy season is starting and our hearts are sinking a little beneath the darkly gathering clouds. I ask Salimo, fixer *extraordinaire*, whether he might, perhaps, be able to acquire some *cajulima* for us.

It's the word 'apples' that feeds my fantasies. How reassuringly European they sound. I see apple orchards in Normandy, apple-cheeked farmers adjusting their stills in mellow stone outhouses, producing an apple brandy that glows gold with October sunshine.

A few mornings later Salimo turns up with a long-necked bottle that looks as if it comes from a London apothecary imagined by Dickens. Inside swirls a golden liquid, hinting for a brief moment at apples, orchards and ancient traditions of the land. But through the twist of cotton fabric that stoppers the narrow neck leaks a smell of something more modern, more industrial. I hand over quite a large sum of money to Salimo and put the bottle away. Performing an illegal and anti-revolutionary transaction is one thing, I tell myself, but drinking in the morning is another.

Later, when the afternoon storm has moved northwards and the town is bathed in the lurid yellowy-green light of the evening sun, before the mosquitoes begin to buzz up from the pools of water left by the day's downpour, our three geologist friends arrive. They're looking for coal in Niassa, moving camp regularly from one piece of wilderness to another, carving roads through the bush, searching for the underground wealth that would mean so much to a cash-strapped country like Mozambique. Piet is a South African, an anguished exile, fair-haired and sturdy, with boundless physical energy; Bernie a tall, skinny, softly-spoken American who likes to play the harmonica, and small olive-skinned Luigi is a homesick Italian. We've invited them to supper.

'That smells OK,' says Piet. 'Is it potato curry again?'

'No.'

'Bean curry?'

'No. It's potato AND bean curry. But look what we've got ...'

I've managed to find five glasses, of varying sizes, and now I get out the apothecary bottle and carefully pour a shot into each glass. In the last rays of the sun the liquid looks not so much golden, as orange. A strong smell of engine oil and metal permeates the room.

Luigi sniffs at his glass and puts it down on the table.—'No, I cannot,' he says.

'Namby-pamby Italians,' says Piet, lifting his glass. He swallows, utters a strangled cry, and downs the rest in one gulp. His face flushes pink and beads of sweat pop out on his forehead and course down his face: 'Christ, man! That's a killer!'

Piet's right, as we discover later. Meanwhile Christopher's thinking of a practical way to ingest the alcohol. 'Let's try it like you drink tequila,' he suggests. He cuts up some limes and shows us how to spread our hands and tip a little mound of salt into the hollow at the base of the thumb muscle. 'Lick up the salt, take a swig of the drink, then suck on a lime quarter,' he instructs. Luigi still prefers not to, but the rest of us give it a go. The salt and the lime juice go some way towards disguising the powerful taste of rusty metal. But not far enough, I decide. I don't care if I'm called a namby-pamby: I'd rather be alive.

A couple of weeks later Christopher hears in the hospital about the deaths of two young men in a nearby village. The story goes that a *cajulima* still was found behind one of the huts, made out of an old oil drum. That Saturday all the teachers in Escola Ngungunhana are called to a meeting where we're harangued by the Provincial Head of Education on the evils of drunkenness. To be drunk is to sabotage the revolution, he cries. Down with drunkenness! *Abaixo bêbedo!* I think I'm probably the only one of the teachers who knows about the *cajulima* victims. A number of my colleagues look puzzled, as well they might; as far as they know, the province has been drink-free for the last two months. But ours not to reason why, and *abaixo bêbedo!* we chorus obediently.

Christopher thinks that the two dead men were more likely poisoned by the rusty flakes of the decaying oil drum than by the alcohol distilled from the cashew apples.

Camarada

Camarada n., S/C: Forma de tratamento inicialmente associada aos guerrilheiros da Frelimo, generalizou-se no periodo pós-Independência, inclusivamente para funções de administração pública (ex., camarada-director, camarada-chefe) ou simples relações sociais (ex., camarada-motorista, camarada Marta). Extensão semântica do termo no PE. O termo caiu em desuso, sendo actualmente utilizado sobretudo no seio do Partido Frelimo. Est. neutro. N.

Comrade, noun, social/cultural. Form of address originally associated with Frelimo guerrillas, it was used more generally in the post-Independence years to encompass posts held in public administration (for example comrade director, comrade boss) or just ordinary social relations (for example comrade driver, comrade Martha). Semantic extension of the European Portuguese term. The term has fallen into disuse, and is now used only by the Party faithful. Non-gender specific. Nation-wide. (See ***Moçambicanismos.***)

In the immediate post-Independence years of the 1970s when I was working in Mozambique as an English teacher in the north of the country (see ***Cooperante***), I was *camarada professora* or *camarada Sara*. Thirty years later I find that I am *dona Sara* in Maputo, and in the rural north, *a mamã*. I understand *a mamã* to be a traditional term of respect, and rather than feeling nostalgia for my earlier comrade-self, I'm happy with the shift—accurate enough—to mother-self. Later I discover from the pages of *Moçambicanismos* that *a mamã*, rather than being, as I'd thought, an old term pushed aside by revolutionary discourse and now regenerated in these post-post-independence times, had its own revolutionary meaning. It was the affectionately respectful title given to the first lady or the wife of a minister. The illustrative example given by lexicographers conjures up Graça Machel as *a mamã Graça*. I learn that the term began to be more widely used, as a title for ordinary as well as for high-up women, from the time when *camarada* began to fall into disuse.

In official speeches and in the pages of the daily paper *Notícias* and the weekly magazine *Tempo*—whose glossy covers provided invaluable material for home-made lampshades for us *cooperantes* in the commodity-poor north—Samora would sometimes be spoken and written of with a conscious theatricality that had its roots both in local culture and in the ornate formalities of the colonial tongue. He would be *o nosso dirigente* (our leader), *o dirigente maximo* (the top leader), or his full name spoken with relish: *o nosso Presidente Samora Moisés Machel*. But while other Party bigwigs such as the ministers and the provincial governors were known as 'comrade' followed by their surnames or their official title, Samora was also and as frequently referred to as *camarada Samora*, or as plain *Samora*.

'Our concern was to establish among rank-and-file soldiers, cadres and leaders, an atmosphere of total confidence and brotherhood in which the word "comrade" should have its full value.' Thus Samora Machel, in 1974, in a speech in Moscow to the Soviet Academy of Sciences, described how the army, the Mozambique People's Liberation Forces (FPLM), eschewed permanent posts just as they eschewed a hierarchy of tasks, 'since all of them are intended to serve the revolution.' He favourably contrasted the discipline of an army in which full value was given to the concept of 'comrade,' with that of the 'discipline inspired by fear' of the colonial army, and also with the 'blind submission' of civilians to village elders and chiefs in traditional village life.[1]

But by 1980 Samora had become highly suspicious of the word *camarada*. In a blistering speech attacking racism, tribalism, corruption, and banditry in the city of Beira, he said that the schools were dens of indiscipline and disrespect where teachers were addressed by pupils as intimates and as 'comrade teacher.' 'We don't want that,' he thundered. 'There is no "comrade teacher." There is no "comrade boss."'[2] From schools he moved to hospitals and other workplaces in his pursuit of false comrades (see ***Ofensiva***).

1980: a turning-point. Six years in charge of the construction of a new country after a victory that perhaps had come sooner than he'd expected, and now the beginning of complications taking root, of fractures showing. Comrades are no longer, necessarily, comrades. Six years before his death. But in people's hearts he himself remained *camarada Samora*: comrade, brother and friend.

O termo caiu em desuso: the term has fallen into disuse. Some other words and phrases that the lexicographers of *Moçambicanismos* tell us have fallen into disuse: *bandidos armados* and *bazuca. Bandidos armados* or armed bandits was the name given to those who belonged to the anti-Frelimo group (see **Renamo**) that was set up by the Rhodesian CIO (Central Intelligence Organisation) and then, throughout the 1980s, supported by apartheid South Africa. In the early post-independence days when they made hasty forays over the border from Rhodesia to lay some mines or blow up a school or health post, they weren't much more than armed bandits, but they soon became a well-armed force with huge destructive powers. Calling the Renamo fighters *bandidos armados* was perhaps an attempt to downplay their significance and strength.

A *bazuca* was the dark green one-litre bottle of Laurentina beer which because of its shape and egregious size was popularly named after the shoulder-held rocket launchers or bazookas developed by the US Army in World War Two and used by the Frelimo guerrillas during the armed struggle.

Thirty years later, I notice that, in addition to the disappearance of *camarada*, *bazuca* and *bandidos armados*, there's another once-ubiquitous word that I haven't heard spoken: *o povo*, the people (see ***Povo***).

Cão-Tinhoso/Mangy-Dog

Maputo 1978, and I was searching for anything that would give me some kind of a handle on a place where I found it difficult enough to understand the official language—Portuguese—let alone any of the other languages I could hear on the street. I'd allowed myself a brief moment of self-congratulation when I managed, on the second day after arrival, to buy a small bar of soap. Roughish soap, jungle green, but soap nonetheless. It would be some months before I would realise that this had been less a miracle of understanding between the shopkeeper and myself and more a miracle of coincidence: the only commodity then available to buy in the shops was, as it happened, soap. Meanwhile I was baffled by what I was hearing. It sounded completely different from the Portuguese I'd been assiduously listening and responding to as I sat with earphones on and my finger hovering over the stop and play buttons on the recorder in the language lab on Rosebery Avenue in London. I struggled on a daily basis with the news stories in *Notícias*, but they were all a bit, well, Marxist-Leninist. I thought that perhaps if I tried to read some Mozambican fiction, a novel or perhaps some children's stories, I would find another way into the language, and a window into the minds and, I hoped, the hearts of the people who spoke it.

What I found was *Cão-Tinhoso*, or Mangy-Dog. The collection of stories *Nós Matámos o Cão-Tinhoso—We Killed Mangy-Dog*—by Luís Bernardo Honwana was the only Mozambican work of fiction you could find in a Maputo bookshop, and made up one third of the fledgling state publishing company's list, the other two thirds consisting of a comic book featuring the character Xiconhoca, a flared jeans-wearing, ghettoblaster-toting wide-boy we all loved to hate (see **Xiconhoca**), and the Portuguese translation of the English original *The Struggle for Mozambique* by Frelimo's first President, Eduardo Mondlane, with an introduction by Samora Machel.

I discovered much later that Honwana's title story, 'We Killed Mangy-Dog,' had been translated into English and first published in the *London Magazine* in 1967, around about the time that its author, aged twenty-five, was arrested by the Portuguese authorities and thrown in jail. The whole collection, translated by Dorothy Guedes, appeared a couple of years later in the Heinemann African Writers Series. Had I known this and read it in English in 1978 I think I would have found Honwana's allegorisation of the colonial era illuminating, the way the story shows not just the casual brutalities of colonialism but also its insidious demands for soul-destroying compliance.

But oh how I struggled. Even with the help of my *Mirador* dictionary—a slightly-larger-than-pocket-size kind of Tardis of a dictionary—I couldn't grasp the meaning of it. I knew some Italian *cooperantes* who were discussing it in their fortnightly reading group, but I didn't dare ask any of them to explain it to me in English, for in their high-minded way they were analysing it in Portuguese rather than in their own language. In contrast to Mondlane's straightforward narrative of oppression and resistance, Honwana's story of poor trembling rheumy-eyed Mangy-Dog with his suppurating sores, his feeble arthritic legs and his poor trusting doggy heart came to represent for me all that I experienced as unsettling and incomprehensible about the People's Republic of Mozambique.

Capulana

Worn tied around the waist or across the chest by women throughout southern and eastern Africa, the *capulana* is a rectangular piece of cotton cloth colourfully printed with patterns, pictures and text. Often bought in pairs; one *capulana* clothes the body while the other, tied across the back, holds your baby tight and snug against you.

You can stand in the middle of *Casa Elefante* on Avenida 25 Setembro in downtown Maputo and see, covering every inch of wall space, hanging flat against the wall or folded and piled in shelves, thousands of *capulanas*. It's an Aladdin's cave of *capulanas*; they gleam in the gloom of the shop's interior. Abstract blocks and swirls of colour alternate with representational designs: a handsome black impala against a scarlet background; trumpeting elephants; a line of blue-speckled *galinhas do mato* (guineafowl, or bush hens); a jigsaw piece-like outline of Mozambique showing the main towns. Others celebrate national events: 9th Congress 2006 in bright red letters on white; FRELIMO: *unidos na luta contra a pobreza*, united in the struggle against poverty, bordered with a criss-cross pattern of drums and maize cobs in green, red and black; a history in pictures you can rub between your finger and thumb and tie around your waist.

C

CFMAG

2010: In London I visit the Bishopsgate Institute opposite Liverpool Street Station where, Jill Sheppard told me, Polly Gaster last year deposited boxes full of CFMAG stuff. CFMAG: the Committee for Freedom in Mozambique, Angola and Guinea-Bissau. Polly set it up in the late 1960s after spending time working with Frelimo in Tanzania, and ran it first from a room in her north London house and then from an office on the floor above The Other Cinema in Little Newport Street, tucked into a corner between Charing Cross Road and Shaftesbury Avenue, a couple of minutes from Leicester Square tube. Soon after Mozambique won independence in 1975, CFMAG was transformed into MAGIC, the Mozambique, Angola and Guinea-Bissau Information Centre, and, under Jill's management, moved to Percy Street off Tottenham Court Road; Polly left for Mozambique.

A huge print of an old photograph covers the whole of one wall in the stone-floored entrance hall of the Bishopsgate Institute and shows an audience of late Victorians—the men in dark jackets with wide lapels and the women in pale buttoned-up blouses—enjoying a humorous talk, according to the caption below, in the Great Hall. They're not roaring with laughter, so perhaps the talk was only gently humorous. Now as then, the Bishopsgate Institute offers the working population of the East End and City of London a range of talks, concerts and courses programmed to take place outside working hours. Nowadays Chinese and Japanese are offered in the languages curriculum, salsa and belly dance in performing arts, and art history, film studies and wine-tasting in leisure. I see in the brochure that an ex-student of mine is teaching the creative writing courses. Glass-and-steel skyscrapers tower over the Institute's neo-Gothic turrets, the shapes of the turrets' pointed spires echoed by the great snout of the Gherkin nudging skywards behind them. The Institute's Great Hall is given over on a daily basis to the various types of accounting exams required of those working their way up to the top floors of the surrounding skyscrapers.

I walk past the Great Hall where rows of empty desks await the arrival of the morning's candidates, and down a green-tiled corridor towards the library. A fractured light falls through the glass dome of the ceiling onto a scattering of readers at the mahogany tables below. I move on through glass doors in a glass wall into the archive area. Here they specialise in labour history and the history of the East End and also offer a safe berth, and final resting place, for the written records of a number of late twentieth century radical groups or groupuscules. At the moment I'm the only reader. It's some time since I've done any archival digging, and I've forgotten what a panacea it provides against biographers' blues. The devil that lives in my head and whispers, who do you think you are? What gives you the right to write about Samora Machel? is silenced by the cheerfully pragmatic welcome I get from the librarian: hello Sarah, we've brought up the first lot of files you requested.

It's not just that here, in the library of the Bishopsgate Institute, looking at these papers is the most natural thing in the world to do. No, it's more than that. It's the best and the only thing in the world to do. The muttering devil is routed. The librarians validate what I'm doing, just as, I realise, my research validates what they're doing. The gunmetal grey box files that contain primrose cardboard folders carefully tied with cotton ribbon, which the librarian hands over to me one at a time, become the site of a mutual silent exchange of validation and respect. I must recommend this to all my writer friends as a specific against despair.

After CFMAG disbanded itself in 1975 the office correspondence was stored in an attic; an attic beneath a leaky roof. I pull apart pages of minutes of meetings and reports from conferences. Water-stains obscure whole paragraphs, and on many of the pages the ink has seeped through onto the reverse. A strong smell of damp hits the back of my nose. Some documents seem to have been typed onto paper with a shiny surface coat, and for a moment I wonder if they're faxes, but then I remember: faxes weren't invented in the early 1970s. These are cyclostyle master sheets, which you used to fit onto a printing drum and ink up before running off the number of sheets you wanted. The shiny surface is disintegrating where the typewriter keys bit into it. My fingers are dusted with sticky 'a's and 'e's and 'o's and random parts of words.

My own past wafts out of the archive of musty cyclostyled sheets. All at once I recognise a different typescript, which belonged to the golfball electric typewriter that was acquired when CFMAG became MAGIC and moved to Percy Street. I was in my early twenties then and looking for something meaningful to do with my life. I see myself sitting at a desk smoking a roll-up and drinking instant coffee out of a chunky white mug decorated with a clenched fist in black and beneath it *Venceremos!* in red cursive lettering. I was wearing my working gear: jeans and a white shirt with sleeves rolled up under my favourite article of clothing, a tanktop from Oxfam made of knitted patchwork squares in different shades of red. On a flat table by the window lay large sheets of thick paper. Next to them a scalpel, squared ruler, blue pencil and a large pot of cow gum stood ready. We were producing an issue of the quarterly magazine *People's Power*. Behind me the electric typewriter rattled and pinged as Jill finished typing the article I was waiting to paste up.

Venceremos! As well as minutes, reports, newsletters and press releases, organisational details of solidarity conferences and the End the Alliance campaign of 1973, when CFMAG organised protests against the visit to England of the sinisterly bespectacled Doctor Caetano, Prime Minister of Portugal, I found five years' worth of correspondence between Polly Gaster and the Frelimo people, first in Dar es Salaam, and then, when representatives were sent to other countries, in Algiers, Bucharest, Cairo, Havana and Lusaka. Their official letters end with three phrases: *A Luta Continua!* The Struggle Continues! *Independência ou Morte!* Independence or Death! *Venceremos!* We Shall Overcome! African dust trapped in the folds of flimsy airmail paper has turned to mould. I find I'm sitting back holding the bits of paper at arms' length but nonetheless as I breathe in I can still sense, or so I fancy, the spores of mould drifting up my nostrils.

Letters in English from Information Secretary Jorge Rebelo, in French from Foreign Affairs Secretary Marcelino dos Santos, in Portuguese from Presidential Secretary Joaquim Chissano, who would himself become President of Mozambique after Samora's death, and from Armando Guebuza, who would become President after Chissano. Telegrams give arrival details of Frelimo emissaries coming to Britain to address the Labour Party or TUC Conferences. Sometimes the representatives were held at Heathrow and not allowed in, and so someone from CFMAG had to go and fight the immigration officials for their release. The glue that stuck the strips of paper to the telegram forms has long since dried out and the yellowing strips of typed words flutter out and down as I lift them. *A Luta Continua! Independência ou Morte! Venceremos!* Phrases from another era that have become part of a romantic revolutionary language of the past, but that in those days expressed lived experience. The struggle did continue, Frelimo did overcome, and many died on the road to independence, by assassination if not in combat.

Most of the correspondence I'm reading deals with the practicalities of CFMAG's activities as a support group, but now and again expressions of caution reveal a subtext of personal danger. Letters are sent to Dar checking on the credentials of this or that Portuguese or Mozambican who has turned up in Little Newport Street claiming to support Frelimo, and in some of the letters the correspondents are careful not to name the people they're referring to. Jokes about the paranoid Left used to circulate, I remember, and when Harold Wilson said he thought that his offices had been bugged, rumour spread that he was losing his mind. It took forty years for MI5 to admit that Wilson's suspicions had indeed been well-founded.

From one of the gunmetal grey box files I take out some of the English-language publications produced in the early 1970s by Rebelo's Information Office and by the Mozambique Institute (see **Matchedje**) in Dar es Salaam, and it's here, among the copies of *Mozambique Revolution*, that at last I find Samora. Throughout the years that CFMAG is struggling to raise Frelimo's profile in Britain, to win support for them from politicians and journalists, and to try to win audiences for the organisation's spokespeople, Samora is training the guerrilla army in Tanzania (see **Nachingwea**), or is himself deep inside Mozambique. Here he is in a village in a Frelimo-controlled zone in Tete Province in 1971, on the second anniversary of the assassination of Eduardo Mondlane (see **Mondlane**), addressing a public meeting: 'Let us swear that we shall finish that task begun by comrade Mondlane, which is the liberation of our country.'[3]

Samora has been commander of the army since 1966, and he is now, newly elected, the President of Frelimo. He goes on:

> One of comrade Mondlane's greatest achievements was the establishment of unity among our people. But unity is an abstract word—is it not possible to see in practice manifestation of that unity? Even here, in this place, among ourselves? Yes, it is possible. For example, the present political commissar of the Province came from Inhambane. This comrade, responsible for sabotage operations, came from Manica e Sofala. This fighter who is here defending your *machambas* came from Gaza. This teacher who teaches your children came from Cabo Delgado, but he is happy to be here because this is also part of his country, Mozambique. There are here among us fighters from all provinces of Mozambique. They left their parents and their brothers far away, and came to live with you because, being Mozambicans, you are also their parents and their brothers.

'This comrade ... this fighter ... this teacher ...' Samora's skill as a speaker lies in the way he speaks to and about individual people. His speeches are always full of this or that ordinary person: it makes all the other ordinary people feel that he's speaking to and about them. He allows his audience to feel that they are, individually, part of this project, controversial then and still controversial a generation later, called unity. After the speech they kill and roast an ox.

Printed on the next page is a photograph of the village school. The trunks of the forest trees provide the walls, their leafy branches the roof. Some little boys crouch in the front row clutching folders or exercise books, behind them two rows of older boys and young men. About thirty students in all, including a couple of young women and two soldiers. In the middle of the back row stands Samora. One of the students standing on his left, 28-year-old José Jeque, describes how he got to the school.

> In a single day twelve people—twelve women—had been killed in my village. They'd gone to cultivate the fields and they'd taken maize flour to eat during the day. By noon they went to a nearby well in order to use the water to cook. When they were near the well they met the Portuguese troops. The Portuguese commander asked them where they were taking the flour. They answered, 'we are going to cook for us to eat.' That Portuguese then answered, 'what you are going to do is to take that to the terrorists—you collaborate with them—I am going to teach you a lesson.' He shot off several rounds of his machine gun and killed all the 12 women. Their bodies remained abandoned near the well. When I heard this I decided to run away before the Portuguese found me: I entered the bush and went to a FRELIMO base. I was there teaching first class (I had 109 students) before coming to this pilot school where I am now doing third class. Of course I am very happy that I came to FRELIMO. I am only doing third class although I am 28 years old, but this is one of the consequences of colonialism. Our struggle will enable our children to have better conditions.

The students' feet may be bare but their expressions are formal and serious, as befits a photograph taken with the military commander and President of Frelimo.

A luta continua! Independência ou morte! Venceremos!

Chima

Gluey and glistening, *chima* made from cassava (also called manioc or *mandioca*) flour (from the root or tuber of the plant) is pallid, *chima* from maize flour has a yellowish tinge. You pluck a lump from the bowl and roll it into a ball in your fingers, then dip it in a sauce: meat or fish if available, otherwise leafy green *matapa* (see ***Matapa***).

Cooperante

Samora called *cooperantes* 'militants who share a common cause and have put personal considerations in second place in order to help with National Reconstruction.'[4] Samora was always good at making people feel good about themselves; I like to think that he enjoyed doing so, and that it provided some compensation for what must have been the dreary task of chiding and chastising people into line, rooting out, over and over again, the enemy within: the backsliders, the recidivists, the opportunists. He was always generous with his praise for the foreign workers known as *cooperantes*.

Cooperantes came to fill the posts left vacant by the fleeing Portuguese, and as a stopgap while Mozambicans were trained to fill the posts themselves. While fear fuelled the exodus of large numbers of the settlers and colonialists—rumours of bloodthirsty Communists were swirling through the city streets—many of them nonetheless took the time to sabotage what they were leaving behind. They disabled trucks and tractors, they killed livestock and burned crops, and they poured concrete down the lift shafts of the hotels in the capital. But the damage to the economy caused by such acts of sabotage was less than the damage caused by the loss of so many skilled workers.

Cooperantes (of whom I was one) could be divided into two main groups: those from the capitalist or social democratic West and those from the socialist East. The Westerners were mostly under thirty and came alone or in pairs from all the countries where solidarity groups had supported Frelimo and the revolutionary movements in Angola, Guinea-Bissau and Cape Verde against Portuguese colonialism: Britain, Holland, France, all the

Scandinavian countries, Italy, Canada and America. They came, too, in exile from South Africa, and southwards from Tanzania and other recently independent African countries. The clash and clang of ideological dispute ricocheted between and amongst groups of Western *cooperantes*, with Marxists shouting down Maoists, hard-line Communists laying down the law to laid-back libertarians, and quiet-voiced social democrats resisting the haranguing of the ultra-leftists. In between whiles they worked in hospitals and secondary schools, on engineering and sanitation projects, in ministry buildings in the capital, in isolated villages, and in the notoriously austere Frelimo residential schools, and, between bouts of arguing, variously fell in and out of love with each other, smoked dope, idolised Samora, lost their illusions, wept to go home.

Cooperantes from the socialist bloc came in teams, and worked and lived in teams. Who knows if they fell in and out of love with each other, if they smoked dope (very unlikely), if they idolised Samora? I'm sure they wept to go home: they had left behind in Moscow, in Beijing, in Havana and in Pyongyang husbands, wives and children.

Amongst the British *cooperantes* working in the health service the comparative ranking of medical competence was generally agreed to run: Americans, British, Cubans, Italians, Russians. North Koreans came in at the very bottom of the scale. We often discussed other national traits that conformed to stereotypes: serious Dutch, high-minded Italians, wild Finns, gloomy Norwegians, cheerful Danes, and hard-drinking Russians and Cubans. Each socialist bloc group included an interpreter in their number; everyone knew that the interpreter was usually the group's minder, too. If a Russian or Cuban or Bulgarian had been seen weeping in public once too often (after a bout of hard drinking), or if she had shown too much interest in a Western *cooperante*, he or she would mysteriously disappear one night and be replaced by someone new. Did they share a common cause, the socialist bloc *cooperantes*, and did they put their personal considerations in second place? We couldn't help thinking that they didn't have much choice in the matter.

Every Western *cooperante* received a salary of between twenty and thirty *contos* a month (about £320 and £480 respectively), a part of which they were allowed to transfer home. This sum was about twice as much as their Mozambican counterparts earned, and unimaginably more than the monthly income of the vast majority of Mozambicans. But a combination of lack of consumer goods and a commitment to a stripped-down lifestyle, the latter shared across the political spectrum, militated against conspicuous consumption. Samora led by personal example and insisted on the highest personal standards of probity within Frelimo. 'We have a common saying,' he said in one of his earliest recorded speeches (in 1971), 'that he who has steak in his mouth cannot speak.'[5]

It was only when Frelimo's tightly woven control of the country began to fray and unravel in the 1980s under the pressures of external aggression and a failing economy, and, after Samora's death, with the huge influx of aid agency workers with their shiny 4x4s and their wads of foreign currency, that the echo of colonialism's polarisation of rich and poor was heard once more. As an unnamed government official said with sadness to the journalist Joseph Hanlon: 'We Mozambicans are sometimes a bit slow. And it has taken us a long time to learn. But we have finally learned from you [Westerners] the first rule of development: that you must have a house and a car, whisky and a stereo, before you can start to help the peasants.'[6]

Crítica e Auto-Crítica

In 1979 I wrote in my diary: 'Sometimes I think that not much has changed since the days of colonialism: Mozambican society's still divided into those who give the orders and those who take them.'

My third term at Escola Ngungunhana had not begun well. On the weekend before term started, all teachers were summoned to attend a session of *crítica e auto-crítica*: critical analysis and self-criticism. On Saturday morning we gathered in one of the larger classrooms, three or four neat rows of us in old wooden bench and desk combinations, facing our *dirigentes*—leaders—who were on chairs behind a table at the front. I was sitting next to Giuliana, an Italian geography teacher. Alongside the provincial director of education and the two *estruturas* (see **Estrutura**) from the directorate who flanked him sat the three members of the school's *commissão*. I looked around: not all the teachers were present. I couldn't see Rosária, the twenty-year-old daughter of the provincial director.

The provincial director stood up. He was a suspiciously fat man. Samora, Graça, all the Frelimo ministers, such as Rebelo, Vieira, Marcelino dos Santos, were uniformly lean. He gave no welcome but launched into a long admonitory speech. 'You must be vigilant against the enemy within,' he said, wagging his index finger at us. 'You must root out the sabotage from your hearts.'

I was reminded of Mother Mary Colette at my convent school, telling us to be vigilant against the devil, warning us of the sin that lurked in our hearts, treating us as wrongdoers before we'd done wrong. I'd hated it then, and I hated it now. He berated us for our failure to attend meetings, for our reactionary attitudes, for our betrayal of the principles of the revolution, for being *xiconhocas* (see **Xiconhoca**).

I could feel my heart hammering as I raised my hand and begged permission to speak.

'Why are you criticising us?' I asked. 'Here we are, at this meeting.'

I could hear the collective gasp of shock at my temerity. The three members of the *commissão* exchanged looks: will Comrade Sarah never mend her liberal Western ways?

Later we divided up into small groups, each led by a party *estrutura* from the directorate, for a session of political study.

I managed to avoid being in the group led by the director himself.

* * *

Revolutionary dialogue:

'*Apoia a linha política do Partido?*' asks our *estrutura*. 'Do you support the political line of the Party?'

'*Sim, apoio,*' says Inácio from the *commissão*. 'Yes, I support it.'

'*Sim, apoio,*' says my English-teaching colleague Hari, a Zambian.

Doubtless Rosária would also say, '*sim, apoio,*' were she present, but she's not.

For a moment I harbour a mad desire to say, '*Não, não apoio,*' but I struggle with it and root it from my heart. Instead I sigh and say sulkily, '*sim, apoio.*'

Giuliana says: 'I don't think this is a useful question, because as we have just heard, it encourages a conformist answer and rules out critical analysis.' She winks at me. 'And today we are here to engage in critical analysis.'

Inácio looks at her in horror, but after a beat of silence our *estrutura* says, 'Our Italian comrade is right. Although perhaps she lacks some experience of Mozambique.'

* * *

The next morning we assembled once more in our best clothes, as instructed, at half past eight. No one from the directorate was present. Twenty minutes later Inácio admitted that the meeting was scheduled to start at nine o'clock, but we'd been told to come early so as to concentrate our minds. At nine fifteen there was still no sign of our leaders. Next to me Marina the maths teacher muttered that the *estruturas* should try to come on time.

'Are you going to criticise them when they come?' I asked. 'No, of course not.' She was astonished that I should suggest such a thing. 'Why not?' 'We can't criticise *estruturas*. They'd call us reactionaries if we did.'

In those days I thought that the never-ending meetings of *crítica* and *auto-crítica* inflicted on us were based on a theory of collective engagement borrowed from the socialist bloc. But Oscar Monteiro and other analysts suggest something quite different. The practice in Gaza province—and not only in Gaza, but elsewhere in Mozambique—was to spend as long as it took to investigate the relationships that underpinned any problem thrown up within the community, and so resolve them to everyone's satisfaction. Samora was brought up within this traditional culture of everyday discussion and debate, which was reinforced by the Methodist practices brought back from the South African mines by his father (see **Baobab**).

The sacrosanct five-hour minimum duration for meetings was, I suspect, the result of the Party's addition of the ideology of the consensus (see **Pensamento Unico**) to this mixture of tribal tradition and Presbyterian/Methodist church practice.

D

Destacamento Feminino

For the first three years of the armed struggle Frelimo women worked as civilians behind the front line. Then, in March 1967, a small group of women arrived in Nachingwea (see **Nachingwea**) to undertake military training. The creation of the *destacamento feminino*—the women's detachment—of the *Forças Populares de Libertação de Moçambique* (FPLM, the People's Forces for the Liberation of Mozambique) was the subject of vigorous and at times bitter debate within Frelimo. Women's inclusion in the army on equal terms with men stuck in the craw of the Makonde 'chairmen' of Cabo Delgado, who saw it as yet another threat to their own power and influence.

If race (could white people be proper revolutionaries and should they be allowed to join Frelimo?) and education (should young cadres be trained in the armed struggle and sent to work amongst the peasants of northern Mozambique, or should they rather be sent off on scholarships abroad so that they would be ready for a leadership role when independence was gained?) were the two jagged rocks on which Frelimo almost foundered, then the role of women in the liberation war became the whirlpool that nearly sucked it under. President Eduardo Mondlane, military commander Samora Machel and the rest of the leadership somehow steered the ship of Frelimo around this danger too. To the sound of the traditionalists' wailing and gnashing of teeth, women won their demand to receive military and political training and to become part of the guerrilla army.

As well as taking responsibility for the support bases and supply lines for the combatants in the bush in northern Mozambique, the women guerrillas of the *destacamento feminino* pioneered the development of political and social infrastructure amongst the local populations in the liberated and semi-liberated zones. They set up health posts, primary schools and childcare centres where children orphaned or traumatised by the war were looked after.

Josina Muthemba Machel (see **Josina**), whom I heard described quaintly but accurately by the curator of the Samora Machel Museum (see **Mbuzini**) as 'the freedom fighter lady,' was one of those who demanded the right to fight for her country alongside men. She joined one of the early cohorts of young women to receive military training and be sent into the northern provinces of Mozambique.

The historian Amélia de Souto arrived in Nachingwea to join the *destacamento feminino* in 1973, when she was nineteen years old. She found she was the only white girl amongst two thousand black girls, in a brigade of a hundred or so northerners, Macuas and Makondes, whose languages she couldn't speak, and many of whom were illiterate. 'I came from a different place; it was difficult to communicate with the others,' she said, with what I imagined was considerable understatement. 'I represented the enemy. It was a very difficult struggle.'[1]

I talked to Amélia de Souto in her office in the Centre for African Studies at the Eduardo Mondlane University in Maputo. From the corridor outside her office you can lean over the balcony and look down onto a flower-planted courtyard where a carved grey piece of stone memorialises two historians who worked at the Centre for African Studies: Ruth First, killed here by a South African parcel bomb in 1982, and Aquino de Bragança, who was injured in the attack but met his own death four years later alongside his President at Mbuzini. Amélia de Souto is currently working on memory and its function in history. Blonde hair just turning grey, with high cheekbones and candid brown eyes, she's slim and stylish, in jeans and a tailored cotton jacket. She's thoughtful and articulate about the clash between her deep affection for Samora Machel and the critical analysis of his leadership demanded by her duty as a historian. 'I liked him very much personally,' she said at the beginning of our talk. 'All the contact I had with him was extraordinary. ... He was a very human person. Real. Someone that you speak the truth with. Some people were frightened of his directness, but I liked it. He liked to look you in the eye, to say what he thought. If he asked me something, I would just tell him what I thought. I was always very direct with him.' As with almost everyone I spoke to, her voice took on a particular timbre when she was talking about her personal encounters with Samora, and, when quoting his words, mimicked his own warm, intimate tones. It's as if the people who met him and were touched by his charm and charisma still hear his voice in their heads, calling them by name, joking with them, praising them.

Amélia met Samora on a number of occasions during the eighteen months she spent in training with the *destacamento feminino*.

When Samora used to come to Nachingwea he used to discuss things with us—how's it all going, he wanted to know? He'd look, he'd see one white person among 2000, he'd know that maybe there was a problem. He'd say to us all: there are white people who are good, who are in Frelimo. He'd say: things aren't so 'black and white!' He was intrinsically a non-racist person. ... One day not long before independence he organized a meeting with the *destacamento* in our groups of two hundred or three hundred. He wanted to talk about the problems we were going to find in the cities. We were a political force and at independence we'd be posted to the various cities. He talked about corruption there, about people who'd try to suborn and undermine us, try to turn us. We'd have to be careful. He spoke about love. He said: there'll be people who say they love you, but it won't be real love. He called me out: Amélia, Amélia, come here, come here. He wanted to put on a piece of theatre. Samora said: 'I am from Frelimo. You are a woman from the city. We're going to show what reactionary love is. You will try to buy me, so that you can infiltrate the FPLM. We'll show everyone what reactionary love is, and then we'll show them what revolutionary love is.' I said: 'But *camarada Presidente*, I don't know how to do it.' Samora: 'You must call me Samora—we are trying to have a relationship. You must say [*in sexy voice*]: "Samora, come here."' And I said: 'I can't do it.' 'All right,' said Samora. '*I* can perform as the reactionary; *you* can be from the armed forces. We'll swap roles.'

On another occasion one of Amélia's poems, an 'epic revolutionary poem' on the subject of prostitutes and revolutionaries, was part of a drama put on by the *destacamento* for a visit by Samora and his regional commanders. 'Who wrote the poem?' asked Samora, and was told it was Amélia. Later a nervous Amélia was summoned to join the top military men and women for dinner. 'Samora told me he loved poetry, and poets. "They see things with feeling, and sometimes see further than leaders do, because they have a sensitivity for the people, for the things that are around them. We will need many poets in Mozambique...." I told him I wanted to go on writing poems, and express my feelings through them. "You must carry on," he said. "Many of the people who've died in the armed struggle wrote poems. Poets are good people."' (see **Mutimati**)

'I'll never forget that dinner,' said Amélia. 'He said: "If you're not properly organised militarily, one mistake can bring disaster, or death, to everyone. You must make yourself into a poet *and* a soldier. You have to find the balance."'

Amélia ended the account of her time in the *destacamento feminino* by saying: 'I was inspired by the revolution,' and reminded me, as befitted a historian working on memory, of the dangers of subjectivity. 'We try to be objective,' she told me, 'but when you have a personal relationship with someone, it's not easy.'

Difficulties

2010: The journalist Paul Fauvet, co-author of a book about his Mozambican colleague Carlos Cardoso who was murdered in Maputo in November 2000 while investigating the theft of $14 million from the country's largest bank, sent me a list of email addresses of some of the people I told him I'd like to talk to about Samora Machel's life and death. Paul Fauvet has lived and worked in Maputo since 1981. He sends out to interested parties regular English-language email bulletins from AIM (*Agencia de Informação de Moçambique*), the Mozambique News Agency, where he's head of the English desk. A continuous thread running through the twice-weekly bulletins in the late 2000s was the story of the prosecution of Cardoso's murderers, a story with enough farcical elements—such as the escape of the accused through a hole in the wall of the prison—to confirm every Westerner's worst prejudices about levels of corruption in post-colonial African countries. As I read the ongoing despatches I noticed myself tut-tutting: such things would never have happened in Samora's day! And then I ask myself, yes, but ... stuff must have gone on that went unadmitted and unjudged?

When Paul sent me his contact list I asked my conversation teacher Gustavo Infante to correct my Portuguese for errors of grammar or protocol, and fired off twenty emails to *Exmo Sr* this and *Exma Sra* that—Most Excellent Sir or Madam—and one or two to the English speakers amongst the old comrades, asking their permission to ask them questions about Samora. Only two people replied: Sérgio Vieira, Central Committee member and variously Governor of the Bank of Mozambique, Director of the President's Office, Minister for Agriculture, Governor of Niassa, and Security Minister at the time of Samora's death in 1986, and Janet Rae Mondlane, widow of Frelimo's first President, Eduardo Chivambe Mondlane (see **Mondlane**), and now President of the Mondlane Foundation. I emailed all Paul's other contacts again but received no replies.

That same week, coincidentally and, I thought at first, serendipitously, I was invited by two Zimbabwean filmmaker friends to meet a fellow filmmaker working on a documentary about Samora Machel. He was tall, articulate and forceful. As soon as we sat down to dinner in Bob and Annie's house he made two things absolutely clear: he himself had found that no-one would cooperate with him because of the wall of silence built around Samora in Mozambique and, secondly, the generally accepted hypothesis about Samora's death, that the plane crash was engineered by the South Africans, was mistaken.

I pushed him on the subject of the plane crash, and he told me he'd actually taken a course in aviation in order better to understand it. This was fascinating. And impressive. What had he discovered? There was never a decoy beacon set up by the South Africans to pull the plane off course, he said. And the plane had landed on flat ground. Really? I said. 'Everything I've read suggested it came down in the hills running along the border. And indeed I've looked at photos taken by Mozambican photographers at the site of the crash that show the hillside.'

Suddenly we seemed to be quarrelling. Perhaps I'd drunk too much wine. I found it difficult to follow his argument, but I thought he was saying the Russian pilot had deliberately crashed the plane. Well, it was the Russians—pilot and co-pilot—who were originally blamed by the South Africans, unsurprisingly. The South Africans said they were drunk, an accusation that they could reasonably hope would be believed. After all, the pilots weren't expecting to have to fly the plane back from Zambia that night. They were under strict instructions—from Vieira's people—not to fly at night on any account, for fear of attack from the ground. And who ever heard of an off-duty Russian not having a drink? But they couldn't have been very drunk or Samora would have noticed as he gave them their orders to ignore the security instructions about night flights. Pilot error maybe, but deliberate...?

As the quarrelsome evening drew to an end, I wondered: why on earth would the Soviet Union have wanted Samora dead? After all, Samora was still walking the tightrope between West and East. Yes, he'd struck up an unlikely friendship with Margaret Thatcher after helping to broker the deal that brought to an end Ian Smith's white minority regime in Rhodesia, but on the other hand, American money and South African matériel were feeding the anti-Frelimo movement Renamo. Samora was committed to keeping open the lines between Maputo and Moscow, even if relations had turned frosty since his 1982 request to enter COMECON had been turned down. On a practical level: what on earth or in heaven would induce two Russian pilots to turn kamikaze? Perhaps, I thought later, I'd misunderstood the documentary-maker.

The following morning I sent him an email with the title 'no expectations!':

It was very nice to meet you round at Bob and Annie's. I was fascinated by what you were saying about the circumstances surrounding the death of Samora Machel. Am I right in thinking that—at least on technical grounds to do with aviation—you conclude the crash must have been deliberate on the part of the Russians? If so, why? Or have I completely misinterpreted you? My apologies if that's the case.

Perhaps it was a bit rude of me to ask at the end of the evening if you could tell me how to get in touch with Graça Machel/Mandela. There's no reason at all why you should help me. I would quite understand a reluctance to share what is probably hard-earned information—with someone you've only just met! I would be hugely grateful for any contacts you felt able to pass on—but I have no expectations, and certainly no offence taken if you'd rather not. Anyway, I very much look forward to seeing your film when it's released. And hope that we'll meet again.

with all best wishes ...

In his reply he said that the accusation against apartheid South Africa was not 'technically consistent' with the way the plane had vanished from the radar, and referred me back to 'all the stuff' he'd said about the landing and questions surrounding the decoy beacon. But 'all the stuff' he'd said was precisely what I'd been puzzling over. He wouldn't rush to blame the Russians, he went on; he had his own questions which if answered would elicit the truth. What a pity, I thought, that he didn't want to share those questions with me. Finally he warned me that Mozambique was such a closed society that I would have difficulty finding anyone to speak to.

Well, thanks for nothing, I thought. I felt more mystified than ever.

Sérgio Vieira and Janet Mondlane had agreed to answer questions if I emailed them. I did so, into a lengthening silence. I felt my confidence dribbling away and began to think that perhaps the documentary-maker was right about Mozambique being a closed society.

I asked for advice from my friend Jill Nicholls. She's a film director and producer, and makes a lot of films for Imagine and music documentaries for BBC 2 and 4. At the start of a project, she told me, she emails potential interviewees, and then follows up with phone calls. Most people are happy to answer questions, she said, and if they're not then it's usually for some reason of their own, rather than because they hate, scorn, dislike, or resent you. Don't take it personally, she advised.

I speak Portuguese adequately in a face-to-face conversation, thanks to Gustavo and to his predecessor, João Cosmé. João wrote his PhD thesis on the Mozambican writer Mia Couto (see ***Pousada***), and shared with the documentary-maker a belief in the closed nature of Mozambican society. But as João had warned me, when I was planning my 2008 visit, that as a white person it would be impossible for me to walk around Maputo on my own without attracting hostile attention, and as that had proved to be absolutely not the case, I'd ascribed his gloom and doom to Portuguese paranoia. In fact, I noticed in 2008 that although I felt free to walk the streets of Maputo, or rather to negotiate the volcano-like eruptions of stone and concrete that pass for pavements, I was almost invariably, except when Paul Fauvet was out and about, the only white person on foot. NGOs, aid workers, white businessmen from Portugal and South Africa travel everywhere with their bums stuck fast to the seats of their air-conditioned 4x4s.

But the prospect of having to speak Portuguese on the telephone to a stranger, explaining who I am and what I want, fills me with dread. It's bad enough cold-calling someone in English. How fortunate that I don't long for a career in investigative journalism, I think to myself. I force myself to try the English-speaking option. My hands shake as I pick up the phone. It rings and rings: there's no reply from the Mondlane Foundation. Phew. I send Janet Mondlane another email, saying that I shall ring her at a certain time the next day. Next morning's one-liner says: please do not ring me.

Although Jill advised me not to take such rejections personally, I find it hard not to. And I think I've provoked Janet Mondlane's displeasure by including, in my list of emailed questions about Samora, a question about Eduardo Mondlane, asking whether she held the Portuguese security police (see **PIDE**) responsible for his death. I blush at my gaucheness, at the crudeness of the question. I only asked her about Eduardo Mondlane because I thought it rude and unfeeling to ask only about Samora, as if I thought Janet's late husband not worth my consideration. I've noticed before how a *faux pas* (or a forks pass as Terry Pratchett's Glenda of the Night Kitchen thinks it's called) can so swiftly conjure up the shameful memories of other *faux pas* that I wish I could forget.

I brooded on this for a few days but when I received an email from an acquaintance in Mozambique querying my right to write about Samora at all, and telling me, once more, that no-one would talk to me, I began to feel cross, and I put copies of all the pissy emails I'd received on the subject into a yellow cardboard folder and in thick black felt-tip pen I wrote on the front: *pissy emails received*. I then felt much better.

Meanwhile I was reading Jacinto Veloso's account of the assassination of Samora Machel. Veloso was a young Portuguese air force pilot who, in 1963 (a month or two after Samora had fled Mozambique), hijacked the plane he was piloting, an American-made Harvard T-6, and flew it north from an airstrip in Mozambique over the border to Tanzania to join Frelimo. When he and his companion João Ferreira (see **Frelimo** and **Hospital**) landed, with barely a teaspoonful of fuel to spare, they were promptly thrown in gaol by the Tanzanian police, who were understandably suspicious of two young white men flying in from out of the blue and saying they wanted to join an outlawed organisation that Tanzania was, at some risk to itself, allowing space to. Years later, when Veloso was Minister of Security, Samora would introduce him with a big grin to foreign visitors: 'Here's the world's first airline hijacker,' he'd say: 'a Mozambican, what's more!'

In his account of the night that Samora died, Veloso talks of an unidentified eastern European man boarding the aeroplane on the runway at Mbala and entering the cabin and talking to the crew. Must have been a Russian. He could have disconnected the radar, says Veloso. That night the pilot must have thought they were coming in to land at Maputo, for otherwise he would surely have turned on the throttle and pointed the plane's nose upwards, away from the fast-approaching hillside. This story doesn't quite make sense to me, for if the radar was disconnected then how would the cockpit have received any signal at all? South African military intelligence—and Veloso, as one of the lead economic negotiators with South Africa in the 1980s, was well placed to catch the passing rumours—had been sowing stories about disagreements within Frelimo, and stories of Samora's imminent demise. Samora knew that someone would try and kill him. He'd known that for years, and that there would be stories that it was an inside job. Veloso reminds us of the Russian engineer, one of the nine survivors of the crash. Whisked off to hospital by the South Africans, he was for weeks much too ill to be interviewed by the investigating Mozambican authorities. When he was well enough to talk, and the Mozambicans turned up at the hospital doors, they were too late: he'd already been flown back to the Soviet Union.

Suspicious, or what? The radar (see **Tupolev**) is an issue that niggles both the documentary-maker and Jacinto Veloso. Veloso suggests that the Soviet Union wanted Samora to die as a punishment for his betrayal of them with the West.[2] That seems somehow unlikely to me. I emailed Veloso care of his publishers. And again. Silence.

Driving Lessons

Q: Que é uma autostrada?
Q: What is a motorway?
A: É uma estrada destinado para transito de trafego rapido, com separação de correntes de trafego, acessos condicionados e sem cruzamentos de nivel.
A: A motorway is a road designed for the movement of fast traffic, with separate lanes, restricted access and without level crossings.

Niassa, 1978. I decide to take driving lessons. This means attending theory classes in the old PIDE (see **PIDE**) building on a corner of the central crossroads in Lichinga, opposite the post office. 'You used to be able to hear the cries of people being tortured in the cellars,' my Zambian colleague Hari tells me. The building now houses the *guárdia civil*, all four of them. I'm the only woman out of sixteen learner drivers. We sit in three rows and take it in turn to answer the questions posed by the youngest-looking of the *guárdia civil*. It reminds me powerfully of catechism lessons at the Convent of the Sacred Heart in Aberdeen:

Q: Who made me?
A: God made me.

Ten minutes every morning after prayers and before lessons began. I was seven or eight, on one of my periodic returns to

Scotland from Uganda, and a weekly boarder. One Monday morning I left my catechism behind at the house where I spent weekends, where I had used it to slide under the mouth of a glass so as to trap a bee, and had forgotten to return it to my satchel. As I was the only boarder in my class, I had no-one from whom I could borrow a catechism in the evening to learn the next day's lesson. Every morning that week I listened intently to the answers of the other girls as Mother Mary Finbar went round the class. I memorised their responses, praying to the God who'd made me that when it came to my turn it would be one of the short, easy answers I was required to come up with, and not one of the ones with sub-clauses and parentheses. I was terrified that I'd be found out, and each day that I didn't own up to not having my catechism the sin grew worse.

That intensive week of memorising the catechism wasn't wasted. Listening to my Mozambican classmates reciting the responses helps fix in my mind the complicated sub-clauses of the finer points of Portuguese driving theory.

It's definitely Portuguese and not Niassan theory that we're learning, and, as in the catechism, while the questions are short and sharp: What is a motorway? Who made me?, the responses are long and convoluted and seem to come from another world. There are no motorways in Mozambique, let alone in Niassa. In Niassa there are fewer than 100 kilometres of tarred road, and most of that was laid only ten years previously so as to make it easier for the Portuguese troops to move around, and of course to make it harder for the Frelimo guerrillas to plant landmines. Motorways, with their separate lanes and their restricted access, exist in a realm of the imagination, an otherworld where perhaps God drives a fast car.

Every so often our teacher beckons us to gather round a table by the window, on which a model Portuguese town is laid out, with roundabouts and traffic lights and even tiny cars and yellow buses. The other three *guárdia civil* usually join us for this exercise: we manoeuvre the vehicles this way and that to show that we know who has precedence at roundabouts, and when to give way to buses. This is our favourite bit of the lessons.

Our teacher directs us towards the last pages of the Highway Code, to the section designed specially for use in the 'overseas provinces.'

Q: What do you do if your lights fail at night?

A: Light a candle and proceed slowly to the next village.

Q: What do you do if a platoon of soldiers is marching towards you?

A: You stop the car and wait until they have passed.

In 1978 there are no platoons of soldiers in Niassa. Who is there to guard against? Friendly socialist Tanzania lies to the north, and Lake Niassa protects us from not-so-friendly capitalist Malawi to the west. Our concerns are with 'the enemy within,' our own corrupt desires for privilege and wealth.

After five theory lessons I'm allowed out with Aida the driving instructor in her own car, a yellow VW which is also the driving school car. It's the only saloon car in the 50,000 square miles of the province of Niassa. Aida is in her late forties, a widow, a white woman who helped the Frelimo guerrillas during the armed struggle (see **Lichinga**) and later chose Mozambican citizenship.

The car is parked outside the classroom. I manage to start it and change up into second gear to creep over the crossroads. 'Go into third,' Aida tells me. There are no other vehicles in sight so there's no apparent danger, but then a Toyota pickup roars up behind us and overtakes, possibly the first ever instance of any overtaking in Lichinga.

People spill out over the road from the gate to the market compound as we approach at a careful 25 kmph. I spot the two doctors from Guinea-Conakry head and shoulders above the rest of the crowd. No-one gets out of the way, until Aida leans across the steering wheel and hits the horn on the other side, and a path opens up in front of the car. I take my foot off the accelerator. 'Don't slow down,' says Aida.

Now out of the corner of my eye I notice the geologists' pickup by the side of the road—that was what overtook me—and two of them coming out through the gate with their arms full of small packets. That explains their hurry: cigarettes have arrived in town. Then we're past the crowd and an empty road stretches ahead.

As we cruise along in fourth gear at a daring 40 kmph I begin to think: maybe there's not as much to this as I thought. 'Turn off the road here,' says Aida. '*Aquí?* Here?' '*Sim*. Yes. Down the bank on the left.' I edge my way down the steep earth slope in first gear, execute a sharp turn to the right under Aida's instructions and growl up again to the lip of the slope.

'Wait here,' says Aida. 'Now imagine a platoon of soldiers is marching towards you. What do you do?' I know the answer to that one: 'Stop and wait until they've passed.'

'Now imagine you have no brakes.' '*Qué?*' I can't believe my ears. Maybe I've misunderstood. 'No brakes?' This is the first attempt at a brakeless manoeuvre I later become expert at: the *ponto de embalagem*. I hang on the lip of the slope with clutch and accelerator in perfect balance, waiting for the ghost soldiers to pass by. Sometimes they march swiftly, and Aida allows me to let out the clutch and gently step on the accelerator after only a few seconds to lift us up back on to the road. At other times—when perhaps they're staggering back to base at the end of a long day—I hang poised, feet trembling on the controls, for minutes at a time. I learn to do it in the rainy season when the bank is slick with red mud, and in high winds in the dry season when the dust flies thick across the windscreen and it's easy to imagine a platoon of soldiers plodding past on the road, the ghosts of one army or another, the soft-footed Frelimo guerrillas, or the young reluctant conscripted Portuguese, frightened of this inhospitable country with its hostile people and wanting only to go home.

D

One day Aida suggests we drive to the end of the tarmac road on the eastern edge of the plateau. Sixty, seventy, eighty miles an hour. I can't believe how fast the trees and bushes are zipping by. The road ends at Litunde, the easternmost colonial government outpost. It's empty now. The broken green wooden shutters of the whitewashed state house bang against the walls in the strong warm breeze that eddies up from the jungle below the cliff edge. Scarlet hibiscus grows rampant up the stone stairs and twines through the stone balustrades. We walk through the dark echoing rooms, and look out eastwards, where the bush stretches thousands of miles to the Indian Ocean. We go into the overgrown garden and Aida shows me, at the foot of the sweep of stone stairs, half obscured by tendrils of pink and purple bougainvillea, a gravestone bearing the inscription: *Aquí jaz o colonialismo português*—here lies Portuguese colonialism—*1974*.

E

Elephants

2008: In the central hall of the Natural History Museum in Maputo a *tableau vivant* (or *nature morte*) of animals of the deserts and savannas of sub-Saharan Africa gathers around a waterhole. An elephant lifts its trunk to soundlessly trumpet, an antelope pricks its ears as it stoops to drink, while a pangolin digs for termites in the base of a nearby earth castle. The zebra and the buffalo, poor things, as in so many wildlife documentaries, have been selected to represent the victims of the redness of nature's tooth and claw; each has a lioness stuck fast to its back. A notice on a wobbly stand assures you this gathering of dead animals illustrates *um ecosistema*, an ecosystem.

I'm looking for something that I remember from thirty years ago. Now, as then, I appear to be the only visitor. I circumnavigate the waterhole ecosystem, and stop by another wobbly stand to read its notice: *Moçambicanos: Este museu e vosso e para que vos orgulheis dele importa colaborem connosco, ajudandô-nos a conservâ-lo e remetendô-nos especimens para estudo ou exibição. Assim, ele servira melhor o povo.*

'Mozambicans: This museum belongs to you and so that you may take pride in it you must work with us, helping us to maintain it, and providing us with specimens for study or display.

Thus, it will be better able to serve the people.' Perhaps this exhortation in the name of *o povo* (see **Povo**) was here the first time I visited: it's an echo of the past like the stuffed animals in their lifeless ecosystem.

I turn away and at once I catch a glimpse of what it is I'm looking for: angled off to one side of this central hall, such that it's not visible from the entrance, I see a whole wall of preservation tanks, in rows one on top of the other, looking like the tanks of a modern aquarium in which you might hope to see the silver flash and glimmer of a darting shoal of tropical fish, or like the surveillance screens in the security room of a shopping mall, where figures move in and out of camera shot, turning, pausing, disappearing. But nothing moves on these screens.

Elephant foetuses that once swam in amniotic fluid are now suspended motionless in formaldehyde. A label beneath each pale and flaky corpse indicates its gestation age. The smaller ones are partially wrapped in thick white coils of umbilicus. They float as if asleep, a closed slit for eyes, mouths in tiny smiles behind their little trunks, their front legs bent at the wrist.

At one month the foetus is the length of half a thumb. Its thickened snout is the only indication it's going to become an elephant. It sits upright on its teeny tail. At three months it's the length of a whole thumb. Its head has grown disproportionately large, and the snout looks like a trunk. At six months it could stand on the palm of my hand. This one floats near the top of its tank with legs dangling. The curve of its back breaks through the surface of the formaldehyde. The flesh looks like fresh putty. At eight months it measures about ten inches from snout to tail. The ears—ears that on the living elephant trace the shape of the African continent—are little more than a couple of wrinkles against the side of the head, but I can see the hemispheric bulge of eyeballs beneath the skin. And at ten months, when it would still have another year swimming inside its mother's womb, it looks like a fully formed miniature elephant, about a foot long and six inches high at the shoulder.

The bigger foetuses are a darker grey, and rigid. They must be plaster casts. Perhaps when they get as big as this you can't keep them whole in preservative; perhaps the flesh begins to break up. At twenty months the plaster model is the height of a large dog.

I first saw these unborn elephants thirty years ago. Now they're nearly a hundred years old. '*Fetos de elefante, 1911*,' the label says. I read in the accompanying English-language text that they died when their mothers were killed as part of a 'clean up.' 'The existence of this collection is due to the fact that at the time of the First World War, the Agricultural of the Colonial Government decide to 'clean up' the area south of Maputo for agricultural projects.' Pre-First World War, if 1911 is accurate. 'To put this into effect, a team of hunters was established, led by the hunt supervisor Mr Carreira. During the 'clean up' around two thousand elephants were killed, being the most plentiful species in the area. Fortunately the aforementioned Mr Carreira had the happy inspiration to preserve in formaldehyde the foetuses he found. Nowadays it would be unthinkable to carry out such a slaughter.' The word 'slaughter,' I think, is unequivocal, despite its proximity to 'fortunately' and 'happy inspiration.' 'To make matter worse in this crime, that area in question never gained any form of agricultural approval; it is from this sad event that there is today a unique collection in the World.' Here we are plunged into moral relativism: would it have been less of a crime, I wonder, had the land been ploughed and sown? And for how many years would it have had to have been productive for the crime to have been less? In the final half sentence, where 'unique collection' wins out over 'sad event,' I detect a defeat for the unequivocal position signalled by 'slaughter.'

I consider what a weight of symbolism African elephants carry on their broad grey shoulders, and what a weight of history.

Quando os elefantes lutam: 1980–1983. This is Jacinto Veloso's title for his chapter on the devastating effect on Mozambique of the Cold War struggle between the superpowers.

Quando os elefantes lutam, quem sofre é o capim, goes the proverb: When elephants fight, it's the grass that suffers ...

Upstairs I wander from room to room, past shelf after shelf and case after case of things pickled and preserved in jars: lizards, snakes, terrapin, squid, jellyfish. In one room I find models of the biggest cockroaches I've ever seen, nightmare cockroaches. I glance through an open doorway into a workshop where three enormous swordfish are lying on a trestle table in a slanting shaft of dusty light.

As I descend the wide wooden staircase I see the janitor waiting by the doorway to usher me out. It's closing time. At the bottom of the stairs I spot something I hadn't noticed earlier that's neither for study nor for display, whose place within the ecosystem of the Museum is crudely functional: an elephant's foot waste paper basket. Perhaps this unregarded foot, which contains a crumpled can and a twisted tissue, was hacked from the leg of one of the Maputo elephants killed in Mr Carreira's clean-up; perhaps it's all that's left of the mother of one of the blind foetuses that's been suspended in non-amniotic fluid for a hundred years. Perhaps, I think fancifully, in some contrary way it could represent the human side of the Mozambican project, the pragmatic muddle of it, the less than perfect ecosystem of the revolution.

As I step out into the riotously overgrown garden I see the deep greens and reds of a mural by Malangatana (see **Malangatana**), splashed by the light and shade of palm fronds shifting and rattling in the evening breeze, so that it looks as if the figures themselves are moving behind the long green spikes of leaves: eyes and mouths, breasts and bellies, teeth, hands and claws, women, men, reptiles, and monsters, the quick and the dead.

Estrutura

Estrutura n., Ls, 'A reunião não se realizou porque as estruturas não compareceram.'

Dirigente, responsável, pessoa que ocupa um cargo na orgânica governamental ou partidária.

Estrutura, noun (Ls: see below): 'The meeting didn't take place because the *estruturas* didn't turn up.'

Leader, person responsible, someone who holds office in the governmental or Party organism.

The abbreviation 'Ls' in the definition above stands for '*significado*,' glossed as having a meaning in Mozambican Portuguese that's different from its meaning in European Portuguese. In literal terms *estrutura* means 'structure.' You can read it as both literal/political and as a figure of speech: the person is the structure on which is constructed the Party (while Frelimo was the only party) or government (now it's no longer a one-party state). What is the structure of the Party but the bodies of its members? Or you can read it as antonomasia: the person called by the name of the office he or she holds, that office being one part of the structure of the Party; or as synecdoche, with the whole (structure) being used to refer to a single part of it.

Although *estrutura* could be applied to anyone holding an official Party or government post, it was generally not applied to those in the highest ranks (who were sometimes referred to as *grande estrutura*, but more often as *dirigente*) but to those lower down; what in a capitalist democracy you would call middle or lower management, functionaries, or, with added value judgment, jobsworths.

In a speech given in the last few months of the liberation war, Samora called *estruturas* 'the instrument for democratizing our life' and 'the transmission belts that drive the machine' and reminded his audience that they 'are also human beings.'[1]

The example of its use given above—'the meeting didn't take place because the *estruturas* failed to turn up'—captures precisely the hollowness at the heart of some *estruturas*, though of course not all. Countless were the *reuniões* in the years of *pós-*

independência when the *estruturas* arrived half an hour, or an hour, late; or didn't turn up at all. Whether or not they felt they were too important to turn up on time, or at all, they certainly felt they were too important to offer explanation or apology.

One of the worst offences it was possible to commit was *saltar estruturas*: to jump over *estruturas*, or in other words, to fail to recognise and respect the hierarchy of the Party and government.

How my blood would boil when we teachers at the Escola Ngungunhana (see **Crítica e Auto-Crítica**) were kept waiting in the cold early mornings for *estruturas* who would then harangue us on our lack of revolutionary commitment. When it was them who were at fault, I wanted to cry, it was them!

But now, as I learn from the lexicon (see **Moçambicanismos**), *estrutura* has acquired a new meaning: it's what women call a well-formed—*bem formado*—or muscular man. Even more recently, men have begun to use it to describe women. An *estrutura* is now someone considered 'fit'; that is, not so much healthy, as 'hot.'

F

Feiticeiro

Feiticeiro n., S/C. O mesmo que muloyi (pl. valoyi) ou nyanga-muloyi (curandeiro-feiticeiro) quando o feiticeiro acumula as duas funcões. Devido a alguma confusão translinguística e transcultural, importa sublinhar que o feiticeiro não é um espiritista: o feiticeiro ocupa-se do domínio do feitiço, ao passo que o espiritista se ocupa do domínio dos espíritos (swikwembo, sing. xikwembo). Formal e informal. N.

Witchdoctor, noun, social/cultural. The same as *muloyi* or *nyanga-muloyi* (healer-witchdoctor) when the witchdoctor fulfils both functions. Due to a certain linguistic and transcultural confusion it's important to emphasise that the witchdoctor is not a spirit medium: the witchdoctor concerns himself with the world of the fetish and its enchantments, while the spirit medium works in the world of spirits (*xikwembo*). Formal and informal. Nation-wide.

Although *feiticeiro* could be translated as 'sorcerer' or 'wizard'—a *feitiço* is a fetish, so a *feiticeiro* strictly speaking would be someone who works with fetishes, for the purposes of divination, etc.—I've translated it as 'witchdoctor' in order to suggest the *feiticeiro*'s interest in doctoring. While *curandeiro* (from *curar*, to heal) might appear a more accurate name for someone mainly dealing with the doctoring/healing aspect of the work, *feiticeiro* and *curandeiro* are often used interchangeably.

A number of commentators have suggested that where Renamo (see **Renamo**) won the support of local rural populations it was at least partly because it recognised a spiritual hunger that had been ignored by Frelimo. In Renamo-controlled areas in the late 1980s the *feiticeiros* and *curandeiros*, along with the old village chiefs, regained the power they had lost in the post-independence years. From early on Frelimo had embraced science as well as scientific socialism, and while encouraging the celebration of cultural diversity as expressed in dance and song, it came out strongly against other expressions of traditional culture: initiation rites, polygamy, *lobolo* or bride price, the absolute power of tribal chiefs, and the witchdoctors and spirit mediums who played a crucial role in many if not all traditional practices.

From the early days of the armed struggle, Samora Machel often expressed strong disapproval of *feiticeiros/curandeiros* for the way they shored up personal power by playing on people's ignorance and fears. Yet it was only three or four years earlier that Samora himself, if we believe Matias Mboa's account (see **Frelimo**), visited a witchdoctor on the eve of his departure from Mozambique in March 1963. As they walked home on the last Saturday in February with their newly-bought suitcases ready for their escape, Samora suggested 'nervously' that they consult a witchdoctor (Mboa uses the word '*curandeiro*') as to the possible outcome of the adventure on which they were about to embark. Mboa, who refers to himself by his *nom de guerre* 'Thomas Khumalo' in this account, agreed with alacrity. But which one? Samora suggested they go to the one who had cured Mboa of his asthma, but Mboa, playing the sceptic, demurred: it would be better to consult one who didn't know them, for 'they often confuse what the *tihlolo* (the throw) says with what they already know about you.' Mboa had heard of a respected witchdoctor known as Pedro, who lived close to Samora's house in the suburb of Mafalala. They set off, Samora 'softly whistling a light tune, as was his habit.'[1]

They found Pedro in a small circular straw-thatched hut, surrounded by bottles, phials and bowls laid out on red, black and white cloths. They removed their shoes. Pedro was in his sixties, bald and with a wild white beard that gave an air of great charisma and dignity to his long face. A few white hairs sprouted on his naked chest. He addressed the two young men in Xironga. 'You're known as?' he asked, taking up the little basket that contained the divinatory bones and shells. 'Machel and Khumalo,' replied Samora, adding, 'We're friends.'

Mboa describes the trepidatious anxiety that rattles even the calmest of men as they await the witchdoctor's reading of the *tihlolo*. He and Samora were no exception. Their hearts fluttered as Pedro threw the *tihlolo* and watched how they fell. He muttered some words that they couldn't catch, and then he spoke: 'I see you fleeing this land. But you haven't committed any crime. You're full of fear. You're going to suffer much during your journey. But you'll arrive. You won't be caught and imprisoned and this man'—pointing his index finger at Samora—'I see him coming back as a great chief!'

Foreign Policy

The Sino-Soviet split of the late 1960s and early 70s produced a polarisation that the liberation movements which had previously looked to both countries for support found hard to resist. 'A week wouldn't pass,' writes Oscar Monteiro, 'without the news agency of each—*Novosti* or *Xinhua*—requesting the leadership of the liberation movements for a declaration of support concerning various issues.'[2] But Samora insisted that Frelimo was not in the business of supporting one or the other; it was in the business of developing its own struggle for independence and asking that other countries support that struggle. With an enormous effort of diplomacy—in the early 1970s Samora and others of the leadership visited the Soviet Union, Romania, Bulgaria, Yugoslavia and East Germany, and also China—Frelimo managed what was almost impossible: good relations with and military support from both sides.

Chinese military instructors trained Frelimo cadres at the end of the 1960s in the use of light artillery in guerrilla warfare. They shared the spartan conditions of the Frelimo training camps in Tanzania, and taught the Mozambicans the practicalities of self-sufficiency in order to help prepare them for a long-term bush war. When shocked young recruits reported to Samora what it was that the Chinese did with their night soil, he laughed, and warned them: 'Be careful not to get lost in their vegetable patch.'[3] The Soviet Union provided the heavier weapons—anti-aircraft artillery and land-to-air missiles—that Frelimo needed when Portugal intensified the war with aerial bombardment of the northern provinces (see **Behind the Lines** and **Nó Gordio**).

But when in America the Carter Presidency gave way to that of Ronald Reagan, and the Soviet Union cranked itself up for a space race and an arms race, the split between the Soviet Union and China, and its effect on Frelimo and its sister liberation movements in the other Portuguese colonies, became sidelined by the glacial drift of the Cold War. For all the valiant attempts Samora made to carry out Eduardo Mondlane's instruction to increase the number of Mozambique's friends (see **Mondlane**), and for all the support of the other Front Line States—Zambia, Tanzania, Zimbabwe (from 1980), Angola, Lesotho, Botswana and Swaziland—Mozambique, with powerful apartheid South Africa banging at its borders, became a battleground for the ideological clash between East and West.

Formulário

Formulário Nacional de Medicamentos: National Formulary of Medicines, a buff-coloured 100-page booklet published in early

1977 by the *Ministério de Saúde*, the Ministry of Health. It contained a list of all the generic drugs, divided into twenty separate groups, which would be available free of charge in the newly independent Mozambique.

Setting up a Pharmaceutical and Therapeutics Commission in order to develop a national Formulary had been one of the very first actions taken by Helder Martins on his appointment as Minister of Heath on 1 July 1975, one week after the official Declaration of Independence. The Commission reported its findings and recommendations in December 1976.

Efficacy and affordability were the foundation stones of the Formulary's list of essential drugs. In his explanatory preface to the *Formulário*, Helder Martins provided an exegesis based on an intricate intertwining of the practical and the ideological. It began: 'Capitalism's obsession with profitability results in a proliferation of commercial brands of pharmaceutical products without any relation to their therapeutic value. Sometimes the same product is marketed under a profusion of different commercial names...' Even the most committed capitalist would find it hard to quarrel with such an observation.

Ten months later, in October 1977, the World Health Organisation published an 'Essential Drugs' list (Technical Report Series 615), which replicated both the criteria used in Mozambique for selection of the drugs and the final list itself. Although over the years the pioneering work undertaken by the Pharmaceutical and Therapeutics Commission in the very first months of independence has been recognised by a number of historians of medicine, its work has never been fully credited by the WHO.[4]

Frelimo

FRELIMO: acronym of the anti-colonialist broad front *Frente de Libertação de Moçambique*: Mozambique Liberation Front, conventionally written in capital letters. Frelimo: the name of the political party into which the broad front transformed itself at its Third Congress in February 1977. For ease of reading and to avoid confusion I have used 'Frelimo' throughout.

Frelimo was created in June 1962 in Dar es Salaam, under the encouraging eye of Julius Nyerere, the passionately pan-Africanist head of newly-independent Tanzania. 'The winds of change,' sang the SWAPO Singers (the choir of the South West Africa People's Organisation) of Namibia, taking a speech made by the British Prime Minister Harold Macmillan in 1960 and turning it into a protest song, 'are sweeping across the continent of Africa.' But those winds failed, as historian Aquino de Bragança put it, to sweep across Portugal's African empire.[5] Instead Portugal tightened its control of its 'overseas provinces' and bloodily squashed any signs of nationalist aspiration. It became, wrote Oscar Monteiro, 'the duty of the Africans themselves to transform the winds into a hurricane.'[6]

Thousands of Mozambicans lived in neighbouring countries, watching and learning as those countries gained independence. Some of those Mozambicans formed their own nationalist organisations in exile: the National Democratic Union of Mozambique (UDENAMO) in Southern Rhodesia, the Mozambique African National Union (MANU) in Kenya, and the National Union of Independent Mozambique (UNAMI) in Nyasaland (later Malawi).

In 1962 the leaders of these groups took up Nyerere's offer of basing their headquarters in Tanzania but unsurprisingly, divided as they were by region, tribe, tongue and different experiences of exile, they found they had little in common and much to quarrel over, not least the form taken by their dreams of independence.

It was Eduardo Mondlane (see **Mondlane**) who brought them together and persuaded them to unite against the shared enemy that was Salazar's Portugal. He had the support of CONCP, the co-ordinating body for the nationalist movements of the Portuguese colonies, which was led by the Mozambican Marcelino dos Santos, and the support of a number of *nacionalistas do interior* who had recently fled Mozambique. With encouragement from Nkrumah in Ghana as well as from Nyerere in Tanzania, Mondlane presided over the first meeting, in June 1962, of the Mozambique Liberation Front, *Frente de Libertação de Moçambique*, or Frelimo.

When Frelimo was formed in 1962 Samora Machel, working as a nurse on the malaria ward at the Miguel Bombarda Hospital in Lourenço Marques, Ward 13 (see **Hospital**), was already under surveillance by the PIDE's agents (see **PIDE**). Nine months later, at the beginning of March the following year, he got a tip-off from João Ferreira, a Portuguese anti-colonialist who worked for a drugs company, that the PIDE was about to arrest him.

He left the next day, stopping only to tell his brother Jossefate of his plans, and to ask a Portuguese friend to look out for the family he was leaving behind. He made it across the border by night and on foot into Swaziland, from where he managed (while his co-workers covered up for him in the hospital) to cross South Africa before the PIDE was alerted to his disappearance from Lourenço Marques. He probably got to Botswana (then the British Protectorate of Bechuanaland) by bus, just one of the many black men streaming across the countries of white-dominated southern Africa with nothing but their labour to sell.

Eight days later João Ferreira made his own escape in an aeroplane piloted and hijacked for the purpose by another white Frelimo sympathiser, Jacinto Veloso of the Portuguese Air Force (see **Difficulties**). João Ferreira was interviewed by Iain Christie for his 1986 biography of Samora: that version presents Samora's flight from Mozambique both as the inevitable consequence of his increasing politicisation and also as a lonely, but urgent, journey towards his own political destiny.

A rather different story emerges in Matias Mboa's *Memórias da Luta Clandestina* (Memoirs of the Undercover Struggle).

Mboa, I discovered, accompanied Samora on the fateful journey towards Tanzania and Frelimo that began on 4 March 1963. The two men had met in 1960 at evening classes in the house of a Dr Azevedo, where they were both studying for the equivalent of secondary school second grade. At that time Samora was living in the suburb of Mafalala with his family: Sorita Tchaiakomo, to whom he was not formally married, and their three small children Juscelina, Idelson and Olívia. The great pull of Tanzania for the two ambitious young men was the presence in Dar es Salaam of Dr Eduardo Mondlane and his gift of scholarships abroad. Samora, in this story, harbours dreams of studying medicine at the Patrice Lumumba University in Moscow; he dreams of becoming a doctor.

In Mboa's version the two men had been planning to flee for months, but Samora was building a house for his children (Mboa doesn't mention the children's mother), which he didn't want to leave unfinished. In both versions João Ferreira plays his part: he tips off Samora that the PIDE are poised to seize him. But Mboa's narrative of events lacks the urgency of other accounts: the two men go downtown to buy suitcases, and later, at Samora's suggestion—the Samora who would become the great rationalist, the scourge of superstition—they visit a witchdoctor (see **Feiticeiro**) to get their futures told. Meanwhile they discuss some of the iniquities of the colonial state: the differences between the brick and concrete houses of the Portuguese and the wood and zinc of the houses in the black suburbs; the fact that precisely one black Mozambican—Eduardo Mondlane himself—is a university graduate.

Matias Mboa's book is part of a late-developing and slowly-growing body of Frelimo witness memoirs. It was published in 2009, following Helder Martins' 2001 *Porquê Sakrani? Memórias dum Médico duma Guerrilha Esquecida* (Why Sakrani? Memoirs of a Doctor in a Forgotten Guerrilla War) and Jacinto Veloso's 'hedge-hopping' memoir of 2006 (*Memórias em*

Voo Rasante), and preceding by six months Sérgio Vieira's *Participei, Por Isso Testemunho* (I Took Part, And So Bear Witness). In *Memórias da Luta Clandestina*, Mboa—confusingly—writes of himself in the third person, as Thomas Khumalo, his *nom de guerre* (see **Mutimati** for *noms de guerre*, pseudonyms, imaginary writers). For much of the book he employs a heightened poetic prose to memorialise and honour the sufferings of the thousands of Frelimo sympathisers and militants inside Mozambique who fell into the hands of the director of the PIDE, a man who 'could have passed for Hitler if he hadn't been so fat.'

In contrast to the poetic language Mboa uses for the stories of struggle, imprisonment, torture and death, he recounts in a discursive narrative prose the events of 1963, that is, his escape from Mozambique with Samora Machel, and reports lengthy conversations, as if verbatim, as if, indeed, between two characters in a novel. Which is not to question the veracity of what he recounts, but to say that Thomas Khumalo strikes the reader as a character written by Matias Mboa. The Samora of the story likewise becomes tinged with a contagious fictiveness.

A sympathetic Anglican priest known to Matias Mboa, Padre Matias Chicogo of Maciene, provided the two men with an introduction to Prince Makuku of the Swazi royal household. Under his protection and with doctored Malawian travel papers they narrowly escaped arrest by the Rhodesian border police and its consequence, the inevitable handover to the PIDE. Once they arrived in Bechuanaland they were billeted with members of the BPP, the Bechuanaland People's Party, while awaiting instructions from Dr Mondlane in Dar es Salaam. Mboa gives a vivid account of this period: of the two men sleeping on the living-room floor, of waking to the cold dawn wind that blew from the desert, of running out of money for food and surviving on a single cup of tea per day mercifully provided by their hosts. 'The days got longer and longer. They seemed to last for weeks, for centuries ... And our inability to communicate and to understand what was going on made everything much worse. Cold, hunger, and not being able to speak English or the local language. Our Calvary had begun.'[7]

Mboa's story gives us two young men, fancy free. Not in this narrative, nor in any other account that I've read of Samora's flight, do we find any mention of the women he left behind: Sorita Tchaiakomo, who at the time was pregnant with their fourth child N'tewane, and Irene Buque, a nursing colleague of Samora's, who had given birth to their daughter, Ornila, just three weeks before he left.

At last, at the end of April, word came from Mondlane. Places had been found for them aboard an ANC-chartered plane flying to Tanzania from Francistown. 'University was beginning to be a reality,' writes Mboa. Not quite the same story as the one I had imagined earlier: an ANC militant bumped off the plane at the last minute to make way for a solitary young man whose eyes blaze with revolutionary fervour (see **Aircraft**). But not entirely different either.

In Dar es Salaam Mondlane invited Machel and Mboa, along with two or three other recent arrivals, to lunch with him at the Grand Hotel, where he was then staying. He quizzed them on their reasons for leaving Mozambique and, on hearing that both hoped to be able to further their studies either in Tanzania or abroad, he urged them to think again, to consider not what they might offer to a post-independence Mozambique, but what they might offer now, in the struggle to achieve that independence. Accounts differ as to what happened next. According to Helder Martins, Samora was the first to raise his hand when Mondlane asked for volunteers for the army; the ones who immediately followed his example would make up the core of the second group who were sent to Algeria for military training, and Samora—decisive, clear and committed—would be their leader.[8]

Mboa makes the point that it was not an easy thing to give up all one's hopes and dreams just like that. In his version Samora begged Mondlane on everyone's behalf for a little time to consider. That night, we read, Thomas Khumalo (Mboa) was woken up at midnight by Samora, who asked him what they should do. 'Well, although it runs completely contrary to our plans, I think that we should agree to what Dr Mondlane proposes,' replied Khumalo with some conviction. 'Yes, that's exactly the conclusion I've come to, too,' said Samora.[9]

Samora went on, in Mboa's account, to give 'an extraordinarily sophisticated analysis' of the situation: that most of the Frelimo militants came from the centre and the north of Mozambique, so for two southerners such as Samora and Khumalo to go on to further their studies might be seen as regional favouritism.

Was Samora's political analysis already so sharp? I suspect Mboa of projecting onto this early period Samora's and Frelimo's later close concern with Mozambique's regional and tribal differences. Whether that is so or not, Samora's choice of military over medical training was hugely significant. Before the first action was ever taken, before the first shot was ever fired, Samora decided to take arms against Mozambique's sea of troubles. He decided in favour of the armed struggle. 'I was certain that the Portuguese would not give us independence and that without armed struggle the Portuguese would never agree to establish a dialogue with us,' he said.[10]

In a speech given in 2006 at Samora's birthplace, Oscar Monteiro said: 'Perhaps now that more than half a century has passed since the beginning of the end of colonialism, such an ending appears to have been almost natural, an historical inevitability. But at that moment the heroic act wasn't yet to shake colonialism to its roots, but to believe that such a thing would be possible.'[11]

Could Samora at that point, newly arrived in Dar es Salaam, have been conscious of the incipient split within Frelimo? The split that was not between the doers and the thinkers, but between those who saw that very division between doers and thinkers as right and natural, and those who saw it as counter-revolutionary?

At Frelimo's second congress in 1968 (see **Matchedje**), the delegates endorsed the concept of *o político-militar*, the parallel or indivisible nature of the political and the military struggle. Unlike some other liberation movements, Frelimo did not split itself into a political wing and an armed wing, the brains and the grunts, but remained a single united body (see **político-militar**). But in 1963 that line was as yet unformulated.

I think this was the turning-point for Samora, rather than the night he left Lourenço Marques, or the day a month or so later when he stepped onto the plane in Francistown. The turning-point was the moment that he chose to be a soldier.

Frogs' Legs

In his memoir, Sérgio Vieira recounts the following anecdote: 'Curiously, in September 1971 in Hanoi, when President Samora, Salesio, Sande, Mabote and I were lunching in the building where we were staying, we were served with some delicious frogs' legs. Some of our company liked them so much that they ordered more, and more, and more. Discovering that Samora and I were the only ones who knew what it was we were eating, at the end of the meal I said to provoke them: *Mmm, what delicious frogs' legs*. Some of our comrades nearly choked to death on the spot. '*But you liked them, my dears, didn't you?*' Samora pointed out. '*See, you must abandon your prejudices*.'[12]

G

Girassol/Sunflower

When Christopher and I arrived in Maputo in April 1978 we were billeted in a squat turret of a hotel called the Girassol, which looked out from the lip of a sandy cliff over green playing fields towards downtown Maputo and the sea. *Girassol*: turning towards the sun; sunflower. The riot of orange and red that was the garden concealed an empty swimming pool in which lay drifts of dry leaves on the cracked blue tiles.

A short, stocky, loquacious Brazilian economist called Luís took us under his wing. 'Dirty napkins,' he said with distaste as we sat at dinner in the gloomy high-ceilinged dining-room, encircled by mosaics of Portuguese personages in beards and ruffs and dark capes. He shook out his napkin to reveal old egg and tomato stains on the white cotton. 'Dirty napkins are both sign and symbol of a reactionary consciousness.' 'Are they?' Tentatively I suggested: 'Perhaps the hotel workers are too busy with socialist reconstruction to be laundering napkins?'

Scorn and pity warred in Luís's expression. 'I have heard from someone,' and here he lowered his voice and leant over the table towards us, 'from someone quite high up in the Party, that this hotel harbours a hive of reactionaries left over from colonialist times and that any day now it will be closed down.' 'They may not be very clean, but they're beautifully ironed and folded,' I said, as a nervous-looking young waiter who was not at all my idea of a reactionary approached to take our orders. 'Don't be fooled, my friend,' said Luís, as he took the proffered menu.

The neatly typed card offered a range of dishes from fish stew to fried steak but we soon discovered that it made no difference what you ordered, as there was only ever one dish on offer. Everyone got the same thing. I asked if this was part of the same political problem as the dirty napkins. 'Oh no,' said Luís. 'This is not their fault. There are shortages in the markets. Profiteers, you know. I hear,' and again he lowered his voice, 'there's going to be a clampdown.' 'Perhaps the napkins are dirty because there's a shortage of soap.' 'There's never a shortage of soap.'

A group of diners at another table were now arguing with the waiter, whose eyes were brimming with tears. They didn't like what had been put before them. 'Russians!' said Luís with scorn. 'Always complaining.'

Soon afterwards an English doctor offered us the use of his flat while he took a month's leave. The flat was on the fourth floor of a block on Avenida Julius Nyerere, at the end of Avenida Eduardo Mondlane, with a view from its back balcony over Maputo Bay. A week after we moved in we saw that on the shelves of the local *cooperativa* the dark green bars of soap stacked like bullion had been joined by an amber army of Famous Grouse whisky. We invited Luís round for a drink.

'*O povo*—the people—are getting restless,' he said, pouring himself a generous shot of Famous Grouse, and shaking his head sadly from side to side. 'They think Frelimo is to blame for the food shortages.' I thought: how does Luís know what the people think? And then I thought: who, exactly, are the people?

On his second whisky Luís cheered up, and told us of the new mood in the Girassol. 'All the *cooperantes*,' he said, 'save the Soviet bloc, went together to the manager to complain of the poor food and service, and the manager he explained that not a single escudo had he had from any of the ministries to pay for the *cooperantes* for the last ten months. It was not his fault. And now, there is no improvement, but we all talk together, and laugh, and drink whisky.' 'With the Russians?' 'No, no.' Luís shook his head in shocked denial. 'With the Cubans yes. Not with the Soviets, no.'

Thirty years on and the Girassol has reinvented itself as a four star hotel with air conditioning and a varied enough menu to satisfy the most exigent Russian and has spawned a chain of Girassols across the country, reaching as far north as Lichinga (see ***Pousada***).

Grupo Dynamizador

Dynamising Group, or Dynamic Action Group. When the Transitional Government took power in September 1974 (see **Lusaka Agreement**) *Grupos Dynamizadores* (known as GDs) were set up in city neighbourhoods, workplaces, and later throughout the country, to carry out the administrative, political and judicial functions necessary to keep the show on the road. There was no other authority in place. They were made up of local people sympathetic to Frelimo (including those who had worked clandestinely for Frelimo in preceding years), and their creation was a form of political mobilisation, which in turn mobilised the wider population. They helped prevent total social and economic collapse in the sudden, unknown post-colonial world.

H

Homem Novo

The concept of the *homem novo*, the New Man (which included the New Woman), lay close to Samora's heart. The liberation war had been fought not to swap one set of rulers for another, but to free the Mozambican people from the evils that were bred by colonialism, which included, as Samora put it: '... bribery, corruption, immorality, theft, nepotism, favours to friends, favouritism, individualism, servility, prostitution, banditry, unemployment, begging, orgies, drunkenness, drugs, the destruction of the family, social breakdown, insecurity and fear.'[1]

The *homem novo* stood in the front line of the war against the old evils. He was virtuous in thought and deed. He sacrificed private pleasure for political duty, and he led by personal example. Close your eyes and conjure up a picture of the *homem novo*: scrupulously honest, hard-working, hard-thinking, fair-minded, with a kind smile and a ready ear, a soldier, for example, who prefers everyday army fatigues to fancy uniforms, or a politician who wants to hear what the people on the street are saying...Why! it's none other than Samora himself during the final years of the liberation war and in the first years of his Presidency. And when Frelimo the liberation front became a Marxist-Leninist vanguard party in 1977 (see **Frelimo**), the *homem* *novo* became a model for Party members, who were required to possess 'outstanding political and moral qualities.'

In the words of José Luís Cabaço, Minister of Information in the early 1980s, the whole project to create the New Man drew on, 'an austere morality with protestant roots, and a cult of reason.'[2]

Like all austere moralities it claimed its victims, such as single mothers, people involved in extramarital affairs, even one of Samora's own daughters when she fell pregnant at sixteen (see ***Reeducação***).

Hospital

Around the open gateway of Maputo's Hospital Central on Avenida Eduardo Mondlane, street vendors have crammed their rickety wooden stalls. Some of what they offer would gladden the heart of any Western nutritionist: bunches of stout pink-skinned bananas, pawpaws, the ice-white flesh of split coconuts, little piles of brown-husked groundnuts. Other tasty offerings for those visiting the sick might win less official favour: drifts of boiled sweets in twists of cellophane, shiny red and green and orange, are flanked by ranks of soft drinks, bright lime, shocking pink and blazing yellow.

Pools of shade within the low hospital wall are provided by mature mango trees; scarlet bougainvillea and red and yellow canna lilies bloom in the flowerbeds. The faint but sharp scent of green leaves threads through a blanket of dust and exhaust fumes.

Christopher worked at the Hospital Central in 1978. He remembers it well, especially the ward full of patients with amoebic dysentery. He'd never come across it before in the flesh, so to speak, only in the pages of a tropical medicine textbook. An Italian surgeon showed him how to deal with the abscessed livers produced by the disease, how to suck out the contents of the abscess with a syringe, a grey brown sludge that looked like anchovy paste.

I'm walking up Avenida Eduardo Mondlane with Christopher and with the journalist Paul Fauvet, who came to Mozambique at about the same time as we did, and stayed on, witness to all the changes the country has gone through. As we approach the main entrance to the hospital, Paul points to a large banner draped above one of the side doors. '*Clínica especial*' he says, his tone indicating simultaneously both disapproval and resigned acceptance. It's not, as would likely be the case with a 'special clinic' in Britain, a VD or STD clinic, but a clinic where rich people go to jump the national health service queue.

'The government's tried to clamp down,' says Paul, 'but the doctors are determined it should stay.' 'Like doctors the world over,' says Christopher. 'They say,' Paul tells us, 'what's wrong with rich people paying money into the public health service if they can afford it?' Christopher: 'Doctors always say that.'

In 1952, after six months spent as a nursing auxiliary at the provincial hospital in Xai-Xai, Samora Machel moved to Lourenço Marques to join a cohort of seventy-five African nursing students at the Hospital Miguel Bombarda, as it was then called. Samora was educated to as high a degree within the school system as could be reached by '*indígenos*' (see **Assimilado**); he was bilingual, speaking both his mother tongue, Xichangana, and the language of the colonialists, Portuguese, and had a smattering of English. He was ambitious and outgoing; and he was steeped in stories of resistance and of right. He had a heart-melting smile, a handsome face and the ability to make friends, and to attract lovers.

The trainee nurses, who came from all areas of Mozambique, were housed in a dilapidated building that also provided shelter for the hospital's mental patients. One large room was divided down the middle by a wooden partition that didn't reach the ceiling. On one side three long rows of narrow cots formed the students' dormitory; on the other side of the partition lived the mental patients. The latter were noisy at the best of times and when especially excited or distressed they would sometimes clamber over the partition into the students' side of the room. But despite such disturbances the students spent most evenings studying in the dormitory, for they were kept hard at work on the wards all day long. Late into the night, according to Aurélio Manave, who like Samora would escape to Tanzania to join Frelimo, he and Samora and a handful of others would discuss the injustices of the colonial system and exchange stories they'd heard of Nasser and the revolution he'd led in Egypt.[3]

Samora's heroes then were Nasser and Nkrumah, and the black American boxers who'd risen from deprived backgrounds on the wings of their physical prowess. On the little wall space by his bed he stuck boxing photos he'd cut out of magazines. Although Iain Christie, Samora's first biographer, says Samora did not himself box, later commentators suggest otherwise, and claim he became head of the nurses' dormitory after beating the previous dormitory head in a boxing match.[4] His nickname was 'Jack Dempsey,' and in Algeria eleven years later he would settle with his fists the angry rows about race that were threatening to tear apart the group of young Frelimo cadres who were receiving military training. Perhaps Christie was writing too soon after Samora's death; his interviewees might have thought a fist-fighting Samora a little undignified.

Portuguese doctors at the Miguel Bombarda Hospital could strike black nurses and other underlings with impunity, and Samora's brother Jossefate tells the story of Samora grabbing a doctor's hands to stop him lashing out. As Samora lacked neither ambition nor application, it might have been these signs of physical fearlessness, or perhaps his tendency to answer back, or the fact that he had become spokesperson for the student nurses, that led to his failing the final exams. He bit his tongue and repeated the year, passing, with second to top marks, in 1954. He was now a qualified nurse. But he was at the lowest grade, and would stay there unless he somehow managed to get further educational qualifications.

He was appointed 'native nurse' for the health post on Inhaca Island, across the bay from the capital, where he was to stay for three years. A photograph from this period, 1957 or thereabouts, shows him in the dispensary. The photograph is so bleached out that his white smock blends into the white of the wall behind. His left forearm is bisected by the white streak of a wristwatch. His right hand is raised, the fingers, with spots of white for the nails, curled to balance the spoonful of medicine that he's about to give to the man seated in front of him, who lifts his eyes, trustful and patient, towards Samora's face. Samora's looking sideways at the photographer, at us. The light catches the gleam of his forehead, the whites of his eyes. His mouth is used to smiling, but he's not smiling. He's keeping his own counsel.

On the island he fell in love with a local Nyaka girl, Sorita Tchaiakomo, and set up house with her. In 1958 they moved back to Lourenço Marques with their two children, Juscelina and Idelson (Olívia, their third child, was born in 1961, and N'tewane in 1963, after Samora had left Mozambique), to a house in the suburb of Mafalala. Samora took a job back at the Miguel Bombarda Hospital. He wanted to take further training at the 'European' nursing level, the entrance requirement for which was grade two of secondary education. A Dr Adalberto Azevedo offered evening classes, which he held in his father's unused garage, for Africans needing the qualifications that they'd not been allowed to get. It was here in Dr Azevedo's garage that Samora met Matias Mboa, his companion when he fled Mozambique in 1963 (see **Frelimo**).

Over the next few years he continued to move up the school grades, attending a Methodist College in Malhangalene, and then for fifth grade the 'Fernando Pessoa' school of a Dr Jaime Rebelo. This all cost money. He spent just under a third of his salary on getting further qualifications (350 escudos a month out of a salary of 1,300); but even as a 'native nurse' he was earning five times as much as a domestic servant.[5]

With fifth grade under his belt, he was qualified at last for entrance into the one-year 'normal' nursing course, except ... it was open only to 'non-natives,' that is, whites and *assimilados*. In a reprise of his primary schooling, when he had to be baptised Catholic in order to take fourth grade, he now had to become *assimilado*, an honorary white, in order to take the qualifications to be a proper nurse. The historian Fernando Ganhão suggests that this demand on the part of the authorities was the second 'violent alienation' of Samora's sense of self and identity (see **Baobab**), and that it further provoked the spirit of rebellion that would carry him into the struggle for Mozambique's liberation.[6] But ambition, determination, and a capacity for hard work had by now become integral to Samora's being, and these outweighed his distaste for or anger with the humiliations inflicted by the colonialist state. His identity was safe from undermining. He requested *assimilado* status. There seem to be no records of whether he achieved it; the request itself sufficed to let him enrol on the one-year course.[7]

He started attending political meetings. When Eduardo Mondlane arrived in Lourenço Marques in early 1961 on a three month visit, Samora became a regular visitor to the house where Mondlane was staying, under the protection of his hosts, the Swiss Protestant Mission. Mondlane, tall, fluent and charismatic, preached revolutionary change and an end to colonialism, and twenty-eight-year-old Samora Machel, conscious of a range of injustices he'd already suffered, drank it in. Beneath the acacias on the further pavement stood the agents of the security police (see **PIDE**), noting down the names of all the young nationalists, black and white, who visited the Swiss Mission to listen and to learn. Fired up by what they'd heard, Samora and a nursing colleague called Albino Maheche became involved with a group of students from the Commercial School, meeting them to talk and to write leaflets.[8] This might have brought them into contact with student leader Filipe Samuel Magaia, and with fifteen-year-old Josina Muthemba (see **Josina**).[9]

Political activity was a dangerous business, for the Portuguese authorities considered even the slightest hint of a nationalist tendency to be illegal. To state that Mozambique was a country, rather than a province of Portugal, was in itself an act of treason. All dissidents eventually ended up in exile, or in prison, or dead. In August that year Maheche was arrested and questioned, and the next year Samora was twice pulled in by the PIDE, but was released both times for lack of evidence.

Meanwhile he was working on Ward 13, the malaria ward, of the Miguel Bombarda Hospital. His work and his politics were coming together: he saw in the hospital structures a reflection of the Portuguese colonialist world, one in which poor whites suffered as well as, if not as much as, the African population. 'Eminent doctors and university professors are brought in to treat the capitalist's cold, to cure the judge's constipation,' he said, 'while nearby children are dying, people are dying, because they did not have the money to call a doctor.'[10]

Ward 13 was where João Ferreira (see **Frelimo**) sought out Samora in early 1963. He motioned Samora outside to warn him he'd been betrayed by an informant and was about to be arrested and imprisoned. Samora replied apocryphally, prophetically, 'In every revolution there are traitors.' A photograph taken in 2001 shows a grey-bearded João Ferreira, who'd gone on to become a minister in the Frelimo government, standing on the stairs where he and Samora had held this whispered conversation. He recalled their relative positions: Samora, the black nurse, one step higher than the white drugs company representative. In the urgency of the moment they'd breached conventional racial etiquette. Samora would remember this later and tease Ferreira: 'You see, Ferreira, even then I was your chief!'[11]

Political activity was a dangerous business, for the Portuguese authorities considered even the slightest hint of a nationalist tendency to be illegal. To state that Mozambique was a country, rather than a province of Portugal, was in itself an act of treason. All dissidents eventually ended up in exile, or in prison, or dead. In August that year, Machel was arrested and questioned, and the next year Samora was twice pulled in by the PIDE, but was released both times for lack of evidence.

Meanwhile he was working on Ward [illegible], the malaria ward, of the Miguel Bombarda Hospital. His work and his politics were coming together. [illegible] the hospital structures a reflection of the Portuguese colonialist [illegible] [illegible] [illegible] [illegible] the Mozambique population [illegible] [illegible] [illegible] to cure the ruler's consumption,' he said, 'while nearby children are dying, people are dying, because they did not have the money to see a doctor.'[8]

[illegible] [illegible] [illegible] [illegible] [illegible] [illegible] Samora, in early 1963. He [illegible] Samora [illegible] to work [illegible][11]

I

Ilha

Island. Specifically, Ilha de Moçambique; Mozambique Island, lying in the Indian Ocean a kilometre or so off the coast of Nampula province. Once the capital of the country. Crescent-shaped, 3 km long, joined to the mainland at the southern end of its curved back by a long low single-track bridge.

A palimpsest for conflicts over land use, water rights and sanitation rights (see ***Latrinas***). An island divided between the stone town and the reed town.

For the protagonist of the Angolan novelist José Eduardo Agualusa's *My Father's Wives*, Ilha is the end of the road that has led from Angola round the southern tip of the continent and up through Mozambique; home for twenty years to the Italian doctor Rino Scuccato, whose experiences in the northern provinces in the mid-1980s inform his dense, passionate and critical memoir of the Mozambican revolution, *La Deviazione di Rotta* (*A Different Destination*).

Ghost town of the colonial era.

Famous for the beauty of its young women, who wear a face mask of white paste, the *misuril*.

J

Josina

She was my heroine before ever Samora became my hero. How could I, aged twenty-one, resist her, as she looked down at me from the wall of my bedroom in north London, pigtailed and smiling, with her AK47 and her jaunty beret, and a dream of freedom in her eyes?

The poster—made up of pixellated shades of grey on thin yellow paper—is one of a set produced in Mozambique in 1974 to celebrate *dez anos de guerra popular*: ten years of people's war. This particular one, the blown-up photograph of a young woman in brilliant sunshine against an amorphous leafy background, advertises 7 April, Mozambican Women's Day.

The bright sunlight bounces off her forehead and cheekbones, her eyelids, nose and teeth. Her smile accentuates the high cheekbones, which cast a shadow over the lower half of her face. Her eyes, too, are shadows, but you know they're smiling. She wears a beret at a jaunty angle: it slants down to the right, and the ends of two short pigtails peep out on either side. A jumper shows ribbing round its V-neck, and over her left breast a little pocket with an open flap casts a small dark triangular shadow.

She looks no older than eighteen, and she radiates health and happiness. She could be the daughter you're so proud of, she could be a Girl Guide or school prefect, or she could be the older sister who always looks out for you, or the girl in your class everyone wants to be best friends with. Except for the barrel of the AK47 pointing skywards behind her right shoulder. Her right hand curls in front of the shoulder strap that holds the gun in place. She's hooked her thumb behind the strap to ease the weight and to add some balance, like a schoolgirl with a book-filled rucksack hanging off one shoulder.

Smiling girl with gun. This is Josina. She looks like the girl who goes out with the boy everybody else wants to go out with, the good-looking boy who, like her, is clever and kind and smiles at you and the world. This is Josina Muthemba, and she is going out with that boy, and his name is Samora Machel.

A square of two narrow red lines frames the photo, and a short poem is printed in red sans serif above her left shoulder, balancing the gun on the other side. It comes from a poem by Samora, *Josina, You Are Not Dead*.[1] On the poster it is unattributed (see **Mutimati** for a variation on the non-attribution of poetry during the armed struggle), and is entitled only 'Josina': *Quando, como tu,/ uma camarada assume/ tão intensamente/ os novos valores,/ ela ganha o nosso coracão/ torna-se nossa bandeira*: When, like you,/ a comrade embraces/ so ardently/ our new-forged values,/ she wins our heart/ becomes our banner.

Josina Muthemba, born 10 August 1945, came from a family which had long been involved in anti-colonial activities: her grandfather was a Presbyterian lay preacher who preached against colonialism and for a national Mozambican identity. Her father was a nurse in Gaza province and the family were *assimilado*, a status that allowed Josina, unlike Samora, to continue education up to secondary level (see ***Assimilado***). She moved to live with her grandmother in Lourenço Marques so as to attend commercial school, where she became active in NESAM (*Núcleo dos Estudantes Africanos Secondários de Moçambique*), the organisation of African secondary school students which Eduardo Mondlane had helped set up in 1949, and through which a number of young black Mozambicans gained their political education. Is this where she met Filipe Samuel Magaia, army conscript and part-time student? Magaia fled Mozambique ahead of Samora, joined Frelimo and led the first group of young militants to be trained in Algeria.

In March 1964, a year after Samora had fled the country, Josina Muthemba, aged eighteen, made a first attempt to flee Mozambique in order, like him, to join Frelimo in Tanzania. The venture ended in failure. She and her friends, who included the future President Armando Guebuza, managed to get as far as Victoria Falls in Northern Rhodesia, where they were caught and returned to the Portuguese authorities in Lourenço Marques. She spent five months in prison. She was allowed to return to school but was now closely watched by the security police. The following year she tried again to flee with another group of students. This time, by the skin of their teeth, after months spent in refugee camps in Swaziland and Zambia, and after narrowly escaping betrayal by informers and receiving help from secret supporters, some of the group—but not all of them—made it at last to Dar es Salaam. One of Josina's uncles, Matheus Sansão Muthemba, a radio operative, was already there, a member of Frelimo's central committee.

In the first year she spent in Tanzania Josina worked as assistant to Janet Mondlane, the director of the Mozambique Institute, who became a close friend. Josina regularly babysat the Mondlanes' three small children, and moved into their house in Dar es Salaam to look after them when, as sometimes happened, Janet and Eduardo were away simultaneously on fund- and profile-raising trips abroad.

Josina became engaged to Filipe Samuel Magaia, now head of the Frelimo armed forces. When he was murdered in 1966 by a PIDE agent who'd infiltrated the FPLM ranks, Josina was told by her uncle Sansão Muthemba in no uncertain terms to wipe away her tears and keep her mouth shut. Why? Because to weep was a sign of weakness? Because at that time women were seen as secondary to the struggle? Or because he thought his niece might draw unwelcome attention to herself, as another target for the PIDE? Muthemba himself would meet a violent death two years later at the hands of anti-Frelimo rebels (see **Matchedje**). Josina wept in Janet Mondlane's arms, then dried her eyes and soon afterwards was accepted as one of the earliest recruits to the Women's Detachment of the FPLM (see ***Destacamento Feminino***). In July 1968 she was a delegate at Frelimo's Second Congress (see **Matchedje**), where she spoke passionately in favour of women's inclusion in all aspects of the liberation struggle.

With the Second Congress Frelimo entered its most turbulent period. When Eduardo Mondlane was killed by a parcel bomb in Dar es Salaam on 3 February 1969 (see **Mondlane**), Josina moved in to live with and give support to her friend Janet, his widow. By then Josina and Samora were deeply in love. How could they not have been? Two passionate idealists living and working together at the very heart of a dangerous revolutionary enterprise, surrounded by secret enemies, thousands of miles distant from their childhood homes, light-years from their past lives. That's how I imagined it when I was twenty-one, looking at the poster of smiling Josina with her plaits, her cocked beret and her AK47, brave, big-hearted, not much older than me, and already dead.

I didn't know then that Josina had lost her first love, nor that Samora already had five children and two separate families. I found, later, that when I asked people if they and all the comrades in Dar es Salaam in the late 1960s had known about Sorita and Irene and their children with Samora, I never received a definite answer. People weren't sure. Some said they thought it was known but wasn't considered a big deal; others thought they remembered how at independence—with Josina long dead and Samora about to be married to Graça Simbine—people were taken aback (to put it mildly) when Samora produced all these other children. But, they all hastened to tell me, he had then done the right thing. All the children were brought up together in his and Graça's household. It's hard enough to remember the details of events of more than forty years ago, let alone the order in which they happened, and least of all, perhaps, one's state of knowledge at the time. Particularly so when the intervening years are crammed with incident and change: a successfully waged liberation struggle, independence and power, barely a breathing space before the struggle starts again, this time against an even more powerful and determined opponent, deaths, murders, losses, disillusion perhaps. I wasn't surprised that the people I spoke to couldn't remember whether or not they'd known.

In his memoir *Porquê Sakrani?*, Helder Martins tells of hearing about Samora's children and their mothers from Aurélio Manave, nurse and colleague of Martins at the Mozambique Institute in the mid-1960s. Martins, who enjoyed a close relationship with Samora (see **Samora**), raised the subject with him soon after. Samora was extremely reluctant to discuss the matter, reports Martins. He was obviously distressed, and spoke with tears in his eyes. He castigated himself for *um comportamento incorrecto*—bad behaviour—and blamed the colonial system for his attitude towards women. Through Frelimo, he confided in Helder Martins, he'd come to understand how badly he'd treated them.[2]

I remain curious about whether Josina knew. If she did, she didn't tell her friend and marriage sponsor Janet Mondlane. It wasn't the first time she'd had to keep her feelings secret.

Perhaps starting a third family didn't seem problematic to Samora, a Shangaan from the patriarchal, polygamous south of the country? But not only was Samora's family background Christian rather than tribal, but his own political journey had led him to a belief in equality between women and men, which, translated into domestic practice, led to the same end as his Christian upbringing: monogamous marriage.

Marriage was encouraged within the ranks of Frelimo as a means of equalising the roles of women and men and in order to regularise sexual relationships. The men who'd shaken their heads and tut-tutted at the idea of women in the guerrilla army and prophesied tears at bedtime would be wrong-footed by the respectability and high morals of the Frelimo soldiers. Samora Machel, as military commander and as one of the presidential triumvirate, needed to set an example of probity for others to follow. When in 1977 Frelimo turned itself into a Marxist-Leninist vanguard party, it would ban people in polygamous marriages from becoming party members (along with religious believers and owners of means of production). Although before its transformation Frelimo didn't exclude polygamists, it nonetheless began from early days to theorise monogamous marriage as an integral part of the revolutionary New Morality (see ***Homem Novo***), somewhat to the consternation of the Western *cooperantes*, who, back home in the liberal West, had for some years been theorising monogamous marriage as an integral part of an anti-revolutionary old morality that needed to be overthrown as swiftly as possible.

But in the late 1960s the armed struggle looked as if it might carry on for years and years. When would the guerrillas see again the families they'd left behind in southern or central Mozambique? Samora probably thought he might never see Sorita Tchaiakomo or Irene Buque again. Nonetheless I can't help thinking that it was fortunate for Samora that he hadn't actually married either of the two women who were already the mothers of his children. He was free to marry Josina.

In May 1969 Josina Muthemba and Samora Machel were married in Tunduru in southern Tanzania.

Whatever the backstory, and the previous relationships on both sides, everyone says that electricity sparked between them. Photos published with the memoirs that have been trickling out since 2000 confirm this. They were mad about each other. In

Raimundo Pachinuapa's book about the Second Congress one of the photos shows the marriage ceremony: Josina and Samora in battle fatigues, sturdy shoes, matching peaked caps. Maybe it's the actual moment that they exchange vows, for they're looking into each other's eyes, their faces illuminated by joy, Josina's right arm beginning to rise as if she can't stop herself reaching out to touch him. Next to Josina stand her two sponsors, Janet Mondlane and Aurélio Manave, and on Manave's right at the end of the row Marcelino dos Santos looks on with hands on hips. On Samora's left, his two sponsors, a smiling Marina Pachinuapa and Samora's second-in-command Alberto Joaquim Chipande (see ***Behind the Lines***), with Armando Guebuza, arms folded, at the end of the row. In a white suit, elbows crooked and palms up, the man conducting the ceremony must be asking the actual question, do you take ...?, and that's why Josina and Samora are smiling into each others' eyes as they answer, We do!

And the man conducting the ceremony? There may be backstories and subtexts to the falling in love and getting married of Josina and Samora; the marriage ceremony itself contains another narrative that will spool out into the future. The man who married them was Uria Timotei Simango (see **Matchedje** and **Simango**), at that time one of the triumvirate leadership of Frelimo, already implicated by association in the murder of Eduardo Mondlane and already some way along the road that would eventually lead, over ten years later, to his execution in a camp in Niassa.

In November 1969 Josina gave birth to Samito—little Samora. She didn't quite recover her strength but nonetheless, as soon as she felt able, she left Samito to be looked after in Dar and returned to work in Niassa and Cabo Delgado, where as head of Social Affairs she was responsible for the welfare and education of war orphans and for the health and education of all children in the war zones. She also ran the women's section of Frelimo's department of international relations and travelled to conferences abroad where she spoke for Frelimo and for the essential role that women could play in the anti-colonial struggle. But she was beginning to lose weight. She was feeling increasingly exhausted.

It's not clear—versions differ—whether Josina was suffering from liver cancer or from leukaemia. Either would have been fatal. Back in Tanzania she wept to Janet: 'I'm the unluckiest woman alive.'[3] In the middle of 1970 she travelled to Moscow for treatment, but the Soviet doctors suggested only rest and a healthy diet as remedies. At the end of that year she spent two months working in Niassa. Then in early 1971 she returned to the liberated zones, this time for a gruelling tour of Cabo Delgado. The story goes that coming back out of Mozambique at the end of March, she stopped on the banks of the Rovuma and handed her pistol to a companion, saying, 'Comrades, I can continue no longer. Give this to the military commander of the province so that it may contribute to the salvation of the Mozambican people.'[4] Apocryphal words perhaps, but the mention of the pistol rings true, for by then she was too weak to bear the weight of an AK47.

She died in Dar es Salaam on 7 April 1971, aged twenty-five. In a speech entitled 'And I also saw him cry,' given in Maputo on the fifteenth anniversary of Samora's death, Oscar Monteiro recalled how, at the very beginning of a session of the Central Committee in 1972, when Marcelino spoke Josina's name in the list he was reading out of those *camaradas* already fallen, Samora broke into such a tempest of weeping that they were obliged to break off the session.[5]

Samora's poem ends:

How can we mourn a comrade but by holding the fallen gun and continuing the combat?

My tears flow from the same source that gave birth to our love, our will and our revolutionary life.

Thus these tears are both a token and a vow of combat.

The flowers which fall from the tree are to prepare the land for new and more beautiful flowers to bloom in the next season.

Your life continues in those who continue the Revolution.

Guns and tears and flowers: the tropes of mid-twentieth century liberation movement poetry and song. Those who continue the Revolution, '*os continuadores*': it came to mean, simply, 'children.' Beautiful beloved Josina, dead at twenty-five, toting over her shoulder a gun that in the intervening years has come to stand for savage death and the brutalisation of children in a number of African countries, of which Mozambique, with its long post-independence fight against apartheid-backed Renamo, was one of the first.

The anniversary of Josina's death is celebrated as Mozambican Women's Day. Josina, forever young, beautiful and hopeful, has achieved the mythic status of invented heroes (see **Mutimati** again), has become, as Samora's poem declares, '*nossa bandeira*.'

Junod

Henri Alexandre Junod (1863–1934), anthropologist and missionary of the Protestant Swiss Romande Mission, working in southern Africa from the 1890s. For some years one of his fellow missionaries acted as personal physician to the Emperor of Gaza (see **Ngunghunhana**), setting a template for two generations of hostile relationships between the Swiss Protestants and the Portuguese authorities, which culminated in the murder of the head of the Swiss Mission in a Lourenço Marques prison in 1972 (see ***Orientações***).

Junod was a naturalist and a linguist, collected butterflies and folk tales, and published a grammar and analysis of the Xironga language. His study of the Thongas (or Tsongas) of southern Mozambique, *The Life of a South African Tribe*, was published in two volumes in 1912 and 1913. The Thongas are now more commonly known as Shangaan or Tshangaan, which was in those days, according to Junod, a white appellation 'applied in Johannesburg to all the East Coast "boys,"'[6] and thus considered an insult.

The high proportion of Shangaan in the Frelimo leadership—including Eduardo Mondlane, Samora Machel, Joaquim Chissano and Sebastião Mabote—provided both a constant source of disquiet to critics, and, on the other hand, a focus for the constantly articulated strong ideological Party line against tribalism and regionalism (the two blurring and overlapping). Anxious muttering about tribal and regional dominance is still alive and strong in the government of Armando Guebuza (mother-tongue Xironga but born in Nampula). Perhaps a parallel can be drawn with anxieties in Western democracies about positive discrimination and the representation of minorities and the historically disadvantaged or underdeveloped. After all, the push and pull of tribal loyalties is hardly unique to African countries.

K

Kanimambo

Kanimambo n., Le. Kanimambo provém originariamente da lingua Xironga e significa obrigado, estar agradecido. O uso da palavra no PM remonta ao periodo colonial e intensificou-se de forma generalizada nas décadas de 70 e 80 no contexto da euforia revolucionária que o país viveu após a sua Independência. A canção Kanimambo Frelimo ecoou por todo o Moçambique através da voz do primeiro Presidente da República, Samora Machel, e foi amplamente divulgada. Est. neutro. N.

This Xironga word meaning 'thank you' was very widely used in what the lexicon calls the context of the 'revolutionary euphoria' in which the country was steeped after independence. 'The song *Kanimambo Frelimo* echoed the length and breadth of Mozambique through the voice of the first President of the Republic, Samora Machel …'

The lyrics are simple: *Kanimambo, kanimambo Frelimo* (the first word sung slowly, each syllable in its own space, the next two sung faster, the notes descending)/ *Kanimambo, kanimambo Frelimo* (same speed, notes ascending)/ *Kanimambo, kanimambo Frelimo* (as in the first line)/ *Kanimambo-o Fre-li-i-mo*. Thank you, thank you Frelimo.

More than a quarter of a century after his death, people not only remember Samora's voice and describe it as electrifying, embracing, inspiring, but many of them, when they speak of him or quote his words, unconsciously mimic its very pitch and timbre.

L

Latrinas

Imagine: two National Latrine Digging Days, as part of the National Environmental Sanitation Campaign instituted post-independence (see ***Pós-Independência***), with Samora himself wielding a pick-axe and a spade. All the government ministers, some of whom are already pleased to be out of combat gear and makeshift huts and into Western-style suits and offices in the capital with flushing lavatories and people to clean them, are obliged to follow his lead. Where people shit and how they dispose of it: Samora knew how important that was.

Before I visited the Ilha de Moçambique (see ***Ilha***) in 2008 I had been warned that the beaches all round the island were spoiled by people shitting on them. I found this to be an exaggeration: the tide, after all, washes the beaches clean twice a day. But it was the young man showing us round the reed town at the south of the island, where the great majority of the inhabitants live, who put it starkly: we have communal toilets, he told us, but would you rather use a tiny box of a room that two hundred other people use, or would you rather go by the edge of the sea?

Samora is remembered for his insistence on the centrality of manual work (see **Nachingwea**). Cleaning, digging, planting, cooking: human dignity is based upon this work. Everybody should know how to dig a latrine, and if they didn't know, then Samora would show them. But it can be quite annoying to be always told how to do something that you think you know how to do quite well. One of the teachers at Ribaué, a Frelimo school in Nampula province, remembers Samora's visit in the late 1970s: Samora giving a speech that lasted for five hours, and then inspecting the kitchen and finding fault with the method of construction of the cooking fires.

Leão/Lion

In 1978, towards the end of the dry season when game was scarce, a pair of lionesses took up residence in the pine forest on the edge of Lichinga. Their first victim was a man drunk on *cajulima* (see ***Cajulima***). Their second was a woman with a baby on her back. People ran from their huts when they heard her cry out and chased the lioness away, but they were too late. The woman's body appeared untouched, save for five small fine cuts fanned out below her right shoulder blade. She died of a punctured lung: the lioness had placed one paw against her back, and flexed her claws their full five-inch length. The baby was unharmed. A hunting party went out next day and tracked and shot one of the lionesses. They dragged the body into town and hung it by its front paws from the branch of a low umbrageous tree (afterwards known to all as the lion tree) opposite the baker's. As word flew from mouth to mouth, *leão, leão*, everyone came running. My heart was hammering although I knew the beast was dead. Ten feet long from outstretched paws to tip of tail, with muscles stretched and visible beneath the tawny strong-smelling coat: she was magnificent. The soldier who had shot her stood beside her solemn and proud, and then he reached up with a knife to cut the rope that bound her to the branch. As she hit the earth we jumped back, some of us laughed to cover our fear, and we let out a collective sigh of relief, awe and pity.

Lembrança/Remembrance

Não vamos esquecer, we shall not forget, Samora would shout, hands stretched out towards the crowd; *não vamos esquecer*, the crowd would roar back, promising Samora that they won't forget either, pledging their remembrance to his. *Lembrança*: remembrance, the calling up of the past, the re-membering or even re-creating of a past that gives meaning to the present. What's the difference between remembrance and memory? *Lembrança* and *memória*?

Sometimes everyone would sing:

> *Não vamos esquecer o tempo que passou*
> (We shall not forget what happened in the past)
> *Não vamos esquecer o tempo que passou*
> *Não vamos, não vamos esquecer*
>
> *O pai de cinco filhos e chamado um rapaz*
> *A mãe de cinco filhas e chamada rapariga*
> *O fascista de quinze anos e chamado 'o senhor'*
> *Quem pode esquecer o que passou?*
> (The man with five sons of his own is called 'boy'
> The mother of five daughters is called 'girl'
> The fifteen-year-old fascist is called 'sir'
> Who can forget what happened?)[1]

Both Mozambique's colonial past and the more recent history of those who had lost their lives in the struggle needed to be constantly remembered so as to give meaning to the present of the revolution. Remembered, rather than memorialised. Perhaps memorialisation creates a gap between present and past, whereas *lembrança*—remembrance—closes that gap, takes into itself the meaning of the word you can trace within it: 'embrace.'

Lichinga

By October 1979 Samora Machel had been President of the country for four years. He was *o dirigente máximo*: the big chief. He travelled with an entourage of aides and advisers. Five years previously he'd passed through Lichinga, capital of Niassa, on his journey from the Rovuma to the Maputo. He wasn't President then, but a soldier in combat gear leading an army of lean guerrilla fighters. Lichinga had been Vila Cabral; Lourenço Marques was now Maputo. He hadn't returned to Niassa since.

'Quem não conhece Niassa, não conhece Moçambique': 'If you don't know Niassa, then you don't know Mozambique.' Part of the appeal of this song was its nuance of subversiveness. We all knew there was no room for regionalism in the new Mozambique, but at public meetings with visiting *estruturas* from the capital city, we sang it with defiance as if to prove that Niassa was just as good as any other province, and even if sometimes we felt ignored or neglected by the power-brokers in Maputo, well, it was their loss rather than ours.

Just as the local people viewed with suspicion the officials sent up from the south to organise them, so we Western *cooperantes* (see ***Cooperantes***) felt superior to our counterparts in Maputo who, toiling in the ministries, may have been closer to the engine-house of the revolution, but nonetheless led soft lives of urban ease (or so we imagined). In 1979 many of us felt that the failure of Samora, *o dirigente máximo*, to have yet returned to the northern province of Niassa, which was, after all, the site of the early liberated and semi-liberated zones of the independence war and the very cradle of the revolution, indicated his estrangement from the real Mozambique. In the weeks leading up to his visit to Lichinga in October 1979 we sang *'Quem não conhece Niassa, não conhece Moçambique'* with added attitude.

Rumours started flying from mouth to mouth from the moment we were told of the impending visit. By the beginning of the second week *o nosso presidente* would arrive on Wednesday, then on Thursday, again on Friday; an enormous plane, a Boeing no less, had landed at night with stocks of food and his personal cooks to cook it; first he would visit the primary school, no, the hospital, no, the state farm.

L

The town was convulsed in a frenzy of *limpeza*, cleaning. In the Escola Ngungunhana we abandoned lessons and spent our time whitewashing the classrooms and sweeping and re-sweeping the open corridors to clean them of the fine red dust that settled every day.

As the week wore on the pessimists began to find their tongues. The President wasn't actually going to come, he was too busy dealing with the Rhodesia crisis and he'd send some junior minister instead. But such sceptical voices were silenced when a different kind of *limpeza* was carried out overnight. Suddenly the streets were empty of *reeducados* (see ***Reeducação***) and of prisoners in their tattered clothes. The latter were back behind their concrete walls and barbed wire, the *reeducados* swiftly and silently removed to their primitive camps out in the countryside.

Street-cleaning of such a kind silenced the doubters and confirmed the rumours: the President would arrive imminently. The removal of misfits, dissidents and underdogs from the sight of emperors, monarchs and presidents has always featured as one of the duties of courtiers and functionaries, as if the very presence of such people on the streets might somehow tarnish the lustre of the Head of State. The *marginais*, marginals, as they were called, are the ones who cannot or will not be incorporated into the body politic, the ones who in their threadbare townie trousers or their egregious mini-skirts, symbolise the impossibility of the dream of unity.

By nine o'clock on Sunday morning a crowd has gathered on the road at the edge of town that leads out to the airport, the road that runs alongside the walls of the Escola Ngungunhana, where we're all still busy sweeping and tidying. Boys with big hide drums slung round their necks move through the crowd, their hands like fluttering birds bouncing off the taut drumskins. Circles of dancing women in bright headscarves and *capulanas*, yellow and red and blue and green, crouch down and straighten up, they clap their hands and shuffle their feet, they move and sway and call out *ululay*, *ululay*, to the rhythm beaten out by the nimble-fingered boys.

The hospital Toyota races down the road and Melo, the nurse, calls out of the window: the President is coming. A cavalcade of shiny black cars snakes round the corner, slows down, and stops at the edge of the crowd. Out of the fourth car steps Samora Machel, dressed in combat fatigues. He grins and strides through the crowd, with his soldier bodyguards scurrying to keep pace. Now he's a pied piper, stocky and handsome, at the head of an army of women and boys and girls, cheering, drumming and singing. Further up the road outside the garage on the corner a group of men are gathered. More inhibited than the women, they look anxiously at each other for a lead in protocol as the terrifying figure of the President of the country swiftly approaches, but they break into shy smiles as Samora stops and shakes hands left and right. He leans forward to shake hands with the three white men at the back of the group. What's your work? he asks, and, when two of them say they're geologists looking for coal, he asks how much they've found, laughing when he hears the answer, very little. The women have formed dancing circles again while they wait for the President to move on.

* * *

Samora was approaching the mid-point of his Presidency of the country he'd led to independence. During the previous five years he and the comrades had been trying to turn the high ideals of the liberation struggle into an everyday reality, so that *o povo*—the people—could live the freedom that had been won. But two major tasks had been sucking up Samora's time and energy: firstly, drumming up international support for the Mozambican dream by winning over the hostile countries of the West while paying due respect to those countries—from the East—that had offered friendship all along. Secondly, dealing with neighbouring Rhodesia's toxic spillage over the perilously long border (see **Renamo**).

By the time the Presidential Boeing touched down at Lichinga airport on 14 October, Samora had already that year flown to London and Washington, had attended two summits of Heads of the Front Line States (one in Luanda, the other in Lusaka) and had held six or seven separate meetings with Presidents Nyerere and Kaunda. Almost as soon as he arrived in Lichinga, later that very day, before any hospital or school or state farm was visited, he was called away to attend yet another meeting of the Front Line States, this time an emergency meeting: Ian Smith was escalating his cross-border raids, while the fragile Patriotic Front alliance between Robert Mugabe's ZANU and Joshua Nkomo's ZAPU was looking likely to crumble at any moment.

Did Samora believe that if a peaceful transfer of power could be negotiated for Rhodesia/Zimbabwe then perhaps, at last, he would be able to concentrate on the hopes and desires of his own people? As it turned out, the absolute opposite happened. In the independent Zimbabwe that came into being the following year the anti-Frelimo dissidents could no longer be kept going by the old Rhodesian CIO. They would be taken over by the South African secret services and would grow strong on South African money and weapons. Samora would soon have a bloody war on his hands that he wouldn't live to see the end of.

His visit to Niassa in 1979 took place in the lull before the storm. Maybe he thought that he'd have more time in the years to come to visit all the obscure or distant parts of his diverse country; surely he must have thought that, for he couldn't have foreseen how riven by war Mozambique would become, how Renamo would dismantle so many of the ties that bound together its disparate parts.

I wonder now if he needed, then, nearly five years after independence, to shake hands and swap words with ordinary people to remind himself of what it was all for. Why the endless round of meetings with heads of state, of negotiations secret and not so secret with all the different parties with interests in southern Africa, why the bodyguards, the advisers and the lonely splendour of the presidential palace?

* * *

Samora returns to us from the emergency meeting two days later, and we're all summoned to the central park where a wooden platform has been erected. Samora's a showman, a shaman. Although the crowd at first are wary—Samora's flanked by an entourage of grim-faced men in suits as well as by armed soldiers—he soon transforms their nervousness into camaraderie. He reminds everyone of the daily humiliations of life under colonialism. '*Não vamos esquecer*'—we shall not forget—the crowd shouts in unison with their President (see ***Lembrança***). People surge towards the platform. When the soldiers push them back Samora snaps: 'Leave the people alone.'

'Where's Aida?' he calls out, and the cry is taken up by the crowd, until Aida, middle-aged white woman, friend to Frelimo during the liberation struggle and now Niassa's one and only driving instructor (see **Driving**), is found, pushed forward and helped up on to the platform by willing hands. Samora hugs her. 'Here is a model of Mozambican womanhood,' he says, holding up her hand in his. Beneath a helmet of freshly set hair Aida looks highly embarrassed. 'Our very own atomic bomb,' says Samora, to cheering from the crowd. Now he remembers his other friends from freedom fighting days, and calls them out of the crowd one by one: Braz da Costa who supplied the guerrillas with provisions from his farm and had his arms blown off by a PIDE parcel bomb, gentle Alberto from the Escola Ngungunhana, Melo the nurse, all are handed up on to the platform and cheered.

I think that everyone wants to be up there, being embraced by Samora. By choosing these quite ordinary-looking people to stand before the crowd and praising them for their role in the liberation struggle, Samora is creating a kind of collective past:

everyone was in this together. We can all feel good about ourselves, is what he's saying. He's generalising from specific cases, and while that generalisation may not be historically accurate—Frelimo was not universally supported—he makes it into something to be desired. He makes it into an incontrovertible present. Somehow, by singling out these people, Samora has conjured up a unity that we now all believe in. And he has conjured up a future. Samora, the conjurer of dreams into reality.

Samora knows how to win over a crowd. Which is not to say that he doesn't believe in what he's saying. He goes on to promise an end to underdevelopment: more airstrips, more planes delivering food and other consumer goods from the richer south. He speaks to resentments and assuages them. Considering the role Niassa played only a few years earlier, it's not surprising its people now feel left out and rancorous. Samora articulates this, and hands it back, with promises.

I wonder how many people believed in Samora's vision of a large airport busy with commercial activity. Did that matter? Perhaps more important was his desire for it, a desire that mirrored and validated the desires of his audience. It was OK to want stuff! I didn't understand then—protected as I was by my status as transient visitor—how crucial was the availability of exchangeable goods to the health and wealth of the newly emerging nation. Samora knew it was crucial. But could he deliver?

The next day he visits the re-education camp at Unango a couple of hours' drive from Lichinga. There he tells the five hundred and more *reeducados* that they're now free: free to build a wonderful new city on the site of their camp, a city with supermarkets and libraries and a swimming pool, a city that will be built with the help of the willing populace of Lichinga. We'll only hear about this speech some days later and will be puzzled. Where are the supermarkets in Lichinga, the libraries and the swimming pool? My colleagues at the Escola Ngungunhana will take exception to the idea that Lichingans will be helping the *reeducados*. They strike me as less than willing. I notice how people react very differently to these two speeches, in response perhaps to the difference between a live Samora, with his intimate electrifying growl, his stirring singing voice and his irresistible wide-armed appeals, and a Samora textified on the pages of *Notícias* or *Tempo*. Maybe each *reeducado* at Unango believed Samora's every word as he said them. Who knows? It was a closed meeting.

That evening we're summoned to a reception at the Governor's house: iron gates, gravel path, a fountain playing in an open square, and, inside, white-clothed trestle tables set out with plates piled high with fried chicken, fried potatoes, biscuits, cakes, and isolated clumps of bottles: mainly Fanta orange but the occasional bottle of beer and even wine. This is the only trickle of alcohol we've seen for a good six months. We take care to place ourselves close to Braz, famous for his skill at manipulating his East German-made prosthetic arms to hook otherwise out-of-reach bottles of booze. We see the team of Soviet doctors further up the table. Blonde Clara the physician is standing shoulder to shoulder with the new interpreter (or 'interpreter,' see ***Cooperante***), a Georgian in black-rimmed spectacles. I notice they're holding hands. Clara grins at me, and the Georgian smiles uncertainly. At the other end of the table, as far away from the Russians as they can position themselves, stand Li and the Red General and four or five other Chinese (see ***Machamba Estatal***). We wave at each other. Across the table from us stand three delegates from the provincial *assembleia popular*: two women in bright *capulanas*, one of whom has a huge goitre in her throat, like a tennis ball wedged between chin and collarbone, and the other with a tiny sleeping baby strapped tightly to her back, and a man whose face beneath his woollen hat is seamed like old wood.

Samora whirls in when we're all assembled. He frowns when he sees the Fanta bottles. '*Nos não somos crianças*' (We're not children), he cries. 'Bring out the beer and wine.' Minions scurry out and swiftly return with crates of beer and wine. Surely the Governor hasn't been keeping them back for himself? Not possible!

The women opposite us go straight for the sponge cake, washing it down with Fanta, before being served with plates of *chima* and *matapa*, while the old man in the woollen hat slowly eats his way through three platefuls of stew and boiled potatoes. Christopher and I eat as many pieces of roasted meat—meat has been scarce, too—as we can get our hands on, and knock back glass after glass of Algerian wine.

On his way out Samora wanders through the crowd of guests. Clara has wriggled away from her attentive companion, and now she grabs me by the hand, and drags me through the crowd towards him. When he sees us he stops, and holds his arms out wide. Clara steps up first, he hugs her and asks her what her work is and where she's from. She steps back and now it's my turn to be pulled into an embrace. 'And you?' He laughs when I say I come from England. 'Ah! When you go back you must speak to Margaret Thatcher,' he tells me. 'I could try. But I doubt she'll listen.' Suddenly he's serious: 'Yes, that woman's deaf, of course.' (Samora grew to respect Mrs Thatcher. At an informal briefing for journalists in 1985 he said: 'People are surprised that I get on so well with Margaret Thatcher. Look—we know perfectly well that our friends in Britain are people like Joan Lestor in the Labour Party. But the point about Thatcher is that she understands power.')[2]

Samora hugs me tight, hugs Clara again and then he's off, followed by the Governor and his retinue.

While I've been talking to Samora, bottles of whisky have appeared from somewhere on the white-clothed tables. Karel, the broad-shouldered Russian surgeon, fills a tumbler, and pours one for me. He empties his own in three or four gulps and fills another, discards the empty bottle, seizes a full one, and moves purposefully up the table towards the Chinese, who watch his approach like paralysed rabbits. He's followed by the remaining Russians—Clara has departed with the new interpreter—all of whom hold full tumblers of whisky. They raise their tumblers to the Chinese, and break into a melancholy folk song. By the end of it tears are streaming down Karel's cheeks. Sobbing, he fills everyone's glasses to the brim once more. Now the Red General throws back his head and bursts into song, followed a beat later by Li and all the other Chinese.

Lusaka Agreement

The coup by the Armed Forces Movement in Portugal on 25 April 1974 didn't presage automatic and inevitable independence for what Portugal had seen as its 'overseas provinces.' Not at all. Caetano's government had crumbled but it was far from clear who was now calling the shots. Meanwhile the young officers of the Armed Forces Movement had put in charge the notorious fascist General António de Spinola, who had commanded the Portuguese army in Guinea-Bissau in the early 1970s and had been responsible for the murder of Amilcar Cabral, the leader of the Guinean liberation front, the PAIGC.

In early June Portugal's new Foreign Minister, Mario Soares, contacted Frelimo and proposed a meeting. Samora suggested Lusaka, the capital of Zambia. 'It is in Africa that African problems must be discussed.'[3] Frelimo's Executive Committee went into intensive discussion to work out responses to whatever proposals might be forthcoming from the Portuguese, with Jorge Rebelo role-playing as Soares. To be negotiating with the Portuguese was a completely new experience for the Frelimo leadership. They didn't even know the protocol of greeting their counterparts. They decided that shaking hands would be appropriate, recognising the delegates as representatives 'of the free Portuguese people with whom we want to discuss a new era in the relations between our peoples.'

Soares took them by surprise when they met in the State House by crossing the floor with the cry, 'Let me embrace you!'[4] But warm embraces butter no parsnips, as the Frelimos soon found out. Soares, speaking on behalf of General Spinola, had two proposals to make: a ceasefire, and then a referendum. Let's stop the war, he was saying, and then we'll see what people want.

'How can you ask a slave if he wants to be free?' was Samora's response, 'especially if he's already risen up against you, and if you yourself are the slave owner?'[5]

Let's agree on independence, and then, only then, will we stop the war, Samora told them. Independence or nothing, and power to be transferred to Frelimo as the Mozambican people's sole legitimate representative.

The talks were broken off. A risky stand to take, but courageous and uncompromisingly clear.

But the Frelimo leaders knew that courage and clarity were not enough. They needed to know what was really going on in Portugal. Towards whom was the power shifting? Much was obscured by the dust of the death-throes of the fascist state, and it was with a stroke of genius that Samora appointed Aquino de Bragança (who would die beside him at Mbuzini) to go to Lisbon, to look for the scales of the balance of power and find out to whom Frelimo should be talking. Meanwhile Samora himself went to address a session of the Organisation of African Unity in Mogadishu, where he argued closely and carefully for the position Frelimo had taken: an agreement on complete independence and the transfer of power to Frelimo prior to any ceasefire.

It was by no means a foregone conclusion that other African countries would support Frelimo's stand. World opinion was all on the side of Portugal's new Armed Forces Movement. Portugal wants peace, everyone said with an approving smile. Ah, but Mozambique wants independence, said Samora.

The guerrilla army continued to push southwards in Mozambique. The Portuguese troops, not knowing what they were now fighting for and wanting to go home, began to desert or to surrender in increasing numbers. Aquino de Bragança identified Ernesto Melo Antunes, one of the leaders of the 25 April coup and an anti-colonialist, as the person Frelimo should negotiate with. A number of secret meetings were held (in Dar es Salaam, London and Algiers), and on 7 September 1974, back in Lusaka, an agreement, afterwards known as the Lusaka Agreement, was signed by Samora Machel for Frelimo and by Ernesto Melo Antunes and seven others for the Portuguese government. Portugal recognised Frelimo's legitimacy as representative of the Mozambican people and agreed to the immediate transfer of power to a transitional government, with the Prime Minister and six out of nine cabinet members appointed by Frelimo, and to the Portuguese army working together with the Frelimo army, the FPLM, in the lead up to full independence the following year. Samora's boldness had been vindicated.

From leadership of a liberation front and its guerrilla army to leadership of a country: the sudden change of scale is considerable. From Kongwa to Nachingwea to the liberated zones to the whole of Mozambique. In Kongwa, the first Frelimo training camp, there was nothing. Samora with his handful of recruits had to cut the grass to build the huts to live in, had to plant the crops to grow the food to cook over the communal fire, had to whittle branches into sticks to use as pretend guns in drills and manoeuvres. The camp at Nachingwea was larger. More people, more guns. It was here that people from different racial groups and tribal groups came together and were united through their transformation into Frelimo guerrilla fighters: people from diverse backgrounds, but not that many of them. In the liberated zones, working alongside the villagers living there, the numbers were encompassable. Decisions could be implemented, actions made effective.

'The *zonas libertadas* were our university,' was how Katupha described it to me (see **OJM**). 'The conditions under which the combatants were living in the liberated zones, and the principles that guided their lives there, were transferred to urban conditions. It wasn't easy ...'[6]

Luta

Luta; a luta continua!: exp.n., S/C: Slogan político; linguagem da tenacidade e da revolução no Moçambique pós-Independente, tendo-se mesmo internacionalizado no seio de movimentos que na região lutavam contra o colonialismo e o apartheid (casos do Zimbabwe, Namíbia e África do Sul). Formal e informal. N.

Struggle; the struggle continues!: noun phrase, social/cultural: political slogan; expression of tenacity and of the ongoingness of the revolution in post-independence Mozambique, and internationalized through the other movements that struggled against colonialism and apartheid (such as in Zimbabwe, Namibia and South Africa). Formal and informal. Nation-wide.

Luta armada: armed struggle. On 25 September 1964 the Central Committee of Frelimo declared war on Portuguese Colonialism: 'Mozambican People: In the name of all of you FRELIMO today solemnly proclaims the General Armed Insurrection of the Mozambican People against Portuguese Colonialism for the attainment of the complete independence of Mozambique.'[7]

Story has it that the first shot was fired by Alberto Joaquim Chipande, who, that day, led one of the small groups making simultaneous attacks on Portuguese garrisons in the northern province of Cabo Delgado (see ***Behind the Lines***). In the attack by Chipande's group on the township of Chai, seven Portuguese were killed. Their deaths were officially recorded as 'death by misadventure.'

Because Filipe Samuel Magaia was at the time undergoing further training in China, it was his second-in-command Samora Machel who selected and trained the militants who launched the armed struggle. 'We began with a derisorily small force,' Samora Machel told the Soviet Academy of Sciences in February 1974:

> We had on 25 September 1964 about 250 fighters, equipped with old repeater weapons, pistols and a few individual automatic weapons. In each province where the struggle was begun, and in the other provinces, the number of fighters varied between 15 and 25. In front of us the colonial army ranged about 40,000 men, equipped with modern weapons, with air and naval forces, with a broad network of military bases, easy communications ...[8]

Explaining the nature of the armed struggle in a predominantly rural country like Mozambique, he told his audience that the Frelimo guerrillas operated like the alligator, who dragged his prey to the river, where he would have the advantage. 'Guerrilla warfare forces the enemy to fight in the midst of a hostile people.' The progress of the armed struggle was 'an accumulation of small victories.'[9]

Struggle: like many words in the English language, and unlike most in Portuguese, a word whose pronunciation is hard to guess from its spelling. My students in the Escola Ngungunhana found it difficult enough to master the unstressed e in 'armed,' and almost impossible to deal with the surprise of the short 'u,' the swallowed 'l' and the final silent 'e' of 'struggle.' As often as not we would end up talking about the 'arméd strooglay.'

M

Machamba Estatal/State Farm

The plan behind the *machambas estatais*, which were created out of the old Portuguese cotton and rice plantations and from the lands of the immigrant settlers, was to maximise production through new technologies, new machines and shiny new farming methods. In the first five years after independence *machambas estatais* received 90 per cent of all agricultural investment. Money was poured into them like water down a thirsty drain.

It was imagined that managers flown in from the socialist countries (considered to be experts in state planning of agriculture) could make the *machambas estatais* produce enough food to feed the urban populations, and on top of that, to earn foreign exchange through exports. The foreign managers had little or no understanding of Mozambican conditions. When the foreign machines broke down there were no spare parts in Mozambique, nor mechanics to fit them. Meanwhile the local peasant populations saw little benefit in providing labour when they had their own *machambas* to look after with no funds for machinery, seeds or fertiliser.

I remember the state farm in Niassa in the late 1970s, the acres of rich red earth that turned to rich red mud in the rainy season, and in the middle of it, floating on the choppy red waves, the concrete blocks that housed the Chinese team. Rows of new tractors sat outside slowly rusting in the rain.

I felt sorry for the Chinese and used to invite them to tea, through Li the interpreter who attended my English evening classes. They took it in turns to come in groups of four or five, always accompanied by Li and by their stately chief, who bore a striking resemblance to the actor who played a Red Army General in one of the all-singing all-dancing Chinese opera films sometimes shown in the Lichinga cinema. They brought us gifts of Chinese leaf and bean sprouts, and they would eat our egg sandwiches and talk wistfully of their wives back in China and the one child that each of them had.

Malangatana

September 2010: When I ring the artist Malangatana Ngwenya to ask if I can come and interview him he says: 'I am like a river run dry.' Then with a deep rumbling laugh, 'But if you want to come and talk to an old man ...'

'Casa Malangatana, faz favor,' I say to the taxi driver next morning, as Monica and I climb into the cab, 'Rua de Camões.' 'Aiee, Malangatana,' says the taxi driver, his voice warm with affection. 'Do you know him?' I ask. 'Everyone knows Malangatana,' he replies. We leave Maputo city centre, drive through shack-filled suburbs, then turn off onto a dirt road—puddles, rocks, barefoot children—down another dirt road, where at the end we stop outside a red-painted 1930s-style house. The house is a gallery as well as a family home, and everywhere, outside as well as in, you can see Malangatana's hand, from the brown and white glazed ceramic tiles that frame the front door, to the metre-wide carved wooden frieze way above our heads that runs around the roofline, down to eye-level, and the metal scroll that bars the lower windows. At first glance this appears to be an abstract design, but when we look closer we see a repeating pattern of two figures: the stylised heads of a man and woman, beard and curly hair for the man, an upright cock and the curve of balls; headscarf and necklace for the woman, semi-circles of breasts and pointy nipples standing proud. Later Malangatana tells me these are portraits of himself and his wife.

A black iron gate is half open so Monica and I push it and enter a narrow courtyard. A stout white man comes huffing out of the entrance to a dark corridor, shouting orders over his shoulder to a man on his heels carrying a large bag. We venture down the corridor and into an inner courtyard. Another middle-aged white man is hanging around, and he gestures at us to sit at a table on a porch outside what is obviously a studio—in the dim interior I can see huge canvases thickly covered with the intertwined bodies of humans and animals that Malangatana is famous for. Young men and women come in and out of the courtyard and vanish down the corridor and then a screen door opens on one side, and Malangatana, large, and brown and grey like an old badger, shuffles out, grabs my hands and kisses me on the cheek, does the same to Monica, and shuffles into his studio. We sit down again and watch the tortoises: a big one balances itself on the very edge of the porch like the coach hanging over the precipice at the end of *The Italian Job*, another squats behind a pillar, while a smaller one lurks behind an ornate metal frame. When we look away for a moment all three make a dash for a pile of lettuce leaves in the corner. You often see a tortoise with its funny down-turned mouth peeping out from behind something in Malangatana's paintings. Two large canvases, both showing crowd scenes in deep reds and browns, are carried out of the studio past us and taken down the corridor. About half an hour later—by then I'm sitting with Malangatana in his studio—they return. The bank, it seems, has refused him a loan of 20,000 euros without the security of two paintings. Each painting is worth at least twice that. But now, after a flurry of phone calls, the bank has said it doesn't need to physically hold the paintings.

Malangatana mutters at all of this and tells me a complicated story about how he was charged with negotiations between the government and this very bank in the first days of Independence. We sit together at his desk surrounded by paintings on walls and easels and propped against chairs, while Monica stays outside at the table on the porch, working on her laptop. He tells me that he started off painting the stories he'd heard when he was little from his mother and grandmother, but then found he could use the same images to paint the experience of colonialism: 'the big monsters with their strong legs stamping on us and gobbling us up with their sharp teeth.' Samora, he tells me, believed artists to be central to the revolution.

Malangatana summons Monica from outside and tells her to get out her camera. What songs do you know? asks Malangatana. I remember some of the old Frelimo songs, and together we sing *Kanimambo* (see **Kanimambo**). Then we sing the only other one I can remember the words of: *Moçambique esta cansada de sofrer/ Os massacres do carrasco/ Ian-i Smitt-i!* ...: 'Mozambique is tired of suffering the massacres perpetrated by the hangman Ian Smith ....' Then in his beautiful rich bass Malangatana sings me a series of love songs in Xironga, about lying down with your beloved in forests and meadows.

'Samora, for me, is still a leader,' Malangatana says. 'Nothing *melted away* when he died. You can still touch his hands; you can still hear his voice.'

When I ask if we can call a taxi to take us back into town, Malangatana forbids it. No, he wants to drive us back into town himself, in his huge pale gold Ford saloon. As we bump along the dirt road kids and grown-ups call out, *ciao, Malangatana*, and as we wait for the lights to change on the main road drivers slow down and shout out of their open windows—*hoy, Malangatana!* When we say goodbye I tell him we're going to rent a car and drive to Xilembene on Sunday to look at Samora's birthplace. 'Hmm,' Malangatana growls, 'it's a long time since I've been to Xilembene. But no, I've got a commission of 24 drawings to finish by next Wednesday for an exhibition in Portugal ... Still, I'd like to come ...'

I don't believe he will come, but when I speak to him on Saturday he's insistent. 'Shall I hire a car?' I ask. 'No, I'm going to drive you,' he says.

Monica and I retire to bed early but are kept awake for much of the night by a massive party somewhere just behind the hotel. Loud music, loud shouting, loud cheering. We get up at five, after a few hours of patchy sleep. The party ends promptly at 5.30—one moment deafening music, the next complete silence—just as we come downstairs. We've said we'll be at Casa Malangatana by six, but when we arrive we find it all locked up, and curtains drawn. I ring the doorbell. We scuff our heels in the sandy road. I'm about to ring again when I hear knocking from up above and look up to see Malangatana looming at a window and gesturing that he'll be down soon. When he comes out he seems surprised to see us, which alarms me for a moment, but he backs the Ford out of the garage past a man who scowls in our direction as he closes the garage door behind him, and I climb into the front while Monica gets into the back seat.

'I had a dream last night,' says Malangatana, as we bump our way towards the main road. 'I dreamt that I went into town and met Mamã Graça and we had a long talk.' 'What did you talk about?' I ask. 'Hmm, hmm, now what was it?' He gives me a long sideways look and smiles to himself, and turns back to the main road ahead just in time to slam on the brakes before we hit the side of a bus.

Malangatana asks about our trip over the border to see where Samora and his companions died (see **Mbuzini**). We talk about José Forjaz's monument on the lonely hillside, the thirty-five rusting metal poles through which the wind sobs and cries. He tells us its abstraction is controversial. Lots of people don't like it, but he, Malangatana, does. Malangatana's own work is a fusion of modernism and traditionalism, at once both abstract and representational.

We drive through the town of Marracuene, and Malangatana points to the right: 'Matalana. My village. Perhaps later we'll go there.' I'm noticing how erratic his driving is: at random moments he slows down or speeds up, he sometimes veers towards the centre of the road, and then swings back suddenly to the left, almost clipping the limbs of people walking along the verge, of whom there are many. To allow for his bulk the driver's seat is pushed back some distance from the steering wheel, so he steers at arm's length, one hand on the wheel while his left hand jabs at various buttons on the dashboard. 'What's this one for?' he mutters. I suspect that he hasn't had the car for long, and I'm wondering how to ask without appearing rude, when the carphone rings. An angry male voice asks Malangatana where he is, and when Malangatana says that he's driving some friends to Xilembene, we're treated to a series of phrases I don't recognise but that sound as if they run along the lines of 'billions of bilious blue blistering barnacles,' or worse. 'My son,' says Malangatana when the diatribe's over. 'He doesn't like me driving. He thinks I should stay at home.'

At Macia we stop for coffee and something to eat. Monica and I have been up since five and we're feeling weak with hunger. Malangatana lights a cigarette. 'They don't like me to smoke,' he says with a throaty laugh. Then he turns to me and asks casually: 'So who have you arranged to meet at Xilembene? Have you spoken to the Machel family to say that you're coming?' Me: 'What? No. What do you mean? I didn't know there were any family members living out there.' Malangatana droops his droopy eyelids, shakes his head and sighs deeply and says this is a very bad business indeed; it's extremely embarrassing for him as anyone who's there will think it really strange, not to say rude, that he, Malangatana, should just turn up without any notice on a Sunday morning and disturb them.

I'm really upset. I tell him that I thought the place was a museum. Certainly one of our guide books says that's the case, and we saw photos in the Mbuzini museum, showing the tree beneath which Samora's mother used to pound the maize for the evening meal, with a caption saying it was a heritage site open to the public. I had no idea that any family still lived there. 'Of course they live there,' says Malangatana in sepulchral tones. 'It's their ancestral village.'

Monica sees how upset I am. When we go to the loo she whispers that she thinks Malangatana's an old rogue who's deliberately trying to wind me up. Malangatana lights another cigarette when we get back to the table and says that it's all his fault, there's been a terrible misunderstanding, he should have asked me on Thursday, when I told him I was planning a trip to Xilembene, about what arrangements I'd made. Well, yes, I think, he should have, if that was what was required. It's funny how nobody else I've spoken to since Thursday has mentioned family to me when I said what our plans were. A final couple of loud sighs and sorrowful shakes of the head, and we go out to the car. As I hold the door open for him and he heaves himself inside I feel a pang of anxious guilt. He's awfully old and obviously not in the best of health, and here I am dragging him out and making things difficult for him … Then I remember that it was he who insisted on taking us.

As soon as we're in the car he reverts to flirtatious mode, and starts telling us all about a film the BBC made of him painting a mural in his home village. 'I think we'll stop at Matalana on the way back,' he says. 'I'd like to show you that mural. And my *machamba*.' He talks again about his dream. 'Now, just think, what if Mamã Graça were at Xilembene …' 'I spoke to Janet Mondlane yesterday,' I say, 'and she told me Graça had been in Maputo but went back to South Africa last week.' 'Ah yes, of course. Nelson's not well. She has to be with her husband. He's an old man. … But dreams are powerful things, don't you think?'

On and on, left after Macia, through fertile Gaza with its great big bushy mango trees, sturdy cashews, and green fields of sugar cane, and tidy villages of huts and houses with neat little yards and gardens behind green thorn hedges. On the roadside boys hold out their hands to us with plastic bags stuffed with cashew nuts for sale. Tied to lines of string on poles behind them the empty bags dance in the breeze like rows of white flags or balloons. Every now and again someone recognises Malangatana, a cry goes up, and he takes his hand off the steering wheel to give a magisterial wave.

Sometime after 10 o'clock we turn off the main Chokwe road and on to a straight tarmac road to Xilembene, with almost no traffic as it goes only to the village and I guess was a dirt road until recently—leaving behind the mangoes and cashews and sugar cane, into the flat plain of the Limpopo valley dotted all over with termite hills and with herds of long-horned cattle being guarded by little boys with sticks. Just as Samora did when he was a little boy in the 1930s and early 40s.

We come to the village and stop and ask an old woman where we can find the Casa Samora. I really can't work out when Malangatana last visited, if ever. We're told we've gone past it, so we turn around, and yes, we see a compound with some white houses and a plaque in the wall, so we drive in through the gate. Another woman appears, she and Malangatana chat in what I guess is Xichangana or Xironga. Malangatana turns to me with stricken eyes. 'Mamã Graça is at home, in her compound over there.' What? What compound? My heart starts thumping so loud that I can only just hear, distantly, Malangatana's, 'Oh, what will they think? Us turning up here unannounced like this? Oh woe is me!' We drive out, across the road, and in through an open gate into a huge grassy compound, in the middle of which sits a handsome long building, wood and glass and a thatch roof that sweeps down to the ground, with a large shady verandah at the end. Modern African traditional, the kind of building you see in brochures for upmarket safari lodges in South Africa. Behind the glass wall of the central section I can see some figures sitting round a table. They look as if they're having a meal.

Malangatana stops the car in the shade of a low, leafy tree. The very same tree, I realise with a shock, that we saw a photo of, the day before, in Mbuzini; the very tree under which Samora's mother used to pound the maize for the evening meal. He issues hurried instructions: 'We mustn't get out. We must sit in the car until they send someone over and then we'll send in a message asking permission to get out.' This isn't play-acting, I realise. His anxiety is contagious. I feel a flutter of panic as I remember the great importance of protocol in the revolutionary days of the 1970s. I'll say it was all my fault, I tell him. No, no, says Malangatana. I must not say anything. He will explain that he wanted to show me where Samora was born, that he was going to ring up in advance but couldn't because he's lost everyone's numbers. This doesn't sound convincing to me: has he ever had Graça's number, I wonder fleetingly? But what do I know?

We sit in silence. A man approaches over the grass. Malangatana says who we are, the man goes away, then reappears and invites us to get out of the car and come in. What luck that I decided to put on my best skirt this morning—floaty green chiffon from Jigsaw—rather than my workaday H&M trousers. Graça Machel is sitting at the head of the table. Malangatana introduces us and she in turn introduces Olívia, one of her stepdaughters (Samora's third child with Sorita Tchaiakomo, see **Frelimo**), and Malengane (her and Samora's son). She bids us welcome and invites us to sit down and join them for breakfast; places are quickly laid and half a pawpaw put in front of each of us. When Malangatana tells Graça that I'm working on a book about her late husband she doesn't look best pleased. Maybe she thinks I'm some kind of stalker, turning up out of the blue like this. Malangatana moves on to his dream of the night before. 'Well, we were certainly surprised to see you,' says Graça. 'Nobody knows we're here. We couldn't imagine who it was when your car drove in and no-one got out. We were just squinting at it, wondering who on earth it could be, when Olívia said, well, that's very strange, it looks awfully like Malangatana sitting there in the driver's seat—what's he doing here?'

Two men come in, one lined and thin, the other, younger, short and plump and jolly, and fall upon Malangatana with joy. These are Samora's two surviving brothers, Jossefate, who was imprisoned alongside Malangatana by the Portuguese colonial government, and Orlando. While the three of them are singing an old prison song, Josina, who is Graça and Samora's daughter, and another young woman introduced as a cousin come in and shake hands and kiss us in greeting. Suddenly, everyone except us gets up, and they all leave the room. Olívia returns with an aged woman whom she settles gently at the table, and bustles round us with a pot of maize porridge, following it with a tray of scrambled eggs and a big bowl of salad. She invites us to help ourselves to tea and coffee, and then she too leaves us.

I failed to catch the news that all the Machels, mother, children, brothers, have gathered here for a family meeting, and as Malangatana doesn't enlighten us, I don't know what's happening. He and the old woman chatter together. After breakfast we move from the dining room onto the open verandah, and an old man joins us. We hang around. An hour passes and then some more time, and then the two brothers reappear and the younger one, Orlando, points out to me different bits of the compound: the colonial prison, the police quarters, the administrator's house. Then Graça whirls up onto the verandah and wants to know my special interest in her late husband. She's beautiful, elegant in a traditional-style blue and green cotton print blouse and long skirt, and sort of intimidating. I say, hesitantly, that, I worked here as a *cooperante* in the post-independence years. A *cooperante*? Her face breaks into a smile and she grabs my arm, linking it in hers, calls over her shoulder to Monica to come with us, and marches me off the verandah and on a tour of the compound, showing me the old Portuguese administration blocks, the police headquarters, and the site of the hut in which Samora was born. 'Here,' she says, 'is where his umbilical cord fell.' A spindly baobab sapling, planted by President Chissano in 1996 on the tenth anniversary of Samora's death, grows on the site (see **Baobab**).

Back on the verandah the chairs have been arranged in a big circle and everyone's waiting for us. Graça gestures me to one of the two armchairs, and she takes the other one, and we talk some more. She suggests one or two people I might interview. She's efficient, to the point, and gracious. On the far side of the circle Malangatana broods benevolently like an old woolly bear, muttering about dreams and coincidences. Your arrival was more than coincidental, says Graça: it was providential. 'If you'd come yesterday, you wouldn't have found us here. We took a last-minute decision.' Graça tells me she and Samora used to come here three or four times a year, staying always in the small prefabricated house on the other side of the road (where we had first gone in), which was where Samora's parents had been moved by the Portuguese in the 1960s when they wanted to keep an eye on them from the administration block. That's the house that's going to become Casa Samora, a museum open to the public. We've arrived a year or two before the opening.

Graça asks Jossefate and Orlando to show us round the little house. There's barely room to swing a cat. 'Samora had no personal ambition,' the two brothers tell us. 'He wanted nothing for himself until everyone in Mozambique had shoes on their feet.' It remains exactly as it was in the years when Samora was President and came here with Graça. The front door leads into the living/dining room: three small armchairs, a dining-room table with a lace tablecloth covered in a plastic sheet, and a small wooden sideboard. A photo on the wall shows Samora stepping off the helicopter that brought him here in 1975, his first footstep on Mozambican soil after twelve years of exile. His face is lit by a huge smile and he seems to be floating on air, his arms extended like wings as he flies towards his father's open arms. Three doors lead out from this room: one into the bedroom which contains one small (again!—but Samora *was* small!) double bed with an orange and blue patterned cover and matching curtains, Sixties-style. Another door leads to a bathroom, and in the further corner the third door leads to a narrow red-painted kitchen, with a sink, an old and rusty electric cooker, and a deep blue fridge.

When we come out the brothers ask us to wait, so we stand on the porch in the shade of the corrugated iron roof while they dash over the yard to a concrete building and emerge carrying a large framed photograph of a serious-looking white-haired man in dark jacket and tie: their father, Mandhande Moisés Machel. Before we say our final goodbyes, we all sing *Kanimambo Frelimo*.

The journey back takes even longer than the journey out. Every so often Malangatana stops to make a phone call, and we stop to pick up his teacher niece Celeste. We turn off the road and drive down a rutted path, which I'm sure scrapes off a large part of the underside of the car, and we sit in Celeste's garden for a while amongst nut trees and peach trees and tall flowers like purple trumpets. Whenever we stop or slow down someone looks at us and the call goes out *ay, Malangatana!* and people wave and run alongside the car, and the three of us wave back. It's not like royalty—it's less formal than that—but perhaps, I think, this is what it would be like travelling with Elton John: big smiles, adoring crowds. One boy by the side of the road calls out: Wait! Let me call my friends from the church, and thirty or forty boys and girls come running and Malangatana heaves himself out of the car and into the middle of the crowd and everyone takes photos.

It begins to get dark, and within quarter of an hour night has fallen. 'Hmm,' says Malangatana. 'What a pity. I'll have to show you my village another day.' I'm now beginning to wonder how well he can actually see. He keeps on veering towards the lights of oncoming cars like a moth to the flame, and it becomes obvious that he can't tell when cars ahead of us are stationary. For some reason he believes that when he switches on the right indicator he's showing the cars behind us, not that we're about to turn, but that something's coming the other way. In their confusion drivers overtake us as fast as they can as we swerve this way and that. Monica will admit later that for the last hour of the drive she put herself into a kind of Buddhist trance. But I'm in the front seat, listening with only one ear as Malangatana tells me how he misses the days of revolutionary engagement whilst with every other fibre of my being I'm concentrating on keeping us on the right side of the road. He tells me a long story about a massive sculpture of his called *Casa Sagrada da Família Mabyaya*, which he's going to take us to see even though the night is pitch black. If we get back alive it will be by my will power alone.

The next morning I speak to Janet Mondlane on the phone and tell her how we went to Xilembene with Malangatana, and had the good fortune to meet Graça Machel. Then I say: 'Well, the drive back was a little nerve-wracking, and Monica had to call on all her yoga skills to stay calm.' 'What?' cries Janet, 'You mean Malangatana was DRIVING?!'

We never got to Matalana, so we didn't see the place where Malangatana grew up, nor his *machamba*, nor the mural that was filmed for a BBC documentary. He died on 5 January 2011, and he was buried there with full state honours. Although I felt a bit guilty about enticing him out to Xilembene with us that day, I'm glad, in the end, that we did, and not just for the extraordinary gift it was for me. I think he enjoyed it too. It gave him a chance to drive his big new shiny car, to flirt, to smoke cigarettes, to wave at adoring roadside fans, and to talk one more time with Mamã Graça, just as he had in his dream.

Malawi

On a map of Mozambique you can see in the top left-hand corner an empty space like a missing jigsaw piece: this is the southern half of Malawi, plunging deep into the heart of Mozambique, and separating Tete province from Niassa and Zambezia. The shortest route from Blantyre, the capital of Malawi, to Harare in Zimbabwe, lies straight across the neck of Tete province, through the town of Tete itself.

For me and the other few Western *cooperantes* working in Niassa in the late 1970s, Malawi, which mostly lurked invisible on the far distant western shore of Lake Niassa, only showing its black mountains for a brief moment each evening as the sun dropped swiftly behind them, glimmered in our imaginations as a fabled paradise of plenty. We had heard that you could walk into a bar and order a whisky (just like that!); that the shops offered cornflakes, biscuits, Marmite, even bottles of olive oil; that there was always butter to spread on your bread.

To the Frelimo soldiers in the 1960s, trying to open up fronts in Tete province and in Zambezia, Malawi was a logistical nightmare through which all weapons had to be smuggled: in mattresses, in cartloads of fish bought from the Lake shore, or stuffed into sacks of the maize that they'd grown in the training camp in southern Tanzania.

Doctor Hastings Banda, who'd practised for many years as a GP in Britain, and who during the forty-three years he'd spent away from his country had acquired a taste for Homburg hats and old-fashioned three-piece suits along with conservative social values to match, was a thorn in Frelimo's side from the outset, a niggling lesion that would develop into a site of pustulent infection. He'd declared, soon after his return in 1958 to what was then the British Protectorate of Nyasaland: 'When Nyasaland is free I will not rest until the greater part of Mozambique is joined to it. We are all the same people.'[1] To have his irredentist ambitions so thoroughly scorned by independent Mozambique must have considerably annoyed him, year after year.

Samora Machel paid four official visits to Dr Hastings Banda. His first visit, as second-in-command of the FPLM, was in 1965. Banda was then Prime Minister. The first attempts to open up Frelimo fronts in Tete and Zambezia had been unsuccessful and the guerrillas had retreated. Banda's men had captured some of them as they made their way back through Malawi to Tanzania, and had already handed some of them over to the PIDE. Samora hoped to persuade him to release the remaining prisoners. Throughout the liberation war Malawi continued to hand captured Frelimo guerrillas over to the PIDE; Malawi's close links with the Portuguese colonial authorities were strengthened with the appointment of the businessman Jorge Jardim (see **Mondlane**), Salazar's godson, as Malawi's honorary consul in Beira.

The second visit took place in February 1968. Samora, after the assassination of Filipe Samuel Magaia (see **Josina**), was now commander of the FPLM. Dr Banda had become 'President for Life' of the Malawi Congress Party and of Malawi itself. Samora was planning to reopen the Tete front and hoped to persuade Banda to stop offering support to the various anti-Frelimo Mozambicans who'd fled Tanzania to gather in Malawi, where they worked in close collaboration with the PIDE. He was unsuccessful in his appeal.

Samora visited again in November 1984, eight months after the Nkomati non-aggression agreement between Mozambique and South Africa had been signed. Since 1982 Malawi had been harbouring increasing numbers of MNR/Renamo gangs who carried out regular attacks in the provinces of Tete and Zambezia. This too was a fruitless visit.

Samora's fourth and final trip to Blantyre took place on 11 September 1986. In the two decades since his first visit Dr Hastings Banda, now calling himself *Ngwazi*, or Conqueror, had kept up a strong performance as the West's pet African dictator, always ready to go the extra mile for the Portuguese fascists or for the apartheid regime in South Africa.

This time Kenneth Kaunda of Zambia and Robert Mugabe of Zimbabwe were also present; the three of them hoped to persuade Banda to finally put an end to South Africa's use of Malawi as a launchpad for the ongoing war against Frelimo (see **Nkomati** and **Renamo**). The jagged jigsaw piece of Malawi that cut northern Mozambique in two had by now become the major supply route for Renamo's military base, complete with airstrip, in the heart of Mozambique's Gorongosa National Park.

On his return Samora called a press conference at Maputo airport. When asked what he would do if Malawi continued to support Renamo, he said: 'We will place missiles along the frontier and we will close the border to traffic between Malawi and South Africa going through Mozambique.'[2]

Five weeks later Samora Machel was dead.

Matapa

A dish made from cassava (*mandioca*) leaves stewed with crushed groundnuts or cashew nuts. It's sometimes made with pumpkin or bean leaves. A perfect sauce to go with *chima* (see ***Chima***), its dark green colour a pleasing contrast to *chima*'s dead white, its strong flavour, simultaneously bitter and sweetly nutty, offset by the pap's blandness, and in texture its mix of chewiness and crunchiness a welcome accompaniment to *chima*'s smooth stickiness.

The cassava root or tuber is rich in carbohydrates and the leaves rich in protein, although both also contain a cyanide-producing sugar derivative that must be extracted through cooking or soaking. Cassava is grown throughout Mozambique, all the year round.

Matchedje

The first photographs of Mozambique I ever saw were of Frelimo's Second Congress taken by the historian Basil Davidson—the only British person present—and Anders Johansson and reproduced in the centre pages of Eduardo Mondlane's *The Struggle for Mozambique* (see **Mondlane**). Here's a pensive Eduardo Mondlane, founder and first President of Frelimo, in a thin gaberdine coat and flat soldier's cap, his hands in his pockets. He is a tall broad-shouldered man, and the angle of the camera makes him look as if he is looking down over our shoulders, focusing on something in the distance behind us. It is July and the winter sun casts sharp shadows. The straight trunk of a tree on his left soars up and out of the picture, and behind him other shadowy tree trunks, camouflaged in a riot of dappled leaves, march up the slope. In seven months' time he will be dead.

Frelimo's Second Congress was held in July 1968 in Niassa province, in a forest clearing near to the river Rovuma next to a tiny hamlet, no more than a circle of mud and wattle huts, called Matchedje, in the district of Sanga. The central committee, meeting in Dar es Salaam some months earlier, had been divided as to where the Second Congress should be held. Should it be held safely in Dar es Salaam, where the First Congress had been held in 1962, or should it be held inside Mozambique, somewhere in the liberated zones? To hold it inside Mozambique would be hugely more difficult, but it would confound the enemy, encourage Frelimo's friends, and provide a symbol of the path, or *linha*, that the leadership hoped would be clarified and confirmed during the five days of the Congress. President Mondlane cast the controlling vote: 'The Second Congress will take place inside our own country, in the area which FRELIMO already controls and where the FRELIMO administration is now a reality.'[3]

Samora Machel, Head of the Department of Defence, was charged with choosing an appropriate site and ensuring its security. The area chosen was wild, thinly populated, and far from any Portuguese garrisons. A group from Nachingwea training camp crossed the river from Tanzania and prepared an open-air conference centre well camouflaged by the surrounding bush. They lopped branches and gathered grass for thatch and twine, and built sleeping huts, rows of benches for the hundred and seventy delegates, and for the leadership, facing the delegates, some tables for notes and papers, and a thatched shelter. Two handlettered banners, one above the other, swooped between the trees on either side of the shelter: II CONGRESSO DA FRELIMO ran along the top, and below: MOÇAMBIQUE. JULHO DE 1968.

While it was important for Frelimo to publicise as widely as possible that they were holding their Congress inside Mozambique so as to contradict the Portuguese story that within the colony there was no war going on at all, they nonetheless needed to keep its whereabouts secret. Accurate intelligence didn't reach the PIDE until the day the Congress ended, so that when the Portuguese planes finally came screaming overhead the bombs fell onto a deserted site.

It was in the shifting dappled light of the clearing at Matchedje that a number of principles that would become not just the guiding principles of the armed struggle but, some of them, the guiding principles of post-independent Mozambique, were discussed, debated, fought over, and finally adopted. It was agreed that the liberation front would plan for a protracted guerrilla war alongside mobilisation of the people in ever-increasing liberated areas, as opposed to short sharp strikes from Tanzanian bases against Portuguese garrisons. There would no longer be a split between the political and military aspects of the liberation struggle. Within the liberated zones the struggle would prioritise production, education and health. The enemy was not to be defined by his colour, but by his actions. The Second Congress confirmed that the emancipation of women, who suffered a double oppression under the colonial system and under men, was a prerequisite for the revolution, and that women could and should play an equal part in the armed struggle. The women's detachment, the *destacamento feminino*, would play a crucial role in the guerrilla army.

One of the photographs of the Second Congress shows five of the women delegates. Four of them are wearing printed cotton frocks: one's a check print, another a bold flower print. The fifth woman, at the end of the row, is wearing loose cotton trousers beneath a heavy coat. All of them wear traditional headscarves. These women look like ordinary, poor peasant women: their shoes are worn and dusty, and one of them is barefoot.

Raimundo Domingos Pachinuapa, then provincial commander of the guerrilla army in Cabo Delgado, writes of the Second Congress as *a bússola*—the compass point or lodestone—and the inspiration for all that came after (see ***Bússola***). Matchedje, on Mozambican soil, became sign and symbol of what Frelimo was committed to: a people's war that would transform all social relations.

Changes were made, too, to the structure of the leadership. Samora Machel, army leader since 1966, was already a member of the central committee, with, amongst others, the two men who would many years later succeed him as Presidents of Mozambique, Joaquim Chissano and Armando Guebuza. Now, at the Second Congress, the central committee was expanded from twenty to forty members, taking in all the front line commanders, and an executive committee was created, consisting of Eduardo Mondlane, Vice-president Uria Simango (see **Simango**), Samora Machel, Joaquim Chissano and Armando Guebuza (Security and Education Secretary respectively), Information Secretary Jorge Rebelo, Marcelino dos Santos (Political Affairs) and Mariano Matsinhe (Interior Affairs).

Most of the leadership was on the winning side, you might say. There was a losing side, too. Cracks had already appeared in the *frente*, the united front, of the *Frente de Libertação de Moçambique*. Earlier that year a Makonde elder called Lazaro N'kavandame, who had been an early supporter of Frelimo and was now 'chairman' in Cabo Delgado (see ***Behind the Lines***), had begun, from his base in southern Tanzania, to organise against the Frelimo leadership. He'd been profiting from cross-border trade and didn't take kindly to being told, after a tour of Cabo Delgado by Eduardo Mondlane in February, that personal profiteering was not consonant with Frelimo policy. But there were deeper differences: he opposed political power being given to military commanders in the liberated zones; he opposed the military strategy theorised and already being implemented by the head of the army, Samora Machel, of a prolonged guerrilla war based amongst the people of the country; he opposed the inclusion of women in the armed struggle and resented their involvement in the social issues of the populations in 'his' area of Cabo Delgado. What he proposed was a breakaway Cabo Delgado, nominally independent and ruled in a traditional way by the Makonde elders. In March, while Mondlane was out of the country, N'kavandame tried unsuccessfully to organize a Congress in southern Tanzania, in the heartland of the Makonde exiles.

Simultaneously trouble was brewing in the Mozambique Institute, the Frelimo school in Dar es Salaam. The previous year a priest called Mateus Pinho Gwenjere, from a Catholic mission school on the Zambezi, had arrived in Dar es Salaam with a large number of young recruits he'd won over to the cause with promises, it transpired later, of scholarships abroad. When it became clear that not only was study abroad not an automatic step for young students, but that they would be expected to return to Mozambique to play their part in the armed struggle inside the liberated zones, Gwenjere stoked their discontent. Being a priest, writes Raimundo Pachinuapa, Gwenjere was viewed with great respect and all that he said was taken as gospel truth.[4] (Ten years later I would see the same respect afforded to a Jesuit priest in the Escola Ngungunhana in Lichinga; he ably exploited the power that his status gave him.)

In partnership with N'kavandame, Gwenjere tried to persuade the Tanzanian authorities that the white Mozambican teachers at the school were spies. Whether or not the Tanzanian authorities believed this story, they decided to expel the white teachers: Helder Martins, who'd taught courses in medicine and healthcare and would later be Minister of Health, his wife Helena, the ex-Portuguese air force pilot Jacinto Veloso and the historian Fernando Ganhão (for crocodile tears being shed, see **Simango**). Meanwhile in America wild rumours were circulating amongst young Mozambicans that Frelimo didn't want the educated amongst their ranks, and that they were sending students into the liberated zones in order to be slaughtered. These rumours flew across the ocean back to Tanzania. In March the students rioted and Frelimo closed the school.

On 16 June a group of the Makonde exiles in Tanzania stormed the Frelimo offices in Nkrumah Street in Dar es Salaam and killed the telecommunications chief Mateus Sansão Muthemba, uncle of Josina, who happened to be there that morning delivering a message rather than in his radio shack in the Mondlanes' back yard. Those brought to trial for Muthemba's murder used the dock to scream accusations against the Frelimo leadership.

Amidst these claims of spying and treachery the genuine PIDE spies and infiltrators continued their work untroubled. Ganhão claims the PIDE had been receiving reports from an agent within Frelimo since July 1967. Gwenjere seems the likeliest candidate. And it wasn't only the PIDE. One of the respected Frelimo members was Leo Milas, an apparently impeccable revolutionary who was spotted by Jacinto Veloso in Cairo walking around with the collected works of Lenin under his arm on his return with Marcelino dos Santos from the first meeting of the Organisation of African Unity in Addis Ababa. It wasn't until later that people realised that the reason no-one had ever come across him in Lourenço Marques or Inhambane or wherever it was in Mozambique he claimed to come from was that he had never actually been there. He was an American, real name Leo Clinton Aldridge. Probably CIA.

While Mondlane was temperamentally inclined to offer the benefit of the doubt and to think the best of people, Samora was a cannier judge. When the priest Gwenjere had turned up unexpectedly at the training camp at Nachingwea asking permission to say mass for the Catholic recruits, Samora promptly sent him packing.

In the end neither N'kavandame nor Gwenjere succeeded in their plans. If anything, their struggles to change the route of the Frelimo journey served only to strengthen and confirm the policies adopted and clarified at the Second Congress: to fight against the dangers of tribalism, to unite Mozambicans of all races and both sexes against the common enemy of colonialism, to build a new society while struggling against the old. Soon after the Congress they revealed their true colours. In December 1968 N'kavandame organised the ambush and murder of Samora's deputy chief of staff Samuel Paolo Khankomba as he was crossing the Rovuma, and soon afterwards both he and Gwenjere fled Tanzania. In 1970, during the Portuguese offensive 'Gordian Knot' (see ***Behind the Lines*** and ***Nó Gordio***), leaflets signed by N'kavandame urging Mozambicans to see the Portuguese as their friends were dropped over the northern provinces between the bombing raids.

Neither N'kavandame nor Gwenjere was present at the Second Congress in Matchedje but someone was present who would prove very much more troublesome to Frelimo in the long-term: their friend and ally, the Vice-President of Frelimo, Uria Simango (see **Mondlane** and **Simango**).

* * *

At the end of 1978, ten years and a bit after Frelimo's Second Congress, I'm heading towards Matchedje in the geologists' Toyota Land Cruiser on a newly made track gouged out of the earth by a Caterpillar. Piet, the head of the geology team, is an indefatigable road builder. They've been searching for coal for the last year, and have recently moved camp to the very north of the province, up by the Rovuma river—and Matchedje. I'm on holiday and when Piet offers me a trip up to the new camp I jump at it. Matchedje! Crucible of the revolution! Lodestone of *o povo moçambicano*!

I'm sitting between Piet and a man from *migracão*, the immigration and customs department. He's fresh from the capital thousands of miles to the south: you can tell by the neat safari suit he wears and his brown leather slip-on shoes. He's going to look at the pros and cons of setting up a border and customs post at Matchedje.

The road has not yet been levelled. We lurch from ridge to trough to ridge as if we're riding a rocking horse while the 7Up that I drank at the last village slops to and fro in my stomach. Darkness falls and after a while we come to the end of the track and slide onto the thick white sand that covers the karoo rocks, following with our headlights a trail left earlier in the day by Luigi on a Suzuki bike. The sand glitters like snow in the light of a full moon.

In first gear we creep up a steep rise and into a dark forest. Two men on bicycles glide silently into the blaze of our headlights. They're wearing white Muslim hats. String bags bulging with two-kilo bags of sugar hang from their handlebars and two transistor radios are strapped between the saddle and the rear wheel on each bike. They're traders from Tanzania. They crossed the Rovuma at five that morning, they tell us, and now that darkness has fallen they're anxious to find a village to stop in for the night. We don't want the lions to get us, they say. We wish them *boa viagem*, and they get on their bikes and wobble past us, heading south. Lions!

When we reach a deep gully across the track, Piet suggests we get out while he inches the Land Cruiser over the two logs laid over it. We huddle up close to each other, me and the man from *migracão*, with our backs to a tree. I know I'm straining my ears to hear the approach of lions over the revving of the engine, and I'm sure he's doing the same. We leap to scramble back into the cab. Now we climb up into thick forest, moving through trees as still as stone and as tall as cathedral pillars. Dead branches are caught in the lower branches and float like huge broken bones before our eyes, behind a shroud of thick entangling creeper that gleams silver and grey in the moonbeams. Piet switches off the headlights and we creep forward as if under water, into and out of the black shadows cast by the trees over the white sand.

The forest begins to thin out, giving way to low scrub and thorn trees. That's when we see the lion, although we almost miss her. She looks to me like a large dog, trotting out in front of us and pausing for a moment. Piet says it's a wild cat. But the man from *migracão*, not such a city lad after all, clutches my arm and breathes, *leão*. And she's gone.

At the geologists' base camp we find Luigi sitting in a canvas chair by the cooking fire, nodding over a glass of *tres estrêlas*—three stars—brandy. The workers are asleep in their tents, but the cook has left us a panful of rice and a pot of gazelle stew keeping warm on the embers of the fire.

The next morning half an hour of walking along a rough grassy track takes us to Matchedje, where the three soldiers who guard the site rush to shake our hands. They haven't had a visitor in months, they say. The thatched shelters that I saw in the photos in Mondlane's book have long ago disintegrated, but a sun-faded banner still stretches across the clearing from the branches of one tree to another: *O SEGUNDO CONGRESSO DA FRELIMO*. Another one reads: *O PRESIDENTE EDUARDO C MONDLANE*. Not an original banner, then. Mondlane wouldn't have had his name on a banner: in those days personality cults were anathema. Three slabs of concrete form an open triangle around a low hillock on which is planted a flagpole with a Frelimo flag drooping in the hot still air. Three metal plaques engraved with lists of names stand propped against one of the concrete slabs. 'For a whole year we sent messages to Maputo asking for screws so we could fix these to the monument,' says one of the soldiers. 'Eventually the screws arrived, eight months ago, but they're the wrong size for the holes in the corners.' He turns to the man from *migração*. 'Please could you ask again when you get back to Maputo?' 'And please remind them,' says the second soldier, 'we've only got three bullets left for our gun.' 'Gun?' asks Piet. 'Yes, we've got only one pistol between us. Made in China.'

I look at the plaques: lists of names of those who attended the Second Congress, those who came from inside the country, those who crossed over the Rovuma from Tanzania, and those who came from further away. Eduardo Mondlane, Samora Machel, Josina Muthemba, Basil Davidson, *escritor e jornalista inglês*, English writer and journalist.

I take a photograph. Piet, conversing with one of the soldiers, has his arm flung out pointing to the north, describing perhaps an imagined road bridge over the river a few hundred metres away; the man from *migração* is closely studying the toe of his left shoe as if something nasty is stuck to it; Luigi, in dark glasses, is reading the names on the plaques, with his head inclined at an odd angle to the camera shot, such that it looks, weirdly, as if his neck is broken.

We set off on foot through the trees to the river, emerging onto a grassy bank above a narrow beach where two bark boats are drawn up. Between us and the dark tangled woods of Tanzania a hundred metres distant, the brown water of the Rovuma churns and swirls and leaps eastwards. One of the soldiers touches me on the arm and suggests I step back from the edge of the bank. Crocodiles, he says, miming with his hands the outstretched neck and snapping jaws that might rear up from the water and drag me in. The man from *migração* makes a dash for the safety of the treeline.

From the far bank we hear a hallooing, and screwing up my eyes against the sun, I see in the shadows of the Tanzanian trees a figure holding a bicycle. Out of the forest behind us comes a skinny grey-haired old man in a pair of blue shorts, who greets us before jumping down onto the beach. He pushes one of the boats out into the river, climbs in and paddles across. On its return journey, laden with passenger, bicycle, and a mountain of bags tied tight with string, the canoe itself is barely visible in the churning choppy water. The man from *migração* has abandoned the safety of the trees and is standing beside me. We both suck in our breath as the canoe is swept downstream; is he horrified by this unregulated cross-border trade, or does he think, as I do, that we're about to see two people drowned and eaten by crocodiles? The ferryman beaches the boat on a narrow strand downstream.

I turn to my companion. 'Would it be you in charge of setting up the border post here?' I ask. *Sim*, he replies, *sim*, investing the short word's nasal twist with a depth of plaintiveness. 'But I'm not going to recommend it.'

As we walk back through the trees towards the site of the Second Congress our soldier guides complain about the difficulty of guarding the site, with only one Chinese-made pistol between them, no bullets for it, and all their requests for ammunition ignored by Maputo. 'What's to guard against?' Luigi asks. 'Lions,' says one. 'Crocodiles,' says another. 'The enemy,' says the third soldier.

A year or so later Luigi left the Niassa geology team. Kicking his heels in Maputo waiting on his next *orientações* (see ***Orientações***), he was riding a motorbike along one of the *avenidas* when he had a head-on collision with an army truck. It must have been quite soon after Luigi was killed that I saw *The Omen*, with its ominous photograph that foreshadows the priest's death, and when I next looked at the photo of Luigi at the Matchedje memorial, I thought how ominous that photo too had proved.

And when, many years later, I looked up *Matchedje* (see **Moçambicanismos**) to see if any popular meanings had accrued to it over the years, I found something even more sinister. *Matchedje*, I learned, was the name that, post-independence, was given to military trucks. The nickname had a negative connotation, *uma certa conotação depreciativa*, based on the large number of fatal accidents the trucks were involved in. Luigi was the victim of a *matchedje*.

Mbuzini

September 2010: I hire a car and driver to take me and Monica over the border into South Africa, to Mbuzini, the site of the plane crash on 19 October 1986 that killed Samora Machel and thirty-four others. Hernani, the driver, is nephew of one of the receptionists in the Hotel Moçambicano, his car a reconditioned Japanese 4x4. I've been surprised by the number of decent-looking cars bowling along Maputo's *avenidas*; where are the old bangers of my 2008 trip, with their bullet-riddled windscreens and doors that wouldn't stay shut? Hernani explains: a year or so ago Mozambique signed a special deal with Japan for reconditioned second-hand cars that are shipped to Durban and then sold on the Mozambican market for $4,000 or $5,000.

We drive out through Matola, the site, in January 1981, of a raid by South African commandos in which twelve ANC members were killed and which signalled the beginning of the apartheid regime's determined assault on the sovereignty of its hated neighbour. It's now a rapidly expanding desirable residential suburb with high-end Chinese-funded housing estates for the upwardly mobile. We take the northwest highway; huge South African lorries loaded with sugar cane hurtle past us towards the capital. Low grey thorn trees stud the bare brown earth. A winter landscape. The border post of Ressano Garcia bustles with Mozambican day shoppers heading for the low prices of Nelspruit on the other side. Over the border we drive through endless fields of sugar cane and banana plantations, a lush green beneath the long thin arms of irrigation gantries. Busy tractors criss-cross the land where the crops have just been harvested, ploughing it ready for the next planting. I realise we didn't pass a single tractor in our hour and a half of travelling through Mozambique.

Hernani tells us that people still cry when they think about Samora. And what do they think of Graça? I ask. There's huge respect for her, he says. Everyone loves Mamã Graça. And you know what they say about her? He laughs. 'They say she's waiting for Obama!'

We turn south at the border and then circle back eastwards. Soon we are climbing up into the Lebombo Hills. Here as in Mozambique, the harvest stubble has been burned in time for the greening rains; the fields are streaked with firelines. Up and up, the road steep and winding, and past some scattered houses. Elegant long-horned cows pose by the roadside, while little goats scamper away from our wheels.

As the road begins to peter out, we suddenly see, incongruous against the bare parched earth of the hills behind, a signpost saying 'Samora Machel' and displaying the international icon—a sort of stylised Pantheon—for public monuments. Hernani follows a white pick-up towards the brow of the next hill and turns, behind it, into an otherwise empty car park. Under lowering grey skies with a fine rain beginning to fall, we walk up a red brick flight of steps to the memorial and, beside it, the new museum. We see a cluster of tall thin brown pipes above us, and as we approach them we hear an eerie wailing and sobbing. It's the wind rushing through the slits at the top of the poles, overlaying a low hum that sounds... just like the engine of an aeroplane. Two men climb the steps behind us—the two from the pick-up, one tall and well-built and in his 20s, the other smaller, slighter, older: two would-be tourist guides, they tell us, from

Komatipoort. Listen, they say: you can hear the plane with the people inside it crying and screaming just before it crashed. The rust on the poles, says the taller man, is the tears and the blood of the people who died. Thirty-five of them: thirty-five poles. From a few steps higher up we see an inscribed marble plaque set flat in the concrete platform at the foot of the pipes and, beyond, a deep pit, narrowing to a point buried in the hillside, containing twisted lumps of metal wreckage. The platform on which the poles stand forms a kind of trapezoid, pointing into and away from the furrow ploughed up by the plane; it represents the flight path as the plane came down and crashed into the hillside.

We stand in silence in the rain, looking out through the vertical lines of the memorial to the scorched land descending from the hilltops, now obscured in lowering mist, and I think of that October dawn twenty-four years ago when broken bodies were scattered on the slope after the plane, following a decoy beacon, ploughed into the side of the hill here at Mbuzini (see **Aircraft** and **Tupolev**). Is that what everyone thinks? I ask Hernani. That the plane was following a decoy beacon? Oh, it wasn't just a beacon, says Hernani: they set up landing lights here as well. We all know in Mozambique that it was the South Africans who set it all up.

From out of the museum's front door bounces a man who pumps our hands and introduces himself as Jonathan, our museum guide. He speaks fast and loud and locks his eyes onto ours with an intense gaze. Come, he says, and shepherds us into the foyer, where a woman with tickets to sell sits at a desk. Hernani and the two South Africans from Komatipoort argue that as they're guides like Jonathan, and as their intention is to advertise the monument to tourists and bring them here to see it, they shouldn't be charged for entrance. After a bit of thought Jonathan agrees, and says only the two tourist ladies need pay, and it will be 50 rands each, thank you very much.

The narrative is displayed international museum-style on big boards with integrated photographs. Samora's life history: pictures of Xilembene, Samora as a young man, a family tree that includes the names of all his wives, official and otherwise: Sorita Tchaiakomo and her four children, Irene Buque and her daughter Ornila. Jonathan jumps from picture to picture, pointing, explaining, asking, 'You get me? You get what I'm saying?' 'Yes, Jonathan,' we chorus dutifully. 'Here,' he says, pointing at Josina on the family tree, 'the freedom fighter lady.'

A photograph of Samora and Josina holding hands at their wedding ceremony, dewy-eyed and grinning at each other below their peaked army caps, with the white-cuffed hand of the treacherous Uria Simango joining their hands together. The photograph has been cropped to remove Simango himself, but it wasn't possible to edit out his hand.

We move on, to a row of black and white photographic portraits of the thirty-four who died alongside Samora; each person has their name and position printed in gold, and on a shelf below sits a sort of passport with a brief official biography and then empty pages for visitors—friends, family, colleagues—to fill in any details of their lives. The youngest to die was one of Samora's bodyguards, only just turned twenty. The oldest was Samora's old friend and comrade, the historian and revolutionary intellectual Aquino de Bragança, aged sixty-two. I walk along the row, reading the names to myself.

'Come on, tourist lady,' says Jonathan. 'Keep up please.' We follow a visual history of the armed struggle, and look at a section on the South African killing of the ANC-ers in Matola, with photos of Samora, Joe Slovo (see **Aircraft**) and the ANC President Oliver Tambo attending their funerals.

Then we move on to the actual plane crash. Here we read that the pilot 'inadvertently' locked onto a stray VOR beacon, and that the crew then failed to make the required checks about proximity to the ground that would have shown them they weren't approaching Maputo airport. Inadvertently? What does that mean here? Jonathan's eyes bulge with unspoken words as he points to his tightly closed mouth and draws his finger and thumb across it, zipping it tight. But the need to talk is too much for him. He opens his mouth: 'I say nothing. The question of the accident is not yet resolved. It's still under investigation.' 'Investigation,' repeats Hernani, making quote marks with his fingers in the air. All five of us, the two tourist ladies and the three tourist guides, up until now quiet and well-behaved, break into unruly discussion about the extent of the apartheid regime's responsibility for the murder of Samora and his thirty-four companions.

The legend on that particular display board is the only one to be equivocal about South African involvement. On an adjoining wall the findings of the Truth and Reconciliation Committee are prominently displayed: that injured survivors of the crash were left to die on the hillside while South Africans rummaged through the wreckage to gather up all the documents they could find and made off with them in the hours before they informed Maputo of the crash.

We move on into a gallery stacked on either side with file boxes that represent the reams of paper produced by the various investigative commissions, and we read the summaries of their findings. These include those of the medical commission, which found that six of the bodies had been interfered with before the Mozambican delegation arrived at the scene. Small incisions in the necks of the bodies indicated that the South Africans had taken blood samples. Was this while they were still alive? What a horrible thought.

From this gallery we look down into the cavernous final room where the rest of the wreckage of the aircraft lies. You can walk round and touch the torn and twisted chunks of metal, which until the museum opened in 2006 had been sitting in the back room of the local police station. They're laid out on a bed of bright plastic flowers. At one end of the room stands an ox made out of the battered metal of the plane—the going-home ox that accompanies the corpse back to the village for burial—and when you get down the stairs and turn round you see another statue made out of the wreckage: one of Samora himself in army fatigues, with his hand outstretched for visitors to shake. At first I feel too, what?, prissily English, I suppose, to do so, but when I see Hernani, Jonathan and the two South African guides enthusiastically snapping each other shaking Samora's hand, I overcome my diffidence and ask Hernani to take a snap of me as I shake it myself.

Moçambicanismos

Moçambicanismos: Para um Léxico de Usos do Português Moçambicano, by Armando Jorge Lopes, Salvador Júlio Sitoe, Paulino José Nhamuende, published 2002, Livraria Universitária, Universidade Eduardo Mondlane.

Literally, 'Mozambicanisms.' A dictionary of Portuguese or African-Portuguese words and phrases which, inflected by the specific tribal, colonial and revolutionary experiences of the country's people, have a particular significance in Mozambican speech which is distinct from their meaning in European Portuguese. See ***Camarada***, ***Estrutura***, ***Feiticeiro***, ***Kanimambo***, ***Luta***, ***Matchedje***, ***Ntchuva***, ***Orientações***, ***Viva!*** and ***Xiconhoca***.

Mondlane

Eduardo Chivambo Mondlane, founder and first President of Frelimo, was born the fourth of sixteen children in June 1920, in the province of Gaza in southern Mozambique. Educated by the Protestant Swiss Mission, he studied for a year at the University of the Witwatersrand in South Africa and spent a year at the University of Lisbon before travelling on a scholarship to the USA, where he completed his undergraduate studies at Oberlin College of Northwestern University, and went on to acquire a PhD in social anthropology and a job with the United Nations. In 1956 he married Janet Rae Johnson, a white university colleague of Swedish extraction whom he met through church activities.

'I was one of the very first people Eduardo Mondlane saved and protected,' Pastor Isaias Funzamo (see **Research Trip**) told me, 'so he's always there in my heart.' That was in 1949, and Mondlane, just back from South Africa, stood up to a white man who'd thrown the teenaged Isaias out of his house and onto the street.

When Eduardo Mondlane, now Dr Mondlane and an official with the UN, returned to Mozambique in 1961 on a diplomatic passport, one of the places he visited was a seminary at Marracuene, where Isaias Funzamo met him for the second time. Funzamo and his co-seminarists were following the Presbyterian path earlier trodden by Mondlane: 'We read about the Pharaoh, and thought about our own Pharaoh: Salazar in Lisbon. We developed a consciousness about the importance of the general rather than the individual good. We all developed a very strong political consciousness. We believed that one day we would be victorious, like the Israelites.'

This was when Samora Machel met Eduardo Mondlane for the first time, in the house in Lourenço Marques where Mondlane was staying under the protection of the Swiss Mission; this was when the dream of a united front that would fight against the colonial authorities and for independence was first articulated (see **Frelimo**).

Eduardo Mondlane was a man of both physical and intellectual authority, a natural leader. A big man, tall and broad-shouldered, he had a big smile and a passionate belief in social justice. The Swiss Mission Presbyterians had always engaged wholeheartedly with the world: indeed one of their earliest emissaries acted as physician for Ngungunhana and his troops when they were battling the Portuguese in the 1890s (see **Junod**). This was Mondlane's background: idealist, visionary, pragmatic.

He understood the crucial importance of winning friends for Frelimo. He drew on the goodwill of contacts made in the USA—there was considerable friendly feeling towards him within the Kennedy administration—and through the UN. The Mozambique Institute in Dar es Salaam, which was set up and managed by Janet Mondlane to further the education of the young Mozambicans who'd fled their country, received funding for its first year from the Ford Foundation (but not thereafter, following a vigorously hostile campaign in Portugal). In the first years of Frelimo's existence Mondlane assiduously sought friends wherever he could: he made trips to Britain, China, the Soviet Union, Romania, Bulgaria, the Scandinavian countries and Holland, and, in Africa, Egypt, Algeria, Tunisia and Morocco, putting the case for an end to Portuguese rule in the African colonies and for support for an independent Mozambique. He built on a sturdy triangle of support from the USA, North Africa and Scandinavia.

Samora Machel inherited Mondlane's belief in non-alignment and would stick to it even as the Cold War got colder and the gap between East and West widened into a chasm.

Was the assassination of Eduardo Mondlane, killed in Dar es Salaam by a parcel bomb on the morning of 3 February 1969, an inevitable next step after the failure of the efforts to topple him from within Frelimo (see **Matchedje**)? Who was behind it? In his biography of Eduardo Mondlane the Portuguese ex-diplomat José Manuel Duarte de Jésus identifies four groups of people whom he considers would have benefited from the elimination of Mondlane: (1) members of Frelimo or other Mozambican groups who opposed Mondlane's 'independent' line; (2) the Soviet Union, having realised that it would not be able to play Mondlane as its puppet; (3) the China of the Red Guards which saw him as a dangerously independent intellectual; (4) a far-right Portuguese group of people fearful about the spread of liberal ideas. 'All these possible beneficiaries,' suggests Duarte de Jésus, 'are equally possible suspects.'[5]

In Mozambique it's widely accepted that the murder was master-minded by the PIDE (see **PIDE**) with the help of some Frelimo dissidents. 'The enemy knew,' wrote Matias Mboa, 'that Mondlane couldn't resist a book.'[6] The bomb inside a book was a favourite gift of the PIDE to its enemies. For Mondlane they hollowed out a volume by the Marxist philosopher Plekhanov. One can only marvel at the cruel cynicism with which such a book was chosen.

It seems that the package was put together in Beira, carried from there to Malawi, carried through Malawi to Tanzania, taken across Tanzania to Dar es Salaam, and handed to the President of Frelimo for him to open along with the rest of the day's post. Many hands were involved in this gruesome pass-the-parcel.

In his memoir *Participei, Por Isso Testemunho*, Sérgio Vieira, who led the investigation into the assassination, names some names: Casimiro Monteiro, chief of the PIDE in Beira, widely known to have been involved in the assassination of the anti-Salazar Portuguese general Humberto Delgado in 1965, constructed the parcel bomb with the encouragement if not the actual help of the wealthy Beira-based Portuguese businessman, ex-minister and godson of Salazar, Jorge Jardim (see **Malawi**); Jardim's close friend Orlando Cristina (later a leading figure, in Ian Smith's Rhodesia, in what would become Renamo), handed the parcel over, in the Portuguese consulate in Blantyre, to a Belgian priest called Pollet who was a friend of the priest Gwenjere; Samuel Dhlakhama received the parcel on the Tanzanian border and was asked to hand it over either to Uria Simango or to Silvério Nhungu. The commission of inquiry found no proof that Pollet, Dhlakhama and Rosária, the last link in the chain, the person who took the parcel from Nhungu and handed it to Mondlane, knew what they were handling. Uria Simango, who was with Silvério Nhungu when he took possession of it in a hotel room in Dar es Salaam, denied all knowledge of its contents. Later Simango confessed that he knew of the plot to kill Mondlane, while denying his own involvement. There's no record of who bought the Tanzanian and Soviet stamps and stuck them onto the parcel to make it look as if it had arrived authentically by post.[7]

Samora Machel was deep inside the liberated zones in the Montepuez district of Cabo Delgado, with Armando Guebuza and Raimundo Pachinuapa, when he heard the news of Mondlane's murder. 'I heard about it on the BBC,' Samora told the central committee. 'The report said you were discussing the leadership question.' This speech of Samora's was transcribed by his first biographer Iain Christie from a tape of the central committee proceedings. Samora was speaking, Christie tells us, 'in a hoarse whisper, filled with emotion. He spoke in Portuguese but the words 'the leadership question' were in English. He repeated these three words, slowly, in English.' Then: 'Do you know what our first question is when we lose a commander in combat? It is not the leadership question. The first question is: what were the circumstances of his death? When I arrived here I mentioned this and some of you said it was just BBC propaganda. But it wasn't, was it? Some of you wanted to discuss the leadership question, as soon as our President was dead.'[8]

For those involved, directly or indirectly, the assassination of Eduardo Mondlane failed to produce the results they had hoped for. At the funeral of Mateus Sansão Muthemba the previous year (see **Josina, Matchedje** and **Simango**) Mondlane had declared in ringing tones: *Podem-nos assassinar, podem matar-me, mas a luta continua!*

They can assassinate us, they can kill me, but the struggle goes on!

Mutimati

Mutimati Barnabé João, known popularly as Mutimati, was a poet and guerrilla fighter who fell in battle during the liberation struggle, leaving a collection of twenty-seven poems that was published posthumously in 1975, the year of independence, with the title *Eu, O Povo*: *poemas da revolução* (*I, the People: poems of the revolution*).[9] The writer Nelson Saúte says: 'There's not a single child who's sat in a classroom in Mozambique who doesn't know Mutimati's verses. We all learned the grammar of our citizenship while sitting in the shade cast by the mythical fighter Mutimati.'[10]

The title poem, number thirteen in the collection, starts: 'I, the People/ I understand the strength of the earth that cracks open the grenade of corn/ I made of this strength a faithful friend.' A praise song to the combined forces of nature and the People, it ends with the promise that 'I, the Mozambican People/ I am going to know and understand all my own Great Powers.'

Both the organic connection between the armed struggle and the forces of nature, and the way that the experience of oppression can be read on the bodies of individual women and men, are common tropes in the poetry of the Mozambican revolution.

Come, brother, and tell me your life
Come, show me the marks of revolt
Which the enemy left on your body ...

begins one of the best-known of these poems, Jorge Rebelo's 'In our land, bullets are beginning to flower.'[11]

So many of the Frelimo guerrillas were poets that you might have described their approach to the armed struggle as *poético-militar* as much as *político-militar* (see ***Político-Militar***). Poems flowed from the leadership, from Jorge Rebelo, Marcelino dos Santos, Sérgio Vieira, Armando Guebuza, from Samora Machel himself (see **Josina**), and from those working clandestinely for Frelimo inside Mozambique, such as José Craveirinha and

Albino Magaia, both of whom suffered long years in PIDE prisons. Craveirinha, the first Mozambican writer to win the prestigious Prémio Camões (in 1991), was posthumously made a national hero by President Chissano in 2003.

Many poems were written and published anonymously. After all, 'I' is not an individual. 'I,' according to Mutimati and other poets, is the People. Some of these poets also published under pseudonyms. Craveirinha used an array of other names and other identities. But not as many as the great Portuguese modernist Fernando Pessoa (1888–1935), with his 'kaleidoscope of voices within him.'[12] Pessoa referred to his many different identities—some of whom not only showed distinctive writing styles but were totally different kinds of people, with very different biographical backgrounds, one or two of them Englishmen for instance—as 'heteronyms.' '*O poeta é um fingidor*,' he writes in *Autopsicografia*: 'The poet is a faker.' The stanza, translated by Richard Zenith, runs:

The poet is a faker
Who's so good at his act
He even fakes the pain
Of pain he feels in fact[13]

Mutimati, poet and fallen guerrilla fighter, never existed. He was invented by António Quadros, a Portuguese poet, painter and architect who arrived in Mozambique in the year of independence and made Maputo his home.

Seven years after the publication of Mutimati's inspiring posthumous collection, the poet João Pedro Grabato Dias published *O povo é nós* (*The people are us*), a collection of poems that mourns the passing of the revolutionary days of noble acts and high ideals, and skewers the rise of a soft-bodied bourgeoisie. And who is Grabato Dias, this other poet who, like Mutimati, speaks for the People, for 'us'? Look a bit closer and you will find that he is none other than … António Quadros, poet, painter, architect. (To heap confusion upon confusion, the biographer of master-faker Fernando Pessoa is one António Quadros. But António Quadros philosopher and critic, born a decade before António Quadros, painter, poet of the people, fallen guerrilla fighter. 'Our' António Quadros.)

Nelson Saúte was unfazed by the revelation that the fallen poet-guerrilla Mutimati Barnabé João had never existed:

> When, later, I learned that those hieratic poems had come from the heart of António Quadros, painter of murals on the walls of Mozambique's city squares and marvellous enchanter (*encantador fabuloso*) in all his multiple personas... [But] I went on believing in the story. Because it carried such a freight of truth. And when stories are truer than the truth of historical actuality then it's worth anchoring our reason within them.[14]

The final poem in Mutimati's *Eu, O Povo*, is '*Venceremos*' ('We Shall Overcome'). The poet, as if foretelling his own death, speaks from beyond the grave. He begins the poem with the past tense: 'The last thing that I saw was nothing...,' and ends it with the future: 'I won't be able any more to fulfil this task/ But the Struggle that continues is independent of any single man/ And there will be another task for two ears and a tongue./ We shall overcome.'

Mutimati, poet and freedom fighter, is dead: he has passed on into the collective poetics of the revolution.

N

Nachingwea

Nachingwea was the name of the military training camp in southern Tanzania that became the headquarters, nerve centre, and beating heart of Frelimo during the last four or five years of the armed struggle. And the spirit of Nachingwea was embodied in Samora himself, President of Frelimo since 1970; here, alongside training and the elaboration of strategy, Samora and the other leading Frelimos put their weight and strength into the core task of the revolution: the forging of the new man and the new woman (see ***Homem Novo***) and the creation of a new Mozambique.

The camp was set up in an abandoned sisal farm, previously known as Farm Seventeen, seventeen miles from the village of Nachingwea. The old farmworkers' houses, round huts of wattle and mud or simple square reed constructions, became offices for Frelimo's different departments: Training, Defence, and General Staff of the Armed Forces to begin with, and later the Presidency and the Departments of Politics, Foreign Affairs, Production and Commerce. At that point a much larger house made of wood, known as the *escala*, became HQ for the General Staff and for the top Frelimo cadres. All policies, military, political, domestic and foreign, were run from this modest wooden building.

Nachingwea was the third site for Frelimo's military training camp. The first one had been near Bagamoyo; its proximity to the bright lights of Dar es Salaam facilitated the two-way traffic of disaffected dissidents and suspected secret agents that plagued all the Frelimo sites in the early 1960s, and when in April 1964 Samora returned to Tanzania from military training in Algeria—already, according to the historian Fernando Ganhão, 'an undisputed leader'—he was instructed to move the camp away from Bagamoyo and further into the heart of the country.[1] He set up the new camp at a place called Kongwa. Reading about this period you can begin to see a connection between the thirty-year-old nurse turned guerrilla fighter and the soldier, politician, diplomat, head of state he will become. The first task at Kongwa was to clear the land and add to the three buildings already there. Samora would always be an enthusiast for building your own, for which doubtless he was roundly cursed in later years by the people who were sent into remote areas of Niassa (see ***Reeducação***). The majority of the trainees at Kongwa, all of them men, were familiar with working the land and growing their own food—no black Mozambicans, even amongst *assimilados*, were more than a parent or cousin away from living on the land—but preparing and cooking the food was a different matter. Women's work, traditionally. Samora pointed out that if they didn't cook then they wouldn't eat, and, leading by example, was first into the kitchen. A cooking rota was then set up amongst the senior men.

At that stage Frelimo had managed to acquire only a handful of weapons, but that didn't deter Samora from training the guerrillas with the utmost rigour. If they had no guns then they would make their own guns: they stripped branches from the trees surrounding the camp and day after day the trainees marched and turned and presented wooden sticks, and clutching those same sticks crawled on their bellies through the dust.[2]

During the years ahead Samora would display the practicality, toughness, and leadership through example first seen at

Kongwa, but even more crucial for the future—his and Frelimo's—was his grasp of the importance of unity. Frelimo's political survival, indeed Samora's own political survival until he was killed in 1986, was dependent on a struggle, and then a country, united across differences of tribe, language and race. The army was the crucible in which this unity was forged. In Kongwa for the first time Xichangana-speakers from the south, such as Samora himself, presented arms, or rather sticks, alongside Emacua speakers from Nampula and Makonde speakers from Cabo Delgado. As army commander Raimundo Pachinuapa, originally from Cabo Delgado, later wrote: 'We had to have a place where we could organise in terms of national unity. This place was the army, starting with the training centres. It was in the army that national unity was forged, that tribe, race and region were killed. But it's not the army itself that achieves those goals. It depends on the way the army is structured and led...'[3]

In Kongwa Samora set about broadening his own political education. He read Mao Tse-tung and Vo Nguyen Giap for their analyses of a people's war and the relationship between fighters and peasants, and he read anything he could find on Mozambique's own history and the history of Portuguese imperialism. At this time Frelimo's head of military affairs, Samuel Filipe Magaia, was himself receiving further training in China. It fell to Samora, his deputy, to select, prepare and train the small group who crossed the Rovuma and entered Mozambique in September 1964 and fired the first shots that launched the armed struggle for national liberation.

Once the armed struggle had begun it became obvious that the Frelimo fighters needed to be gathered in the south of Tanzania, close to the Rovuma river, not just in order to facilitate the passage of armed guerrillas into and out of Mozambique but so as to be as close as possible to what Frelimo was now committed to: the creation of semi-liberated and liberated zones inside Mozambique from which the war would be waged with the support of the populations of those zones. Tunduru became a medical base and a camp for orphaned children and civilian refugees from Mozambique; Nachingwea became Frelimo's operational headquarters.

At the beginning of everyone's military training, Oscar Monteiro wrote of his time at Nachingwea,[4] each person was encouraged to recount to their training group a *narracão dos sofrimentos*, an account of their sufferings under colonialism, in order to liberate the individual from personal rancour. Samora theorised the process as leading to *um reacerto*, a reassertion, of history. The commonalty of experiences expressed in these 'narratives of suffering' served to illustrate, in personal terms, what Samora demanded of every guerrilla: that they understood and believed that their enemy was the system, rather than the individuals within it. When, early on, a white baker in Cabo Delgado was attacked because he was white, by a group of guerrillas, Samora was swift to come down on them. It never happened again.

Sometime in 1968 the priest Mateus Gwenjere (see **Matchedje**) turned up at Nachingwea, offering to bless the Christian men before they went off to fight. Samora, convinced by then of the endlessly divisive nature of religious belief, ordered him out.

The numbers at the camp grew, augmented from 1970 by the women of the *destacamento feminino*, and as the population increased so too did the work of clearing the land, building, planting crops, digging latrines and pools and irrigation ditches, a rehearsal for working inside the liberated zones in Mozambique. Samora reclaimed the value of manual work from the lowly status assigned to it (see ***Latrinas***) and recognised its bonding powers: *fundir o nosso esforco, quando suor de cada um se funde no suor dos outros*, he wrote: to merge our strength, when the sweat of each one blends with the sweat of others.[5] 'Show us your hands,' he would say. He wanted to see callused palms, sign of honest work and open hearts.

He watched, judged, intervened as groups and individuals within groups struggled to learn new ways of seeing themselves—young women and men who had been brought up to accept without question the old ways as the best ways—and new ways of seeing each other.

Samora's confidence grew and flourished at Nachingwea in the 1970s. The people involved in Mondlane's murder in 1969 had been routed, the great Portuguese military offensive of 1970 (see ***Nó Gordio***) had failed utterly, and Samora, approaching forty, was in peak physical condition. He had grown wise from the experiences of the tumultuous years that had gone before, and by all accounts was psychologically acute and emotionally responsive. Perhaps his own experience of personal grief (see **Josina**) had deepened his empathy with others.

It was not that the end of the armed struggle was in sight. On the contrary, when the end came, it came suddenly. But the camp at Nachingwea was sufficiently large and complex to be imagined as a society in microcosm: it provided a vision of what could really be. 'We entered Nachingwea as Makondes, Makuas, Nianjas, Nyungues, Manicas, Shanganas, Ajauas, Rongas, Senas; we came out Mozambicans. We entered as Blacks, Whites, mulattos, Indians; we came out as Mozambicans ...' Nachingwea was 'the filter and the mould of consciousness,' the 'laboratory and forge' of the Mozambican nation.[6]

Ngungunhana

Nineteenth century Emperor, known as the Lion of Gaza, who fiercely resisted Portuguese attempts to extend the territory under their control northwards and westwards, in the European 'scramble for Africa' that was given impetus by the Conference of Berlin in 1884. (For down-time for his warriors see **Ntchuva.**) The Emperor Ngungunhana was captured by the Portuguese in 1895 and sent into exile on the island of Terceira in the Azores (see

Azores). For another two years his army, with Samora Machel's grandfather, Moisés Malengane Machel, an officer in its ranks (see ***Antepassados***), continued to fight the Portuguese under the command of Maguiguane Khosa, suffering a final defeat in 1897. The Emperor Ngungunhana died on Terceira in 1906.

Niassa

Niassa, land of red earth and green pines, of a lake as wide as an inland sea through whose deep, clear waters swim iridescent shoals of cichlids, whose shores are guarded by silent grey-skinned baobabs, and across whose surface the Nyanja have poled their long wooden fishing boats for centuries. Niassa, land of wild beasts: lions, elephants and the shy, fretful porcupine.

'Quem não conhece Niassa, não conhece Moçambique' ('If you don't know Niassa, then you don't know Mozambique') (see **Lichinga**). From 1891 until 1929 Niassa, and the neighbouring province of Cabo Delgado, were run by a British-financed charter company, the Niassa Company, with its own rules, regulations, tax system and postage stamps. In 1964 the *Junta das Investigações do Ultramar*—the Council for Overseas Research in Lisbon—published a volume entitled *O Desconhecido Niassa* (*Unknown Niassa*), for the benefit of the ignorant colonial authorities. The book, in blue board covers and containing sections on geology, climate, demography, ethnology, and photographs of some of the earliest maps of the territory, proved a useful resource for Samora Machel, who came from the south of the country and had never visited the northern provinces before the launch of the liberation war. He took it with him and studied it on his first forays into Niassa and Cabo Delgado.[7]

Along the narrow footpaths that wind through the thick forests of eastern Niassa, Samora Machel led a group of Frelimo guerrillas in November 1965. He needed to implement the strategy of working with the support of the people—*o povo*—to vanquish the Portuguese, setting up simultaneously a basic structure for civil society after independence. Earlier that year the guerrillas' infiltration of western Niassa—the lakeside and north of the *planalto*—had been a disaster. The Portuguese, with an army garrison in the provincial capital of Vila Cabral (now Lichinga) on the *planalto*, gunboats at Metangula on the Lake and napalm-dropping aeroplanes in the Niassa skies, retaliated swiftly to Frelimo's appearance, and the lakeside people, the Nyanja, fled in their thousands, heading north to Tanzania or finding sanctuary on Malawi-owned Likoma Island in the Lake. Frelimo, finding there was no *povo* left to win the support of, retreated.

Now Samora, on his first incursion into Mozambique since he'd fled into exile in 1963, returned with a small group of guerrillas and made for a village whose inhabitants, they'd heard, would be sympathetic. But the Portuguese had arrived before them and Samora and his men, desperate for water and food, were obliged to march on, some of them shouldering the packs of those who had fallen to the ground with exhaustion.

Eventually the small column of exhausted guerrillas arrived at another village where the headman, Chief Mataca, was also sympathetic to the liberation struggle. (This Mataca must have been the son or grandson of the turn-of-the-century Chief Mataca, described in *O Desconhecido Niassa* as a veritable Ngungunhana of the North, in a state of 'constant rebellion' and requiring a series of 'campaigns of pacification' to keep him under control. The book shows a photograph of him in robe and neck scarf, looking intransigent).[8] But perhaps the Portuguese had been nosing around this village too? Samora put on a traditional white robe and hat and, disguised as a Muslim headman from elsewhere in the province, smuggled himself into the presence of the Chief.

Reading an account of Samora Machel's first military sortie into Mozambique I'm reminded of the stories of the British POWs who disguised themselves as German officers. Where those attempts were rarely successful—the skeletal skinniness of the figures inside the heavy greatcoats giving the game away—Samora succeeded not once but twice, springing Chief Mataca from the administrative post where he was held after being arrested on suspicion (correctly) of having had dealings with the guerrillas. Which is not to suggest that Samora was a master of disguise; to the Portuguese conscripts one 'native' would have looked much like another one in a long white robe and embroidered Muslim hat. But playful though this seems—to dress up as a traditional Muslim and pinch someone from under the noses of the army—Machel was risking death or worse if he'd been handed over to the PIDE, just as some young British POWs were executed as soon as they were caught.

I read the postscript to this tale of derring-do in Iain Christie's biography: the commander of the Portuguese troops in eastern Niassa in the early 1960s and the man who ordered the arrest of Chief Mataca was a certain Lieutenant Ramalho Eanes.[9] Eanes became President of the Portuguese Republic in 1976, and on a state visit to Mozambique some years later was reminiscing with Samora about the fighting in Niassa. He said that the night he seized Chief Mataca his soldiers under cover of darkness had looted some bicycles and other goods belonging to the villagers. 'When I saw this,' he told Samora, 'I felt terrible because this did not match up to our military dignity.' Samora turned to the assembled VIPs: 'This man,' he said with a flourish of his arms, 'sounds like an officer trained by Frelimo!'

Many stories are told of both the discipline and the *politesse* of the Frelimo guerrillas during the armed struggle. Father John Paul, who lived in Niassa and was in charge of the lakeside Anglican mission at Messumba from the late 1950s until he was expelled by the colonial authorities in 1970, recounts some of these tales. The Portuguese were highly suspicious of the Anglicans, who had a tendency, unlike most (but not all) of the Catholic missionaries, to speak out and indeed write about the terror tactics employed by the Portuguese against Mozambican civilians; in order to be allowed to stay in the country they had to be extremely careful not to be seen supporting Frelimo. Frelimo soldiers, John Paul recalled, would slip into the mission grounds of Messumba under cover of darkness, only to hang around for ages while they laboriously filled out, by lantern light, receipts in triplicate for food and goods; eventually he pointed out to them that such careful accounting was endangering everyone's lives. Samora insisted on scrupulous honesty in all Frelimo's dealings with civilians: indeed the bitter internal row with Lazaro N'kavamande that nearly tore Frelimo apart in 1968 and led to at least two of the murders of its leaders began with N'kavamande's sense of entitlement to personal profits from the trade carried on between Mozambique's liberated zones and Tanzania (see **Matchedje**).

By the time the Portuguese decided to get rid of all their troublesome Anglican priests Father John Paul was viewed with extreme suspicion by the Niassan authorities, who had eventually realised why every second Wednesday their troops could travel on the road from Vila Cabral down to the Lake without fear of triggering land mines: the Frelimo guerrillas would ensure that the road was safe as that was the day when Father John Paul came up from the mission to the provincial capital to do his fortnightly shopping.

John Paul was the first person to introduce me to Niassa, for his *Mozambique: Memoirs of a Revolution* was one of the only two English-language books about recent history that I could find before I went to Mozambique in 1978 (the other was Eduardo Mondlane's *The Struggle for Mozambique*). I recently looked again at his preface to the book and was reminded of his passion and his admirable outspokenness. In his preface, dated 1974, he wrote:

> I have read glowing accounts of Portuguese rule in Africa written by MPs and others who had been completely hoodwinked by Portugal's 'public relations,' and I have been astonished at their naivety.

When the Mucumbura massacres coincided with the White Fathers' withdrawal from Mozambique in 1971, I hoped that this might open the eyes of the politicians and the public here to the true state of affairs in that country. But in 1973, England was celebrating her Ancient Alliance with Portugal, and fêting Dr Caetano in London. Her Majesty, 'head' of the Established Church of England, was required to entertain a Prime Minister whose Government was responsible for the oppression of millions of people in Africa. As a British subject and an Anglican, I found this distressing and repugnant.

The then Foreign Secretary and the Archbishop of Canterbury returned bland answers when I addressed to them pleas that at least her Majesty and the Duke of Edinburgh might be allowed to hold themselves aloof from this political jamboree ...[10]

I would have liked to meet Father John Paul, and regret the fact that I did not think sooner about tracking him down. He died in 2009.

In the immediate post-independence years Niassa and the neighbouring province of Cabo Delgado shared the kudos of having honourably suffered the worst excesses of the Portuguese military onslaught: boys snatched from villages and prodded with guns into highstepping along the roads in front of the troop columns as expendable mine-seekers, napalm drops on villages near the Tanzanian border just in case they were harbouring Frelimo soldiers, and then the intensification of the war in 1970 (see ***Nó Gordio***).

But by the late 1970s Niassa was developing a less honourable notoriety: it became known as the province where people who had fallen foul of the new government were sent in order to be re-educated. Who were they? Men and women, at first mainly from the southern towns, whose lifestyle—prostitution, pimping and petty criminality of one kind or another—was at odds with the new revolutionary morality. Such behaviour perpetuated, it was claimed, colonialist systems of exploitation. The liberated zones had become re-education zones (see ***Reeducação***). And in 1983 it all got much worse (see ***Operação Produção***).

Quem não conhece Niassa, não conhece Moçambique.

Nkomati

The Nkomati (or Incomati, or Inkomati, or, in South Africa, Komati) river rises in the eastern highlands of South Africa, runs eastward through Swaziland to the border with Mozambique, where it turns northwards and runs parallel to Mozambique's Lebombo mountains up towards Komatipoort and Ressano Garcia, the two border posts on either side of the frontier between South Africa and Mozambique. Here the Nkomati sets off northeastwards into Mozambique in a meandering semi-circular journey of over 300 km, curving southwards to empty its waters into the Indian Ocean just north of Maputo. By rail from Maputo to Ressano Garcia is only 67 km, but the Nkomati river, named after the siSwati word for 'cow' for its waters that never run dry, follows its own route, swelling as it is fed by river after river flowing south across Mozambique's central plain.

16 March 1984. A bright Friday afternoon at the end of the rainy season. Between the railway track and the south bank of the Nkomati river, the South Africans have set up an encampment of huge white marquees. On the track itself a stationary train, with one carriage painted white. A military guard of honour drawn from both sides, the Mozambican and the South African, stand to attention awaiting the arrival of President Samora Machel and Prime Minister P.W. Botha, who are meeting here to sign the Agreement on Non-Aggression and Good Neighbourliness between their two countries that will become known as the Nkomati Accord.

I imagine it as a scene in a fantasy novel: the forces of good led by the embattled Samora and his trusty knights, Foreign Minister Joaquim Chissano, Minister of Justice Oscar Monteiro and the former Portuguese pilot and head of Security Jacinto Veloso; the forces of darkness represented by P.W. Botha, his Foreign Minister Roelof 'Pik' Botha and their team of slab-faced, pink-skinned, crew-cutted Boers. They meet against a background of uniforms and gleaming guns, of white pennants fluttering beneath a clear blue sky and, in the background, a little boy prodding the flanks of a few skinny cows along the riverbank, a grizzled old man asleep in the shade of a mango tree, and a baldheaded ibis flapping into the northern distance, following the course of the Nkomati river.

As all readers of fantasy novels know, the signing of such truces and accords is followed inevitably by betrayal.

Inside the white-painted carriage Samora Machel and P.W. Botha sit on opposite sides of a lustrously polished table through the middle of which runs the invisible line that is the frontier between the two countries. Both men are in full military regalia, Samora in a pale dress uniform with elaborate piping made specially for the occasion: he is insisting that this is a meeting of equals. Each page of the document is initialled by Jacinto Veloso and Pik Botha, who then step back to allow the two principals, Samora from inside Mozambique and P.W. Botha from inside South Africa, to sign the Accord.

By this date Renamo controlled large areas of the Mozambican countryside (see **Renamo** and **Malawi**); their targeting of roads and railways combined with their terrorist tactics against civilians, which led to villagers abandoning their fields and villages and crowding into the towns for protection, had led to a famine the previous year that had caused something in the region of 100,000 deaths in the provinces of Gaza and Inhambane alone. The chaos made Frelimo's friends abroad jittery. Aid was drying up.

What had happened to the dream of freedom? Samora's vision of the patchwork fabric of Mozambican society stitched together out of diverse multi-coloured parts of different tribes and cultures was being ripped to shreds by Renamo's depredations. Peace was desperately needed, otherwise the Frelimo project would fail.

This was what drove Samora to Nkomati and an agreement with South Africa. They needed, he said, to find a *modus vivendi*, for neighbours were not a matter of choice and 'we cannot change geography.'[11] Pragmatic words; but the real pragmatism was the need to slice through the umbilical cord between Renamo and the apartheid state.

And what did South Africa want in return? Primarily South Africa wanted an end to Mozambique's support for the ANC (African National Congress). What Paul Fauvet calls the 'key clause' of the Accord stated:

> the High Contracting Parties shall not allow their respective territories, territorial waters or air space to be used as a base, thoroughfare, or in any other way by another state, government, foreign military forces, organisations or individuals which plan or prepare to commit acts of violence, terrorism or aggression against the territorial integrity or political independence of the other, or may threaten the security of its inhabitants.

South Africa had long been obsessed about Frelimo allowing the Russians to set up a naval base in the port of Nacala, a groundless fear as Frelimo had no intention whatsoever of allowing that. The pledge 'to forbid and prevent in their respective territories the organisation of irregular forces or armed bands' who intended to commit the acts of violence, terrorism and aggression was directed at the ANC on the one side and Renamo on the other. Fauvet again: 'This was a simple quid pro quo: South Africa would stop its military support for the MNR (Renamo) if Mozambique stopped its support for the ANC.'[12]

For Mozambicans and ANC members alike, the concept of equivalence between the ANC and Renamo was anathema, for the ANC, unlike Renamo, was an indigenous revolutionary movement with clear political aims, as Frelimo had been in the days of the armed struggle. The Nkomati Accord seemed to promulgate the view held then by many of the Western media: that the ANC was a 'terrorist' organisation with no political legitimacy. It would be another sixteen years before Nelson Mandela became the most sought-after best friend on the planet.

The ANC felt betrayed by Nkomati (see ***Soledariedade***). Julius Nyerere and the other Heads of the Front Line States were shocked and disappointed. And not everyone in Frelimo was able to be as upbeat about the Accord as Samora. Fauvet reports Luís Bernardo Honwana's account of a meeting of the leadership two days prior to the signing of the Agreement: 'Honwana recalls Machel declaring, "We have obliged the enemy to sign," but it was clear that many in the room found that hard to believe. Machel tackled that latent tension with the rhetorical question: "is there anyone who doubts that the Nkomati Accord is a triumph for the Mozambican revolution?"' Only the journalist Carlos Cardoso dared put up his hand. The others remained silent.[13]

Samora's combination of pragmatism and optimism led him to believe that by signing at Nkomati Mozambique was taking a step towards the peace it so desperately needed, a position that some months later, when the original hurt had faded, was accepted by the ANC. As the ANC President Oliver Tambo said at a press conference: 'I'm not sure that in their position I'd have gone quite so far, but it must be accepted that the South African regime had decided to destroy Mozambique, to kill it as a state, and the leadership was forced to choose between life and death. So if it meant hugging the hyena, they had to do it.'[14]

It could be argued that the long-term effect of the meeting on the banks of the Nkomati river (the fact of it rather than the details) was to pave the way towards black majority-rule in South Africa. But at the time no-one foresaw that. No-one believed that it was a triumph. Samora was isolated, and he isolated himself further by declaring: 'I am the president of a sovereign country. I don't have to explain myself to anybody. I do what I want.'[15] He must have felt desperately lonely, talking loudly of triumph and seeing all around him only turned backs, blank faces and lowered eyes.

And in practical terms? Mozambique kept its side of the bargain, such that only a handful of ANC individuals remained living and working inside the country, but Renamo's assaults not only continued but increased in frequency and intensity. Maputo was regularly plunged into darkness as Renamo upped its attacks on the power lines; people were too terrified to move from one place to another for fear of being caught in an ambush in which they would be hacked or burned to death.

It turned out later that for the South Africans the signing of the Nkomati Accord was only ever a cynical public relations exercise aimed at Western governments. Of course, the apartheid regime itself was riddled with secrets and power games: while the two Bothas and others may, or may not, have wished to decrease their country's bankrolling of Renamo, there were others who were determined it would continue. Jacinto Veloso records General van der Westhuizen, the leader of a group of generals in military intelligence, summoning Afonso Dhlakama (later General Secretary of Renamo) to Pretoria a few weeks prior to the Accord and telling him they had no intention of abandoning him.[16] They ensured that six months' worth of supplies were sent to Renamo bases inside Mozambique in the weeks leading up to the Accord.[17]

Samora's pragmatism had come to nothing. His optimism had been shown to be utterly misplaced. There had been no bargain. He had embraced the hyena and it had savaged him.

Nó Gordio/Gordian Knot

Codename for the military operation launched against the Frelimo guerrillas in Cabo Delgado by the newly-appointed Portuguese military commander General Kaulza de Arriaga in May 1970 (see ***Behind the Lines***), the very month Samora Machel was elected President of Frelimo. The General deployed 35,000 troops, 15,000 tonnes of bombs, and dozens of planes and helicopters. It was meant to wipe out Frelimo once and for all; its failure to do so provoked a crisis of morale in the Portuguese military. With hindsight it can be seen as a turning-point in the armed struggle.

Ntchuva

Ntchuva, n, Ln S/C: Tipo de jogo popular entre jovens e adultos; consiste na movimentação de pedrinhas (ou caroços) através de pequenos buracos ou covas feitas no chão ou em tabuleiro de madeira, consoante regras específicas. Praticado em muitas outras regiões de África e do mundo, foi também jogo favorito nos tempos de lazer de Ngungunyane e seus guerreiros. Da língua siSwati intjuba> *Venda* ndzichuva> *Xichangana, Xironga, Xitshwa* ntchuva>*PM. Est. neutro. N.*

Popular game played by young people and adults: it involves moving pebbles (or fruit pits), according to specific rules, in and out of shallow holes or dips made in the ground or in a wooden board. Played in many other parts of Africa and the rest of the world, it was the favourite game of Ngungunhana and his warriors when they were resting from their campaigns. In siSwati: *intjuba*; in Venda: *ndzichuva*; in Xichangana, Xironga, Xitshwa: *ntchuva*. Mozambican Portuguese; general usage. Nation-wide.

I've only ever seen men, squatting on their heels, never women, playing *ntchuva*, more often than not with the metal tops of Coke bottles or other *refrescos*, these coming more easily to hand in the sandy north of Mozambique than fruit pits or indeed pebbles or small stones.

O

Ofensiva

Offensive: a military term applied to the social, political and economic campaigns launched by Samora in the mid-years of his Presidency, 1979–81, with a series of wide-ranging public speeches in which he analysed the structures and functions of different aspects of the state, and looked closely and critically at the behaviour and morality of its citizens (see also ***Homem Novo***).

Initiating one of the first *ofensivas* in a speech in December 1979 that addressed problems of disorganisation in hospitals up and down the country, Samora spoke in military metaphors: 'How are we going to organize victory in our hospitals? ... Before a battle, the principle is to reconnoitre the ground and the enemy positions ...'[1]

A month later, in the very first month of the new decade, Samora used metaphors of planting and housework. 'What do we want to do in the next two years?' he asked. 'Are we going on as we are? To sow and reap a good harvest, one must first clear the ground. One must turn the soil, one must weed and water, and then we shall have a good harvest. For our house to have a pleasant, homely and lively feel, we must clean it every day, clear out the dust that affects our lungs ...'[2]

With the end of Rhodesian aggression (before it was realised that the brains behind the MNR/Renamo had moved south to a new and richer base in South Africa), and with the end of the economically crippling effect of the sanctions imposed against Ian Smith's illegal regime (see ***Pós-Independência***), Mozambique could afford to take a good look at it itself, shake itself down, sweep itself clean and think about its own future.

In these turn-of-the-decade *ofensivas* Samora targeted false egalitarianism (see ***Camarada***), indiscipline, laziness, laissez-faire, meaningless bureaucracy: a whole range of behaviours that stemmed from a misunderstanding of what liberation from colonialism really meant. He demanded that people dress smartly at work, that they be courteous to members of the public, that they show respect for authority, that they work with enthusiasm. 'Our state apparatus is corrupted,' he said, talking about *o inimigo interno*, the enemy within:

> It is sick, full of parasites, some clinging to the skin and others internal ... We shall be ruthless with the undisciplined, the incompetent, the lazy, the negligent, the careless, those who go in for red tape, for inertia, those who fall into the trap of routine, those who despise the people, misappropriate state property or squander the property of the people. ... The person responsible for letting rice, maize, milk, batteries, beans, cloth and cashew nuts, intended for the population, lie rotting in the warehouse is a criminal. It is the action of the enemy...[3]

Not everyone was happy with the reintroduction of hierarchies, nor with being told they had to wear a suit and tie, or tunic, to work. 'Decency and good taste' were urged upon women: 'It is unacceptable to come to work in a headscarf.'

Samora came back, fiercely, to housework: 'In the first place we shall purge our ranks, we shall clean up the state apparatus. We are going to sweep our house out. The broom will reach into every corner.'[4]

Pre-empting the charge that some of these directives aped European lifestyles and ignored African cultures and customs,

Samora delivered a blistering attack on romantic notions of 'Africanness.' First he listed some of the victories of the revolution: the right to work, to education and health services, to food and decent clothes, to soap and razors, and he went on,

But our friends in the West say that if we go about well-dressed, if we shave, if we have decent housing, we shall lose our African characteristics. Do you know what African characteristics are? A skin, a loincloth, a wrap-around cloth, a stick in hand behind a flock, to be skinny with every rib sticking out, sores on the feet and legs, with a cashew leaf to cover the suppurating wound, jiggers in the toes—that is the African. That's what they see as African characteristics.[5]

Yet the *ofensivas* were offensives against more than just bad behaviour and misunderstandings of what it meant to be a revolutionary. They targeted corruption, opportunism (see ***Oportunismo***) and criminal activity of all sorts. And they looked forward to a better future for everyone.

In the words of the journalist Joseph Hanlon, 1980 was the year of promise.[6] This was the year Frelimo launched the *Plano Perspectivo Indicativo*, a plan for economic growth which radically rethought the economic policies of the first five years of *pós-independência*. These policies had been based on socialistic models and on widespread nationalisation. Opinions differ as to whether they were implemented for pragmatic or for purely ideological reasons. Jacinto Veloso emphasises the latter. 'At the time,' he writes, 'it was the consensus that private business was the exploitation of man by man, that rewarding a good worker was corruption, that the theft of goods from the state or from the company was a "deviation" to be solved through "self-criticism" and that the national wealth should be equally divided between good and bad workers ...' The climate at Independence, as Veloso puts it, was one that limited individual initiative.[7]

But Hanlon suggests a mixture of factors: 'Most factories, shops, farms now run by the state had simply been abandoned at independence; the few things that were nationalized were taken over for special reasons—the banks because of fraud, the coalmines because of safety lapses etc. Only land, rented housing and social services (health, education, law and funerals) were nationalised as a matter of policy.'[8]

Whatever the historical reasons, and in whatever ways it had been interpreted, by 1980 the limitations of a rigidly state-controlled economy were beginning to be seen. Socialism does not mean that the state should be tied up selling matches and needles, Samora told everyone, or selling tomatoes and kerosene, or selling razor blades and running barber shops. People remember different examples. As always, when Samora was speaking passionately he extemporised, and his extemporisations did not always make it into the official printed text (see ***Pensamento Unico***).

Whatever examples he used, his meaning was absolutely clear, and is clearly remembered thirty years later. Early in 2011 the General Secretary of Frelimo, Filipe Paunde, in rebutting a proposal for increased nationalisation, called up those very sections of Samora's March 1980 *ofensiva*: 'At the beginning of the 1980s, Samora launched the *Plano Perspectivo Indicativo*, which foresaw the existence of the private sector by stating: the State can't carry on selling needles and managing corner shops, but has to concern itself with major projects.'[9]

Samora spelled out the responsibilities of the state:

> The state must be concerned with directing the economy and reviving major development projects ... The state must devote itself to building large dams and irrigation schemes, to the electrification of the country, to augmenting information on our agricultural, mineral and fisheries resources ... The state must devote itself to the main social sectors: education, health, housing and justice. ... The state apparatus must ensure the conditions for increased production and improved quality of products, and must inspect factory output. It must ensure that there is no shortage of raw materials or spare parts in the factories essential for our development and for production of goods for the people. For this reason, we repeat, the state cannot waste its energies in managing a shop, a canteen, a bar, a boutique, a cobbler, a small workshop, a garage, a hairdresser ...[10]

'Here is the Frelimo vision of 1980,' writes Paul Fauvet, 'on the eve of the ten year development plan:

> the State will direct the economy, manage the 'commanding heights,' and leave petty production and trade to the private sector. At least some people in Frelimo, probably including Samora, had always thought along these lines—but there just weren't very many Mozambican capitalists around in 1975, and the vast majority of the Portuguese had scurried out of the country.[11]

But by 1980, writes Joseph Hanlon, 'there were [now] local entrepreneurs with the confidence (in themselves and in Frelimo) and experience to take over businesses which had been abandoned five years before.'[12]

'Unfortunately,' says Paul Fauvet, 'much of this speech (March 1980) was never implemented, because the war overwhelmed Frelimo as from 1981, and many good intentions remained on paper.'[13] Nonetheless, this *ofensiva* had a profound effect on the way that people conceptualised the revolution and their own part in it. Within five years of Independence, complacency had been settling on people like a warm blanket: Samora snatched that blanket off and forced a chilly reappraisal.

The last of the *ofensivas* was perhaps the most sensational. By the end of 1981 it had become obvious that the war was by no means over; it had simply changed shape and the direction it was coming from. Despite this—or perhaps because of this, since they had become more than ever crucial to Mozambique's future—Samora turned his attention to the army, the security police, the ordinary police and the militias. In a speech delivered in Maputo on 5 November 1981, he delivered a devastating critique of their behaviour towards the people they were meant to serve and protect: he spoke of the bribes, the violence, the demands for sex, the lies and the secrecy, the corruption from top to bottom. He denounced the armed forces of his own state as exploiters.[14]

It was said that when news of the speech reached the leaders of the socialist bloc countries they could hardly believe their ears.

'No leader of any other socialist country had ever castigated his own security forces in this way,' wrote Paul Fauvet. 'Were such statements not the height of recklessness? Was Samora Machel not inviting a coup d'état? But there was no coup.'[15]

OJM/OMM: *Organisação da Juventude Moçambicana/ Organisação da Mulher Moçambicana*

Mozambican Youth Organisation and Mozambican Women's Organisation, two Frelimo affiliates. At the founding conference of the OMM ('*oh-emmy-em-e*') in March 1973 Samora Machel said in his opening speech:

> The emancipation of women is not an act of charity, the result of a humanitarian or compassionate attitude. The liberation of women is a fundamental necessity for the revolution, the guarantee of its continuity and the precondition of its victory. The main objective of the revolution is to destroy the system of exploitation and build a new society which releases the potential of human beings, reconciling them with labour and with nature. This is the context within which the question of women's emancipation arises.[16]

As the historian Malyn Newitt has pointed out, these words provide 'a useful summary of the social objectives of the Frelimo revolution.'[17]

During the second national conference of the OMM in 1976, the first after independence, Samora whirled from session to session, listening to the details of the proposed changes to family law—rights to joint ownership of property, child maintenance, monogamous marriage, responsibilities of fathers towards their children—and demanded full transcripts every night of the debates that had taken place.[18] The Mozambican woman as represented on a poster of that period wears *capulana*, blouse and headscarf. Her left hand rests protectively on a woolly-hatted baby tied on her hip, while her right hand waves aloft a hoe. 'Mozambican woman,' runs the text, 'liberate us by increasing our understanding of productive work, dynamising the class struggle, forging the revolution.' It's from women that we learn. Women, in this scenario, are our leaders.

Samora remained passionately interested in both the OMM and in its equivalent for young people, the youth organisation OJM. What had perhaps started in the training camps of Tanzania and in the liberated zones of the north as a pragmatic recognition of what women and young people could bring to the struggle became increasingly a personal commitment and, even, a personal dependence. Being closely involved in these two organisations offered, Samora believed, a way of keeping in touch with the people, something that became increasingly difficult during his presidency, and a way of keeping alive the radical ideas that it was so easy to lose sight of in the day-to-day exigencies of government.

José Mateus Katupha (later Minister of Culture during Chissano's presidency), was in the leadership of the OJM during the last years of Samora's life. I spoke to Katupha (as he's known) in a meeting-room on the 7th floor of the headquarters of Petromoc, the state-owned oil company, where he's the newly appointed CEO. When I'd rung him, nervously, thinking he'd be too busy to see me, he'd said at once he'd be happy to talk to me, and greeted me with a big smile, asking after common friends in London, ex-*cooperante* doctors with whom Katupha stayed in the early 1980s when he was doing an MA in linguistics at the University of London, at SOAS.

It was there, in London, that Katupha first met his President on one of Samora's diplomatic visits. Katupha, who ran the Association of Mozambican students in Britain, had written to the Dean of Eduardo Mondlane University to ask if he could stay on in Britain and do a PhD. Samora came into the hotel room where he was meeting the students and took a slip of paper out of his pocket. 'Is there someone here called Mateus Katupha?' Repeating Samora's words Katupha's own voice took on the warm, affectionate tone, mimicking Samora's own voice, that I heard in the tones of all those who loved Samora. 'I hear he's not wanting to come back to Mozambique. Here,' Katupha crooked his finger in imitation of Samora's gesture to him all those years ago, 'you come with me.'

Katupha told me that he and the other members of the secretariat of the OJM were very close to Samora in the year and a half before he died. 'We were like some kind of car exhaust—an opportunity for him to let off steam! And to air thoughts that he thought other people perhaps wouldn't welcome.' Oh, so do you think he felt isolated? I asked. 'Yes,' said Katupha. 'Undoubtedly.'

And what sorts of things did you discuss?

The war. We talked about that. And the army. And land reform, for example. Samora asked us to gather material for a book on the complexity of the armed forces. He wanted us to provide a picture, through interviews with people, of the way the army worked. He told us to interview the different commanders. The other thing we discussed at length was the issue of the inheritance of land, and how some people would argue that there should be no succession, people shouldn't be able to inherit land, while others would say: but my father's left some land and it's not right that I can't inherit it. The problem of land and property was an ideological conflict within Frelimo.

Here Katupha stopped and laughed. 'And I don't think that Frelimo has yet resolved it!'

Would you say that he was using you and your OJM group as a way of exploring ideas himself? I asked. 'Yes,' said Katupha. 'He was doing exactly that. I think he found us good company for that, because our meetings with him were intimate and informal. One of his characteristics—and it was good in some ways but bad in others—was that he was very direct. Almost confrontational. He would tell you exactly what he thought.'

I'd heard about this aspect of Samora's *modus operandi* from a number of people, and had wondered whether their response to it depended on whether he was speaking truth in private, or in public. 'I remember,' said Katupha, when I was in the Soviet Union with him, I think in 1983, Andropov told him that they didn't look very kindly on his overtures to the West, and he said: "Look here! All I've been doing up until now is look after my own people." The same thing happened when he said that he was going to negotiate with the South Africans (see **Nkomati**). There were people in the party who didn't agree with him. He said: "Come on, you want us all to die? I'm the general here. Let's go and discuss this." He'd take hours, sometimes days if necessary, to discuss matters. After that, he'd want everyone to be on board.

Katupha and his friends and comrades of the OJM were with Samora the day before he flew to Mbala. 'We were the last group of people to be with him in Mozambique. It was a terrible shock for us the next day,' he said quietly (see **Aircraft, Mbuzini, Tupolev**). He thought for a moment, and then said, 'When I look back on that time, I feel that he was preparing us to take over. He was looking to the future. It was a deliberate exercise on his part to gather together these young people to teach them and show them how to think about and analyse things.'

I thought it was time that I should go. I was sure Katupha had important stuff to be doing. One last question just before I left: what about now? How do people think of Samora now? 'Now,' said Katupha, 'you find people in bars listening to recordings of Samora's speeches. People feel that Samora is *alive*. They feel the loss of him *now*. There's this big gap now between those who have and those who have not, and when you listen to Samora denouncing corruption, it seems that he's speaking today. People think: oh that guy Samora, he should be here now!'[19]

Operação Produção

The story of *Operação Produção*, or 'Operation Production,' begins at the end of April 1983 at Frelimo's Fourth Congress. Samora was in a combative mood, his 'magnetic presence,' in Paul Fauvet's words, dominating the Congress.[20] One of his unscripted contributions took the form of an exchange with an ageing veteran from the armed struggle who complained of the lack of medical care for wounded soldiers, and suggested that Frelimo had been infiltrated to the highest level by its enemies, some of whom, he said, were members of the central committee, some even on the Council of Ministers.

Samora listened to this criticism of party members, mulled it over during the night, and returned to Congress the next day with a refinement of the terms: infiltration was not so much the problem, he said, but corruption. Some leading people in Frelimo, ministers even, were too fond of the soft life, had become 'slaves to their furniture, slaves to their residence.' It would be better for everyone, he went on, if people who were not up to their jobs would honestly admit it, and ask to be transferred, but he knew only too well that ministers might not want to give up 'their right to ride in a white Volvo, with a little flag of the Republic fluttering from the bonnet.' He asked the question: 'Power corrupts, doesn't it?' And answered it himself: 'This name of Minister, Secretary, Governor also corrupts. They've become used to it.'[21]

This was Samora in heroic mode, taking on powerful people at some risk to himself, just as he had taken on the army and its generals in 1981 (see ***Ofensiva***). Samora was no coward; he was willing to make enemies even amongst his ministers if that was the price to be paid for upholding the high moral standards of the revolution.

But his attack on those corrupted by the comfortable trappings of high position was only one of Samora's off the cuff interventions at the Congress, and the people targeted by another of his improvised speeches were considerably less able to escape the consequences of his moral disapproval than the ministers with their stereos, their whisky and their chauffeur-driven white Volvos. By the time of the Fourth Congress Samora and his government were under threat from all sides. In January 1981 a group of South African commandos had come over the border and right into the Maputo suburb of Matola, where they killed twelve members of the ANC. *Que venham!*: Let them come!, said Samora in a defiant public speech in February. 'Let all the racists come here, and then the great majority, the twenty-three million South Africans can take power there! Let them come, and let the end of apartheid draw ever closer! Let them come! And we'll bring war to an end once and for all, for everyone!'[22]

They had indeed come, and they kept on coming. Less than a month after the Congress, on the night of 23 May, South Africa targeted Matola once again, this time with a bombing raid that killed six people and left thirty-nine wounded. They narrowly missed an oil refinery and hit instead the Somopal jam factory, where three of the six casualties worked. Later the South Africans claimed that they were conducting 'operations against the ANC,' and also that they had broadcast a warning to the Mozambican authorities. Tapes at Maputo air control confirmed that the South Africans had indeed transmitted a message, but as they had done so after, rather than before, the bombing raid, it was more of a report than a warning. Within the week an unmanned South African spy plane was spotted over the bay of Maputo. It was shot down.

Samora must have felt both rage and frustration at the increased provocations over the border from South Africa and at the simultaneous escalation of terror tactics by Renamo to the north, deep inside the Mozambican countryside. Renamo, with the support of money, arms and military training from South Africa, had come a long way since its inception as a ragtag bunch of malcontents and Frelimo expulsees organised by Ken Flower, the head of Rhodesia's CIO (Central Intelligence Organisation), to dash over the border and chuck grenades at a health post or primary school. South Africa was now funding a considerable army deep in the heart of Mozambique, which was dedicated to the terrorising of peasants in order to drive them from their villages.

The crisis in food production that was one of the consequences of this situation was a subject of discussion at the

Fourth Congress, and it inspired another of Samora's improvised contributions: expel from the cities people who were not in regular employment and send them off to till the land.

Many of the plans and schemes that were continually bubbling up in Samora's energetic mind as he wrestled with what must at times have seemed like hopelessly intractable problems of government never saw the light of day. Lack of human resources, a lumbering bureaucracy, and timidity on the part of individual *estruturas* (see ***Estrutura***) when it came to taking the initiative, were some of the reasons for the gap between idea and execution. Alas for everyone that *Operação Produção* did not fall into that gap and vanish.

After the Congress Samora would not drop the idea. 'Only those who work can stay in the cities,' he proclaimed at a rally on 21 May.[23] By then the definition of those targeted for expulsion into the countryside had broadened to include 'the unemployed, the under-employed, parasites and marginal elements.'

What was he thinking? How could he have become so far removed from the lives of ordinary Mozambicans that those who lived outside the formal economy, such as it was, could be called 'parasites'? What was making him fall back into a crude form of Maoist doublethink, that at once held up manual labour as the highest work of man and woman, and also as a punishment? What had happened to his common sense? His pragmatism? His ability to listen?

In early July *Operação Produção* was put into effect by the Minister of the Interior, Armando Guebuza. 'Non-productive' proved to be an elastic concept. The *Operação* became in some cases an apparatchiks' charter for the settling of old scores, and in others, the manifestation of a bureaucracy at once inflexible and nervous of doing the wrong thing. Once a person was named, or denounced, it was almost impossible to disentangle themselves from the bureaucratic coils that would drag them from their homes. Single mothers were denounced as prostitutes, unemployed school leavers as parasites, street traders as *marginais*; in Maputo and the other cities the net was flung wide and its catch was bundled on to overcrowded planes to Niassa. That province, infamous already for its re-education camps (see ***Reeducação***), became, on a passing presidential whim, a dumping ground for thousands of bewildered urban southerners.

Even were such a policy justifiable in human terms, where were the pangas and the hoes for clearing the bush and tilling the ground, where was the food for people to eat until they were able to produce the food themselves, where were the houses, and the health posts? As Paul Fauvet says, the 'grossly misnamed' *Operação Produção* was 'one enormous abuse of power.'[24] While the Mozambican press vociferously denounced individual violations of the official guidelines when they came across them, journalists were unable to criticise the concept as a whole. Not just because they would have been reprimanded, but because they were paralysed by their years of loyalty to Samora and to a revolutionary government that had always been under attack.

Operação Produção did not last long. Samora was brought to his senses by listening at last to some of his closest friends and advisers (including his elder brother Boaventura) who warned him of the damage being done to Frelimo's reputation. Meanwhile the Governor of Niassa, Sérgio Vieira, threatened to put trucks on the landing strip to stop the arrival of any more planes. On a visit to Zambezia province in August Samora saw for himself the devastation caused by Renamo in the central provinces and the army's failure in all too many instances to fight back effectively. It was obvious that *Operação Produção* was a diversion from the real threat to Mozambique. It was abruptly ended.

But no mechanisms were in place to return the displaced citizens from Niassa to their homes and families. More urgent perhaps for the government were the growing numbers of people threatened by death from famine in the provinces of Inhambane and Gaza towards the end of 1983, provinces where the Frelimo government was fast losing control.

In 2008 I found Lichinga's central market, which in the immediate post-independence days barely merited the name of market as so little trade took place in it, buzzing with commerce. In a maze of narrow pathways snaking from the original covered building hundreds of stalls offered bedsteads and bicycles, flip-flops, *capulanas*, kitchen knives, batteries, mosquito nets, mattresses, plastic bowls and buckets, shiny black wellington boots. Here the traders were all men. Pairs of them squatted on their heels playing *ntchuva*, on the wooden board with its four by eight rows of shallow dips balanced on a stool between them (see ***Ntchuva***). On the high stone counters of the covered market the women displayed their produce on strips of old plastic sacking: neat hills of coloured beans, clusters of fat cloves of garlic, pyramids of shiny tomatoes. Behind the market a mêlée of pickup trucks in various stages of unloading, motorbikes weaving in and out, and dusty buses. One of the buses promised Maputo, three thousand kilometres south, for a destination.

Two or three people told me that many of the traders and small business people swept up in *Operação Produção*'s dragnet twenty-five years earlier had simply stayed on in Niassa and now a second generation was injecting energy into the commercial life of the province. It was here that I first heard the story of the Jehovah's Witnesses (see ***Reeducação*** again), sent to Niassa soon after Independence; I imagined them walking through the war-ravaged landscape of Mozambique to emerge from the wilderness at the very end of the millennium to reach their old homes at last.

And I thought that the period around *Operação Produção* was a time in the wilderness for Samora too. 1983 was also the year in which Frelimo introduced the *lei de chicotada*, public flogging for a range of minor crimes such as theft and small-scale black marketeering. It was the year that Frelimo extended the death penalty to cover other crimes besides treason. In April a man found guilty of large-scale prawn-smuggling, Goolam Nabi, and two thieves who'd robbed a bakery were publicly executed by firing squad. Samora seemed to have stepped off his own moral path and lost his way.

Operação Produção showed that he could be both autocratic and cruel. Although he castigated Frelimo ministers for being corrupted by material wealth, and lambasted them for abandoning the ideology of hardship and self-sacrifice that had been forged during the liberation war, the objects of his ire were protected by their positions, for there was no wider pool of educated, experienced cadres to draw upon. The victims of *Operação Produção* had no such protection, and while it lasted only three months—whereas his battles with the apparently infinite corruptibility of people in positions of power were a lifelong commitment—the fallout lasted well beyond his death.

Oportunismo

Samora, in October 1976, sixteen months after Independence: 'The method of operation of the power-seeker is opportunism, *oportunismo*, and his main characteristic is corruption, *corrupção*. He is like a chameleon who is white on a white wall, and then turns red on a red wall. They are the ones among us who most obtrusively wave the FRELIMO flag.'[25]

Orientações

Orientações: haver/ter/dar/receber orientações: exp.vb., S/C, 'No GD ainda não ha orientações da nação.' Veja tb nação: significa governo central, Maputo. coloq, N.

Orientations, directions, directives, guidance: to have, give, receive these: verbal phrase, social/cultural. 'The GD (Dynamising

Group) hasn't yet received any directives from the *nação*.' See also *nação*: central government, Maputo. Colloquial, nation-wide.

When Malangatana (see **Malangatana**) and the other *xibotsos* or former political prisoners were ordered to Tanzania in 1974 it was to receive *orientações*, 'so as to ensure that we wouldn't improvise things.'[26] This was related to *a linha do Partido*, the Party line (see ***Pensamento Unico***).

Orientações come always from the centre, having been formulated collectively by one Party or government body or another. Until they are received, no action can be taken, for to act on one's own initiative, prior to receiving *orientações*, is to risk going against them. It is to risk acting in a counter-revolutionary manner.

But if you look at the verb *orientar-se*, from which the noun is taken, you see that there can be another interpretation of the giving and receiving of *orientações* besides the hard-line one. Isaias Funzamo (see **Research Trip**), pastor in the Presbyterian Church of Mozambique and lifelong Frelimo supporter, told me when I met him in 2010 that whenever he faces difficulties in his life three people visit him in his dreams: Samora Machel, Eduardo Mondlane, and the head of the Presbyterian Church who was murdered in prison in 1972 (see **Junod**) by the PIDE. *Aparecem orientar-me*. They come, he said, to show me the way.

P

Pensamento Unico

Consensus; one mind with one thought; unity.

If hours of debate were required for consensus to be reached, then hours of debate would take place. Frelimo had to speak with one voice; who knew into how many fragments it might otherwise shatter?

The process is well illustrated in Helder Martins' description of the painstaking and gruellingly long debates within the Frelimo leadership about national health policy in the weeks just after Independence.[1]

You can see the insistence on consensus as rooted in the belief that all voices should be listened to before decisions are reached or taken; in other words, as an inclusive process not entirely different from either traditional or Protestant methods of problem-solving (see **Baobab**). Or you can see it as a control-driven desire to eliminate contradictions, a cover-up for a fear of difference and dissidence. Is it, once again, a question of scale?

Nowhere are the contradictions more apparent than in the person of Samora himself, who insisted on the importance of *pensamento unico* within Frelimo, the *linha do partido*, and yet, up on the platform, seemed unable to stop himself articulating the ideas that came fizzing and bubbling into his head.

PIDE

Polícia Internacional de Defesa do Estado: International Police for the Defence of the State. Salazar's secret police, who had powers to investigate, arrest, detain, torture and get rid of anyone suspected of being anti-State. They took over from the PVDE (*Polícia de Vigilância e de Defesa do Estado*: State Defence and Surveillance Police) in 1945. In 1969 the PIDE was renamed DGS (*Direcção Geral de Segurança*) by Prime Minister Caetano, although it continued to be universally referred to as PIDE. The PIDE/DGS collapsed with the victory of the Armed Forces Movement coup in Portugal in 1974.

The PIDE/DGS was hugely successful, in Mozambique and the other African colonies as well as in Portugal, in infiltrating agents (Mozambicans in Mozambique, Angolans in Angola and so on) into organisations opposed to the Salazar regime. Frelimo was no more immune to it than anyone else; even at the conference of the World Council of Churches in Geneva, where in 1966 Eduardo Mondlane was presenting a paper on the role of the church in social development, so many PIDE agents were in attendance—according to a Mozambican delegate, Pastor Isaias Funzamo—that no-one dared speak freely.[2]

Many of the assassinations, including that of Frelimo's first president Eduardo Mondlane, were instigated if not actually carried out by PIDE agents. In October 1966, while leading a patrol across a river in Niassa, Filipe Samuel Magaia, Head of Defence, was shot dead by Lourenço Matola, who had been his companion-in-arms in Algeria in 1963 but had been a PIDE agent from the start. Magaia had led the first group of young Mozambicans to be trained in Algeria; Samora led the second; the leader of the third group, António Silva, turned out to be another PIDE agent.

In their prisons in Mozambique the PIDE tortured and killed thousands of Mozambicans. One of their most feared Mozambican agents was Francisco Langa, known as Chico Feio—Ugly

Chico—who, according to Matias Mboa, Samora's travelling companion on the flight from Mozambique in 1963 (see **Frelimo**), had a mouth like a chimpanzee's. Chico Feio took great pleasure in killing his countrymen and women, as slowly and as painfully as possible. Another one of the PIDE's prisoners, Albino Magaia, wrote of him: 'Ugly Chico, Chico traitor. He had eyes of blood. He smelt of blood. He sweated blood ...'[3]

The suspicion with which Frelimo treated the *xibotsos* or ex-political prisoners after Independence grew from the recognition that the PIDE had managed to 'turn' a considerable number of the people they'd held in their clutches. It must have been tough on the *xibotsos*, to suffer so under the colonialists and then to be kept at arms' length by Frelimo; but sure enough, after lying low for a while, some of them bobbed up to the surface in the ranks of the MNR/Renamo (see **Renamo**).

POLANA

2008: The black and white marble-tiled terrace of the Polana Hotel, on Avenida Julius Nyerere, looks out over a stone staircase down to the smooth blue of a swimming pool and to the choppy glinting blue of Maputo Bay beyond. Frangipani trees line the staircase, their waxy star-shaped flowers glowing white against dark green leaves; from the well-watered lawns huge palm trees rise up. Balustraded balconies in cream-painted plaster decorate the elegant curve of the hotel's seaward façade. The Polana advertises itself as offering a taste of 'the grandeur of the colonial past.'

As I sipped a cold Laurentina I noticed that all the guests around me on the terrace were white-skinned, while the waiters, kitted out in white trousers and starched white jackets buttoned up to the neck, were all black. Then I noticed guards in khaki uniform with little green peaked hats positioned—strategically? randomly?—here and there on the garden paths and by the stone stairs. In case of a sudden uprising by the waiters? Or part of the grandeur of the colonial past?

Overweight white men in baggy shorts and expensive trainers sat at the tables around me hunched over their mobile phones. The one nearest to me, a crewcutted American, said loudly into his phone: 'We don't want the government to be our payroll master.' He was talking about a Bayview Hotel—shades of Lyme Regis or Worthing—in Mocimboa da Praia. He was issuing instructions to a minion to employ local workers through the village chief or district administrator. 'I've had enough of these problems,' he suddenly shouted. A young woman carrying a punch folder joined him at the table. He acknowledged her with a nod of his bullet head and she started leafing through the papers in her folder. 'In the employment guidelines it says direct recruitment is allowed,' he said and snapped shut his phone. He turned to the young woman and ordered her to arrange a conference call for later in the afternoon.

In Graham Greene's *The Human Factor* the British spy Maurice Castle remembers spending two nights in the Polana with his Black South African girlfriend, soon to be wife, Sarah, after she's been smuggled into Mozambique from out of the clutches of BOSS, the South African security police. Greene provides no dates, but it must have been 1967, for seven years later there are 'new chaps in power in Mozambique' but Lourenço Marques is still Lourenço Marques, it hasn't yet become Maputo, which puts the present day of the novel at 1974, the time of the transitional government. The novel's Operation Uncle Remus—initiated by the White House just in case the world's supply of gold and diamonds dries up as a result of conflict in southern Africa, and involving both the South African and the British secret services—'is purely a product of the author's imagination,' says Greene in his author's note, wryly adding a caveat from Hans Andersen: 'out of reality are our tales of imagination fashioned.' Greene draws the horse-trading over southern Africa so deftly and presciently—Castle is advised by his superiors to go a bit carefully on sharing with South Africa the information he has on Chinese interests, for 'the day may come when we need the Chinese'—that it's hard to imagine that even though he was seventy-four when he published *The Human Factor* in 1978, he was not himself still prowling the outer threads of that murky cobweb of intrigue.

An attempt by the South Africans in 1980 to kill two birds with one stone as Samora Machel and Robert Mugabe flew together into Maputo airport didn't work out as planned. The operative driving the Peugeot 404 that was stuffed with explosives couldn't get through the airport security; obliged to turn back, he got lost in Maputo and abandoned the car outside the only landmark he knew—the Polana hotel.[4]

Político-Militar

O político-militar: I find it difficult to translate this into English, as it seems to turn itself into a qualifying adjective when really it's a noun that means the idea or concept, or the realisation of the idea or concept, of the organic intertwinedness of the political and the military outlook or strategy. The phrase is so integral a part of the armed struggle, elucidated and defined by Frelimo's central committee in October 1966, that it carries little meaning outside that context. When I looked it up in *Moçambicanismos* (see **Moçambicanismos**) I wasn't surprised to find it absent.

Samora Machel said of political-military training that it was 'the forge of national unity, of a common way of thinking, of a patriotic and class consciousness.'[5] Fernando Ganhão used the phrase as a noun with which to define Samora himself: by 1969 Samora *was* the political-military (person, or figure), *o político-militar*, that was needed to lead a people's war.[6]

Pós-independência

Pós-independência or *os anos de pós-independência*, post-independence or the years of post-independence, loosely describes the four or five years after independence; in other words the first half of *o tempo de Samora*, the time of Samora, which describes the eleven year period of his Presidency, 1975–86. Both *pós-independência* and *o tempo de Samora* are of course retrospective labels: while people lived through the post-independence years and the time of Samora they did not name them as such. The years of *pós-independência* came to an end as Renamo became increasingly active within Mozambique (see **Renamo**).

They were years of an ever-tightening economic squeeze. The cosy financial deals that linked the colonial administration to apartheid South Africa—whereby Portugal benefited by being paid in gold for the black miners it exported—were not on offer to revolutionary socialist Mozambique. As well as withdrawing the gold subsidy, South Africa reduced the number of Mozambican workers in its mines, and, overall, cut down drastically on its use of the port of Maputo for imports and exports.

Even more economically significant to Mozambique was the relationship with another of its neighbours, Rhodesia, under the illegal regime of Ian Smith. Just as Zambia had suffered from closing its border with Rhodesia so as to implement the UN-agreed sanctions, so now did Mozambique.

Samora offered Mozambique as a base to the (not exactly united) Zimbabwean freedom fighters, and closed the long border with Rhodesia early in 1976, suddenly and swiftly. Story has it that the Minister for Transport, Luís Cabaço, heard the news and protested, 'But Mr President, we've got a plane on its way to Salisbury right now!' Samora: 'Well, call it back!'

The consequent cost to Mozambique was estimated in a United Nations Economic and Social Council report at between £70 and £82 million in the first twelve months, and between £54 and £67 million per annum afterwards.[7] The port of Beira, through which the oil had flowed into the pipeline to landlocked Rhodesia, became a ghost town (which perhaps partially explains Beira's less than 100 per cent support for Samora and Frelimo in later years). Those countries that had taken the decisions to impose sanctions against Smith's Rhodesia failed to follow their mouths with their money. Britain offered a paltry loan of £5 million, with strings attaching it to British goods and services.[8]

In the years of *pós-independência* Mozambique suffered less from the political hostility of its two minority-ruled neighbours than from a devastating economic isolation, which in turn was exacerbated by the exodus at Independence of large numbers of technicians and skilled workers (see ***Cooperante***). But the years of *pós-independência* were also, simultaneously—and, in retrospect, astonishingly—years when visions took form and ideas blossomed.

At midnight on 25 June 1975 Alberto Joaquim Chipande, the man who had fired the first shot in the armed struggle on 25 September 1964, raised the flag of independent Mozambique in Machava Stadium on the outskirts of Maputo. The symbols on the flag, a hoe crossed with an AK47 above an open book, symbolised the achievements of the past and hopes for the future. The prototype of a new society had been formed during the ten years of armed struggle in the schools, health centres and training camps in Tanzania and in the liberated zones of northern Mozambique. Frelimo had wanted to pull the *povo* out of the poverty and ignorance to which they'd been consigned within the colonial system of government: theory and practice would come together through universal literacy, universal healthcare and the working of the land to feed all citizens. But it was one thing to execute one's vision amongst populations that were small and discrete, another to carry it through nation-wide.

The next five years were years of huge changes, years of high-octane energy, of optimism and of incredibly hard work. The task was to transform education, health and production. In the Ministry of Education under Graça Machel, Amélia de Souto, now a historian at the Centre for African Studies at Eduardo Mondlane University, then straight out of guerrilla training (see

Destacamento Feminino), worked as political *responsável* for the nationalisation of schools in all the southern provinces. Her working day started at seven in the morning and ended an hour or so before midnight. She was twenty-one years old, and by no means the youngest. They were all learning on the job. Everything was moving so fast that there was barely time to think. It was gruelling, but, she said, 'to quote Pablo Neruda: *I can say that I have lived*.'[9]

Many of the newly appointed ministers were flying by the seats of their pants in those first few months, desperately trying to get a grip on what the Health Minister, Helder Martins, called the 'frightening realities' of the new situation.[10] He himself, with the backing of the Council of Ministers and the Central Committee, instituted a country-wide campaign of participative preventive medicine, a hugely successful mobilisation—*mobilisação*—behind two campaigns in which Samora himself played a central and very public role, leading his ministers with pickaxe and spade on the two National Latrine Digging Days (see ***Latrinas***). The National Vaccination Campaign, organised through Frelimo members, dynamising groups (see ***Grupos Dinamizadores***) and the OMM and OJM (see **OJM/OMM**), achieved coverage of 96 per cent. 11 million were vaccinated against smallpox, 1.5 million children against the deadly measles, 5 million children against TB, and 2 million women of child-bearing age against tetanus. In June 1977 the WHO described the vaccination campaign as 'a success which has no precedent in any other country'[11] (see ***Formulário***).

Like a number of people who have spoken and written about the Samora of *pós-independência*, Martins believes his grasp of economics was shaky. 'His great dream was for a better life for his people, but without taking into account the fact that development is a slow process, and that if you don't produce, then you can't harvest the fruits of what has not been produced.'[12] Yet in the liberated zones during the armed struggle, Samora had got at once to the heart of the problem when he saw how Frelimo's relationship with the *povo* was undermined by the *povo*'s commercial relationship with the Portuguese, and at the end of *os anos de pós-independência* it was Samora who recognized how the massive weight of the State was dragging the economy to a standstill. 'Why should the State be selling matches and needles, running corner shops and hairdressers?' he demanded (see ***Ofensiva***).

The ending of the state monopoly on trade can be seen, alongside the end of white minority rule in Zimbabwe and its consequence, apartheid South Africa's adoption of the MNR (see **Renamo**), as another sign and symbol of the end of those years of *pós-independência*. I think it was not that Samora 'wasn't very sensitive to economic questions,' as Martins and others suggest; I think he had to have the leapfrogging vision that would keep the ends in view shimmering somewhere beyond the daily grind. He held a vision of how Mozambicans could live, and would live, in a state of modest prosperity, of equality and justice; he needed to protect that vision against the daily depredations of getting there. He needed to believe in it to protect it from those who thought it was all too difficult, if not impossible.

The years of *pós-independência* were the years when the careful and cautious were pushed and prodded and inspired by Samora's determination and faith: faith that the dreams were achievable.

Amélia de Souto recalls an episode from the end of this period, when the euphoria of *pós-independência* was beginning to drain away, when there was still so much to be done but people were getting tired, and when new, previously unimagined difficulties seemed to arise every day. 'It was 1980 or 81,' she says,

a time of crisis, of food shortages and other problems. The OMM were meeting [Amélia had volunteered as a secretary], and a lot of problems were being raised. Samora couldn't attend all the meetings, but he wanted to hear all that went on. Whatever time it ended, we had to make a resumé of that night's proceedings, and then deliver the full transcript the next day. At 2 am he turned up with his bodyguard, with a cardboard box full of food. 'I know you haven't eaten, and I'm worried about you,' he said. There was coffee, sandwiches, fruit. 'You want strong coffee?,' he asked, pouring it out for us into mugs. He'd brought it from the presidential palace. No-one else ever thought to see if us secretaries were OK, to see that we had food and drink if we were working all night. Only Samora. And again at 5 am he sends someone to see that we're OK. No other Minister ever took the trouble.

Amélia pauses and sighs. 'This is the difficulty and the danger of memory,' she says. 'You try to be objective, but when you have a close relationship with someone, you can't be objective, it's just not possible ...'[13]

Pousada/Inn

2008: On the plane going north I open this week's *Tempo* and see there's an article about a young businesswoman who's taken over the Pousada de Lichinga and is going to transform it into a destination of choice for tourists.

When we moved to Lichinga in 1978 Christopher and I stayed at first in government lodgings and walked to the Pousada de Lichinga every day for lunch. The *pousada*: the inn. Basic by name and basic by nature. It was a concrete, boxy, 1930s-ish building opposite and just up from the post office on the central crossroads of the town. In my memories of that time all I can conjure up of its interior is the *sala de jantar*, the little dining room at the back of the building which you reached by going through an inner room that was permanently dark. The dining room contained seven or eight small tables covered in fraying brown nylon cloths ; it was mostly unused except by the two of us next to a window looking on to the back yard, and in the diagonal corner a French agronomist called François. Occasionally there would be other guests, government officials of insufficiently high status to be lunching with the governor or any of the provincial directors of services.

Lunch at the Pousada was the same every day: boiled grey pig's ear that wobbled hairily on the plate next to a spoonful of glaucous rice. Why was it always pig's ear? Where was the rest of the pig? I was adrift in a sea of questions, one of which, what was I doing here? I hardly dared consider. I hadn't started work; the head of the Escola Ngungunhana, to which I was told I'd been posted, had received no instructions and seemed less than enthusiastic. I poked at the pig's ear with my fork so that it wobbled even more and then struggled to hold back the tears that were always brimming and ready to spill over. I felt desperately homesick.

'Un café, s'il vous plait!' François shouted in the direction of the young waiter as he disappeared through the door into the kitchen. Then, furiously, *'Il y a du fromage? Du fruit?'* Nothing happened, and with a final *'Ha! Les merdes!'* and a curt nod in our direction, he pushed back his chair and stalked from the dining room.

The first time this happened we thought he was cross about the slow service. Then we puzzled over why he gave his orders in French. At last the waiter, emerging from the kitchen once François had left the room, explained: there was no coffee, no cheese, no fruit. There had never been coffee, or cheese, or fruit, not since the olden days (see ***Antigamente***). The comrade senhor Frenchman knew this very well.

Like a lot of *cooperantes* working on their own outside Maputo, François was lonely and unhappy. So I realised later. He expressed his unhappiness through a rhetoric of sarcasm towards all aspects of the revolution he had come to help, and this included shouting incomprehensible and impossible demands at the bewildered waiter in the Pousada. I realised too that pig's ear featured so large on the menu because it would have been considered disrespectful to offer the basic peasant food of *matapa* and *chima* (see ***Matapa*** and ***Chima***), green vegetable slurry with maize porridge, and there wasn't much else.

Who got to eat the other bits of pig in this mainly Muslim town was a mystery I never solved.

Lichinga thirty years later, and the Pousada flaunts its clean modernist lines in bright blocks of yellow and white paint. I'd quite forgotten how sunlight falls into the reception area through the tall bevelled windows in the Pousada's façade and illuminates the plain wide stone stairs that lead from beside the desk up to the first floor. A young woman stands behind the desk in a thick mustard-coloured coat buttoned up to her neck. She denies having received my booking, but luckily there are no other guests. She smiles mysteriously to herself while I fill in, at her insistence, a green protocol form. Car registration, mother's maiden name: I remember irrelevant questions like this from thirty years before. Surely these can't be the same colonial-era forms that they were using after Independence? When I've finished she puts it away carefully in a drawer and hands me the key for Room 2.

'It's a low season for tourists,' says the receptionist in Mia Couto's novel *O último voo do flamingo* (*The Last Flight of the Flamingo*), a novel set in post-post-independence times in a fictitious town in northern Mozambique that bears a strong resemblance to Lichinga. The receptionist is joking: there are never any tourists in this town. When I read Justin Fox's *With Both Hands Waving*, his hilarious and vivid account of a road trip around Mozambique in 2002, it somehow didn't surprise me that he and his companions failed to reach Lichinga. They had planned to, but were struck down variously with malaria, amoebic dysentery, sandworm in the foot and proto-psychosis brought on by anti-malaria medication, and had to turn back.

The other two people having lunch in the *sala de jantar* in 2008 are dressed for business rather than tourism and are complaining loudly at the inordinate length of time they are being made to wait for their *sopa de batata*, their potato soup. It could be thirty years ago and François complaining about the service.

I think Christopher and I are sitting at the same table we used to sit at, but thank God we don't have to eat pig's ear. It doesn't even appear on the menu, which is written up in shaky black felt tip, with many crossings out and illegible additions, on a board propped up on a table by the kitchen door. Instead we have *frango*—fried chicken—and chips. It comes long before the other couple's potato soup and is delicious—that hot greased meat taste I remember so well, and tearing at the skinny carcase to get the meat off the bones. Each table has an overlarge arrangement of fraying nylon flowers in pink and purple, on a pale brown nylon tablecloth also frayed at the edges. It's pretty much exactly as I remember it. Were ketchup and salad cream available before? I can't remember, but the plastic bottles are stiff and cracked enough to have been there since Independence. The waiters still haven't been to waiters' school, and snatch your plate away before you've finished, as if they're anxious to get on with the washing up. And then stand huddled in the corner with their backs turned, laboriously filling in receipt books on top of a large metal food trolley that contains only the ketchup and salad cream bottles. But there's beer, which never used to be on offer. I feel a sudden strong rush of affection for the Pousada.

The newly-built Girassol, part of the Girassol chain (see **Girassol**), just round the corner not fifty yards from the Pousada, offers a gloomy foyer behind tinted glass, low ceilings, and air conditioning. A sign on the reception desk boasts internet access, but the unsmiling man sitting behind it is pleased to tell me it's not working.

Room 2 at the far end of the Pousada's upper corridor is light and airy, and has a private bathroom. The matching pine veneer of the bedroom furniture—bed, dressing table, wardrobe—is adorned with fancy lights that don't work and none of the drawers have handles, except for a drawer in the bedstead head that pokes into my back when I sit up on the bed to read. I've reached the bit in *The Last Flight of the Flamingo* when the narrator and the man from the UN he's looking after are being shown to their rooms in the novel's *pousada*. The receptionist has just told them that there's electricity for only one hour per day, and goes on:

– There's also no water in the taps.
– No water?
– Don't worry my dear sir: first thing in the morning, we'll bring you a can of water.
– And where does this water come from?
– The water doesn't come from anywhere: it's a boy who brings it.

When the receptionist shows the UN man to his cockroach-infested room, the narrator notices a 'gooey liquid' dribbling down the walls.

– Is that water?
– If only it was, but as I mentioned, we don't have any water here.[14]

The window catches are broken, so the windows swing to and fro in the night-breeze and the thick shiny leaves of a huge tree outside lap and rustle against each other all night long like rainfall. But the mosquito mesh is newly installed and unbroken, and I know that I would rather be sleeping here than in the recycled air of the upmarket Girassol.

The next morning I notice water seeping up from the edges of the floor tiles in the bathroom.

Breakfast consists of some very small pieces of bread, with jam and butter. Plates but no knives. I have a total memory block against the Portuguese word for 'knife,' so I mime it, and the waiter brings one. Only one. He looks surprised when I ask for one each. We drink instant coffee made with hot water from a battered Frelimo-decorated thermos. No milk today, sorry. I tell the waiter that we were here in *pós-independência*—post-independence. That was a long time ago, he says, shaking his head in amazement. We met the President here in Lichinga, Samora

Machel. Ah yes, Samora Machel, I learned about him in school. I ask how long he's been working at the Pousada. Not long, he says. He's come up to Lichinga from the lakeside, and what he really wants is to go and work in one of the new hotels in Pemba. That's a long way away, I say. Suddenly he breaks into English. They have lots of tourists in Pemba, he tells us. From under the big empty metal food trolley behind him a rat whisks out and vanishes round the open door into the kitchen.

In the reception area our receptionist continues to display a Gioconda-like smile while a young woman with a baby strapped to her back and an older woman holding a mop chat to her in a language I don't recognise. Thick electrical cables snake across the floor and a man up a ladder is removing the front door frame. I wonder if this is part of the refurbishment I read about, but when I ask the Gioconda she doesn't understand me. I explain that although we're leaving today to go down to the Lake we'll be back in four days time, on Monday, and would like the same room if possible, please.

But when we come in through the frameless doorway four days later and find the same three women chatting by the desk, they turn to us in astonishment, as if they hadn't expected to ever set eyes on us again. 'Can we have the same room, please, Room 2?' No, we can't. Apparently the Pousada's almost full up. Who with? we wonder, a sudden influx of tourists?

Instead we're given Room 3, at the far end of the wide corridor from last week's Room 2, into which I see a Portuguese-looking man disappear. Room 3 doesn't have its own bathroom. The lavatory and bathroom are down another corridor and neither of them appears to have a lock or bolt. When I go to wash only a thin trickle of water comes out of the basin tap, and I can't flush the lavatory. I wake in the early hours with stomach cramps, and although I tell myself over and over that they are stress-related and brought on by fear of the possibility of *falta de água*, lack of water—a Mozambique-specific *falta de água* phobia—my body doesn't believe me.

By dawn I'm rushing to and from the unflushable lavatory, and at seven o'clock I send Christopher downstairs to report the *falta de água*. Ten minutes later there's a knock on the door, and the receptionist's adviser/sister—now without a baby on her back—tells me, *já água*, but when we go together to inspect this miracle she shows me that by '*já água*' she's referring to two buckets of water in the bathroom, one of which is standing in the bath collecting drips from the shower head.

How do you wash with water from a bucket if there's no plug in the basin? Especially when your head's spinning with delirium? I manage it somehow.

As well as bowels-turned-to-liquid I now think I might vomit, so I take two Diafixes. My guts judder to a stony halt, and I get the strange hallucinatory clear-edged vision that I used to get when I took Feminax in the days when hyoscine was still an active ingredient. I sit on the cane sofa in front of the reception desk while Christopher stands outside, smoking and keeping an eye out for the taxi that's going to take us to catch our plane to Nampula. La Gioconda's friend or sister continues to toil up and down the stairs with buckets of water on her head. Two middle-aged men pass her as they come down the stairs. One of them is black and the other is the Portuguese-looking one I saw going into our old room.

The Portuguese fellow launches into a list of complaints: what kind of a hotel is it where you can't have a shower when you want? Where you can't even wash your face? Where the bathroom floor is wet with water coming from somewhere?

La Gioconda lowers her eyes and smiles as if she knows the answers to all these questions but has chosen not to share them with anyone else.

'How can you possibly expect to attract tourists?' Do I see a little shrug of the shoulders beneath the mustard yellow coat? A shrug of I-don't-care? Or is it the Diafix making everything flicker before my eyes?

The Portuguese turns away from the desk and sweeps out his arm to include me: How can they hope to bring tourists here? he cries. In my head I hear the echo of François's despairing voice: where's my coffee? Where's my fruit and cheese?

At that moment Christopher comes in to tell me the taxi's outside. *Até a próxima!* I say, standing up. Until the next time! For a moment the two women look startled. Then their faces break into enchanting smiles. *Boa viagem!* they chorus. Safe journey! *Até a próxima!*

Povo

O *povo*: the people. (See also under **Elephants.**) At Independence public discourse was peppered with *o povo*, and if the actual noun didn't feature in the title of one of Samora's speeches—*Fazer da escola uma base para o povo tomar o poder* (Make schooling a base for the people to seize power), or *Transformar o Hospital Central num hospital do povo* (Transform the Central Hospital into a people's hospital)—then you could guarantee that it would appear in its adjectival form: *Estabelecer o poder popular para servir as massas* (Establishing people's power to serve the masses).

Lojas de povo were the people's shops, and a *jornal de povo*, six or eight pages pinned up flat on noticeboards in schools, hospitals and other large workplaces, a people's newspaper. Whereas I found the shelves of the *lojas de povo* in Maputo generously, if almost exclusively, stocked with bars of dark green soap when I first arrived in 1978 (see under **Girassol**), in Niassa six months later the shelves carried no soap but were stacked with an arsenal of cylindrical tins of powdered KLIM (read it backwards). The failures of state centralism, especially in agriculture and in retail trade, were becoming glaringly obvious. What do people want to buy? and how to get those goods into shops? became pressing questions. In July 1979 Samora spoke, in 'Organising our Resources to Resolve the People's Problems,' of the 'absurdity' of a *loja* in a rural area 'having its shelves loaded with tinned beans but devoid of *capulanas*.'[15]

Where once *o povo*, the people, were the focus of so much official thought and speech, a generation later poverty—*a pobreza*—is the central subject. Poverty, from Latin *paupertas* via Old French *poverte*: misleadingly similar in look and sound to the Portuguese word '*povo*,' from the Latin *populus*. Different roots and meanings converging in the reality of the poverty of the mass of the people.

When the Constitution was rewritten in 1990, a year after Marxism-Leninism had been abandoned at Frelimo's Fifth Congress, 'People' was quietly dropped from the People's Republic of Mozambique. (But the flag stays the same: see **AK47**.)

When I check in *Moçambicanismos*, expecting to find this word, like *camarada*, qualified by *caiu em desuso*—fallen into disuse—I find that there's no entry at all for the once ubiquitous *o povo*.

Q

Quelimane

Pronounced '*kell-ee-marn-e.*' Coastal town north of the river Zambezi, once a busy port—and major slave-trading centre—before the river that linked it to the Zambezi silted up. Notoriously swampy and mosquito-ridden.

End point in 1856 of David Livingstone's two-year-long transcontinental trek from Luanda on the western seaboard. He spent six weeks in Quelimane, returning as Her Majesty's Consul two years later, charged with commanding an expedition to further explore the interior.

When Robert Mugabe crossed into Mozambique from Rhodesia in 1975, soon after the assassination in Zambia of the ZANU leader Herbert Chitepo, and while most of the rest of the ZANU leadership (see **Tongogara**) were detained in a Zambian prison, he arrived as an unknown. The Frelimo leadership had no idea of his provenance, nor of his position within the fractured body of Zimbabwean resistance (see ***Soledariedade***). They gathered him up and packed him off to Quelimane to work as an English teacher while they checked out his credentials.

R

Reeducação

Niassa 1978: How casually we accepted the concept of re-education, although even then, in the 1970s, it was a word that clattered in our ears with Stalinist echoes. Re-education teaches people to think in a different way from how they have thought before, teaches them to think in a way that is approved by a government, or a party. Or, rather, it insists that they think in that way. We are all taught to think in one way or another, and we all tend to accept as right or true those beliefs with which we have been brought up, or with which we have been educated. So what's the difference between education and re-education, I've been asking myself, beyond the fact that we educate the young, and re-educate the adult? Perhaps the difference lies in the possibility of dissent: while education—ideally, but neither always nor universally—allows it, its absolute prohibition lies at the heart of re-education.

Grammatically, *reeducado* or *reeducada* means a man or woman who has been re-educated, but in Mozambique the word was used to mean someone currently undergoing re-education: it described the women in miniskirts and tight t-shirts bumming cigarettes on the street corners of Lichinga, who looked as if they came from not just a different country from the local women in their patterned cotton *capulanas* (see ***Capulana***) with their babies swaddled on their backs, but from a different world entirely; and it described men in worn-out townie shoes waiting miserably in the hospital to be treated for the TB and sleeping sickness they would catch again as soon as they were back in the re-education camps. It described the Jehovah's Witnesses and their families, who, accepting no authority other than their God, refused to join in with *Viva Frelimo!*.

Frelimo preferred to call the places where they sent people for re-education '*centros de reeducação*'—centres—rather than '*campos de reeducação*'—camps—as sounding more educational and less punitive, but '*campos*' was widely used. And they were indeed camps: spartan and basic camps in the bush far from any amenities.

I think now that my casual acceptance of re-education came in part from an unwillingness to believe that my hero Samora Machel would act with deliberate injustice. In the early days, too, re-education was a short-term experience, except for the armed struggle dissidents and enemy agents, whose very existence was never publicly mentioned (see **Simango**). Being sent to a re-education camp was a matter of bad luck, to be endured like other forms of bad luck, and certainly not as potentially terminal as being incarcerated by the colonialist authorities.

* * *

Revolutionary dialogue:

Alvaro, a student in 8th class, approaches me one Tuesday lunchtime to ask me, as his class teacher, to sign him off from school for the rest of the week. He's already got the deputy head's signature. I'm about to sign when I read the details on the *guia*: 'the bearer of this *guia* is permitted to leave school for three days in order to travel to Nampula and give support—*dar apoio*—to the family of his uncle who has been bitten by a mad dog.'

'Bitten by a mad dog?'

'Yes, *professora* Sara.'

'But there's no rabies in northern Mozambique.'

Alvaro hangs his head. 'There are mad dogs in Nampula province,' he whispers. I sign the *guia*, but at the end of the day I search out the deputy head, João, and ask him why he typed out a fraudulent permit for Alvaro.

'You don't understand, *camarada* Sara.' João enjoys telling me I don't understand things. 'Alvaro's uncle has been sent to re-education.'

'Oh, I'm sorry.'

João shrugs his shoulders and turns away. I'm mortified that I haven't realised how shameful re-education is.

The next day one of the girls asks where Alvaro is, and is answered by a chorus of cheerful cries that he's gone to Nampula to the family of his mother's sister because his uncle has been sent to re-education. And I wonder whether the mad dog was invented by Alvaro and the deputy head solely for my benefit, to protect the sensibilities of someone who comes, after all, from a capitalist country and therefore can't understand the revolution. Then I realise: no, both Alvaro and João thought I would be more likely to sign the *guia* on account of an impressively dramatic mad dog than on account of common-or-garden re-education.

* * *

Re-education camps were the sites of terrible injustices, as Samora himself found out on a 1981 tour when he found, in the Ruarua camp in Cabo Delgado, a group of old guerrillas. It made him sick to his stomach to see them there, he said:

> Just because someone was six hours late for work he was sent to the re-education camp, because he was absent for four days, or for a small fault, he was sent for re-education alongside the traitors, criminals, corrupt elements and scoundrels ... some of our freedom fighters (who) because of some minor fault or deviation, had been detained for six years in the re-education centre... They had been detained for six years ... six years![1]

Ruarua was closed, and in Niassa the camp commandant was arrested by Governor Aurélio Manave after Samora had found old, sick people there in 'medieval' conditions, subjected to brutality and abuse. The Jehovah's Witnesses had been singled out for specially cruel treatment.[2]

Samora did not view the camps, or centres, as places of punishment. Rather, he saw them as offering a chance to their inhabitants to regain honour and dignity, and to transform themselves into active, worthy members of society. 'Our policy of re-education is correct,' he insisted, in the same speech about Ruarua. 'It is an achievement and a revolutionary measure. The re-education camp has already produced good results for our revolution. It has produced men from the human wrecks left by colonialism. It has liberated the minds of men who had been trained only to kill ...'

In a newspaper article a year after his death, the writer Lina Magaia was remembering some of the occasions when Samora had spoken to her intimately. One day in 1982, she recalled, he said: 'You know, Lina, I don't want to die. I love life. I believe that man is a creature with endless potential for change (*é um ser transformável*), and that with education, and when necessary, with re-education, he develops and becomes a useful part of society, and becomes more human.'[3]

Grand ideas, but I doubt they would have impressed the women in Niassa re-education camps who at Independence had been swept up off the streets of Maputo and Beira on the orders of Armando Guebuza, Minister of Internal Administration under the Transitional Government (and see ***Operação Produção***), in one of the first acts of government that expressed Frelimo's deep anxiety about female sexuality in general and prostitution in particular.

* * *

Revolutionary dialogue:

Christopher and I and *doutora* Moira are spending a weekend at the geology camp down on the lakeside near Metangula. The camp is set back half a kilometre from the shore, amidst tall grasses that sway like metronomes beneath the weight of the gourd-shaped nests that weaver birds have fashioned high up on the stalks. The path is narrow and single file. When we arrive we find a disciplinary meeting in progress. The previous night the police raided the camp and found in the workers' tents five women from the re-education camp up on the plateau. The women were taken away, the workers left to be disciplined by the geology team.

'They were wild women,' says one of the workers.

'They had slept with lions,' pipes up another.

'They were so fierce we couldn't refuse them,' claims a third.

Piet, the South African exile who is head of the geology team, begins to lecture them on the anti-revolutionary nature of commercial sexual transactions, raising his voice over their not-so-low mutterings of 'we couldn't help it,' and 'they forced us to do it.' The three of us slip out of the tent and walk back through the high dry yellow grass to the beach.

Later, as the hills of Malawi rise up black against the setting sun, we pass round a bottle of Algerian wine and watch the Nyanja fishermen, outlined against the crimson sky, pole their canoes down the lake towards Metangula.

'Those poor women were only doing it for cigarettes, I expect,' says Bernie, an American. 'I feel really sorry for them.'

'You're such a liberal,' says Piet.

'They can't have much to brighten their lives stuck in a re-education camp two thousand miles from home.'

'I know. But if they're casualties of the revolution it's not our place to remedy that.'

The grass behind us rustles and the weaver birds' nests dip forwards and back as a troop of monkeys with long tails held high over their backs emerge and skitter past us to drink at the water's edge. Scorpio clambers up the night sky and the moonlight lays a path across the water to our feet.

Piet's right, I think, but I wonder if he's trying to convince himself as much as us. His words echo harshly in the velvet silence of the night.

* * *

Re-education was a wide-ranging concept that covered people who were sent into villages in the countryside as well as those sent to the camps, or centres. At Independence the artist Malangatana Ngwenya (see **Malangatana**) experienced this milder form of re-education along with all the other *xibotsos* or ex-political prisoners of the colonial authorities. After undergoing six months of political-military training (see ***Político-Militar***) Malangatana was sent north to one of the communal villages (see ***Aldeias Communais***) in Nampula province. Samora sent him off with the words: 'These new experiences will feed into your art. You'll discover all sorts of new things.' Malangatana bore no grudge: rather the opposite. He told me that his experiences working amongst the villagers in Nampula province had indeed enriched his art. I was still puzzled as to why it had been deemed necessary to re-educate all the ex-political prisoners; it seemed to me that they had suffered enough at the hands of the PIDE and brutal prison guards. But that was not how Malangatana saw it.

'While I was in Nampula province, sent by the Party along with other ex-political prisoners to work in the communal villages,' Malangatana told me, 'an exhibition of photographs was held in Maputo, which included some of mine. Indeed one of my photos won second prize. Samora was there and he stopped and admired some of my pictures, not knowing that they were mine. "Whose are these?" he asked, and when he was told, he said, "Ah, so it's Malangatana. Where is he?" People told him I was in Nampula. "What, he's still in Nampula? When's he coming back?"'[4] Which struck me as a bit rich, considering Samora had sent him there in the first place. Malangatana recounted it without a trace of bitterness.

Notwithstanding a level of acceptance amongst many of those who were re-educated in this way, the fact that re-education camps were sited mainly in the north of the country, and especially in Niassa and Cabo Delgado, coloured the forcible sending of anyone to the north, even if it was not to a camp. When Ornila, Samora's daughter by Irene Buque, fell pregnant at the age of sixteen, and she was obliged by Samora to marry the baby's father, the two of them were promptly expelled from Maputo and packed off ... to Niassa. What had once been the liberated zones had now become punishment zones.

Renamo

In *Chronicler of the Winds*, Solveig Nordlund's 2006 film of Henning Mankell's 1995 novel (first published in Swedish as *Comédia Infantil*), we watch a scene in which a Renamo-ist enters a village and snatches a baby from a woman who's been too slow to run away. The man exhibits the iconography of insanity: staring eyes, crazed smile, wild hair. He's high as a kite: on drugs or bloodshed or both. He holds the baby up in the air over her head as she crouches in the dust, baring his teeth in a grin, then drops the baby into the wooden mortar in which only half an hour before the woman had been crushing peanuts for the evening meal, grabs the pestle, and, roaring with laughter at the mother's screams, pounds the baby to a pulp.

The film shows us this one event performed by a single Renamo-ist. In real life such barbarous scenes were enacted in their hundreds and thousands, throughout the decade of the 1980s, after what was then known as the MNR—standing for Mozambique National Resistance, its English-language title reflecting its origins in English-speaking Southern Rhodesia—had been adopted by apartheid South Africa. The South African security forces taught the men of the MNR to go into villages and round up the little boys and force them to kill their own parents, and incorporate the numbed and soul-destroyed children into their own ranks; they taught them to force the men of the village to watch their wives and daughters being raped; they taught them to force women at gunpoint to cook and eat the butchered bodies of their husbands and fathers.

One of the most notorious atrocities took place in July 1987 in the village of Homoíne in Gaza province. The final death toll reached 424. All the patients in the hospital were dragged from their beds and killed, including seven women and their newborn babies, whose corpses were found heaped together in a pool of blood.[5]

First person accounts of those terrible years are unbearably painful to read. So much cutting and slicing and crushing of vulnerable human flesh. Cristina Menos described a Renamo raid on her village in Sofala province in the centre of the country: 'One of the bandits took a knife and sliced off my right ear. He began to laugh and said I could call on Frelimo. My mother began to scream, and tried to flee. The same man grabbed her, cut off both her ears and threw them on the ground.'[6] In *Dumba Nengue* the writer Lina Magaia collects more eye-witness accounts of Renamo attacks than one would ever want to hear. 'Peasant Tales of Genocide' is the subtitle.

Ears, noses, lips, breasts, hands and feet: all could be, and were, hacked off to leave the person mutilated and forever marked. It was as if the very idea of a Mozambican identity, Samora's dream of unity, had to be chopped into little bits in the soft bodies of peasant women and men and their children.

Prior to 1980 it was not at all clear to the general population who these *bandidos armados*—armed bandits—were. Ever since Independence an organisation calling itself Africa Livre (Free Africa) had been broadcasting anti-Frelimo propaganda from somewhere or other: Rhodesia? Malawi? No-one was sure. Later, I discovered that Africa Livre was formed by a group of Portuguese and Mozambican soldiers from elite units in the defeated colonial army along with anti-Frelimo dissidents, and was based in Malawi.[7] It was quite different from the MNR, although it would join forces with them in 1982, but at the time the distinction was obscure. And the MNR? In 1974 Ken Flower, Director General of the CIO (Central Intelligence Organisation) in Rhodesia, created a group which he called the 'Mozambique Resistance Movement.'[8] The group was drawn from Mozambican anti-Frelimo refugees in Rhodesia and black soldiers from the Rhodesian army (thus differing from the racially-mixed Selous Scouts). Their job was twofold: to destabilise newly-independent Mozambique through acts of sabotage and terror, and to gather intelligence on the ZANLA guerrillas (see ***Solidariedade***) whose bases were inside Mozambique. By the time it moved to South Africa people were calling it the MNR. Then, as it gained a toehold and then a foothold inside Mozambique in the early 1980s, it began to go by a non-English name, as if it were a genuinely homegrown movement: *Resistência Nacional de Moçambique*, or RNM, or Renamo.

In some areas of the country they soon became known as the 'locust people.' As one old man explained to the journalist Joseph Hanlon: 'They eat everything—food, clothes and us—until we have no more. Then they go and eat elsewhere.'[9]

My own experience of Africa Livre/MNR/what will become Renamo happens on the journey I take from Lichinga to Maputo at the end of 1979. I hold the romantic notion that I can follow in Samora's footsteps from the Rovuma (I've already travelled the Rovuma/Lichinga leg with South African Piet, see **Matchedje**) to the Maputo, the river which gives its name to the capital. Samora's triumphant journey south in 1975 is such recent history that it hasn't yet been written about and it will be some years before I realise that Samora didn't march on foot from the Rovuma to the Maputo—of course not, it would have taken months—but helicopter-hopped southwards. By then I also realise that it wasn't exactly triumphant: Samora had a lot of persuading to do and had to marshal all the oratorical skills he had honed over the previous ten years to persuade the populations of the towns in particular—Sofala, Quelimane, Inhambane, the snakepit of Beira where Simango and Jardim (see **Malawi** and **Simango**) were poisoning the air—that Independence meant liberation, and was cause for joy rather than fear. I fondly imagine we're retracing that historic journey.

It's not until we reach the Zambezi river that the vague rumours of an anti-Frelimo group that we've been hearing for the last eighteen months begin to take form and detail. Miles upstream in Tete province the Cahora Bassa Dam is providing South Africa and Rhodesia with hydro-electric power; in front of us huge clumps of green matter jostle each other on the river's swift flow, showing a flash or splash of deep purple as they twist and turn. The water churns brown and cream in the narrow gaps between. It's like a living moving mat of grass and leaves. Someone knows what the clumps are: water hyacinths. How on earth will the wooden steam ferry fight its way through such a vegetable thicket to get to us?

We're probably smoking a joint. Or sucking on mangoes. Or both. Three blokes and me, leaning against the Toyota Land Cruiser that we've driven this far. We're all *cooperantes*: me, my English boyfriend Christopher, South African Piet, and American Bernie. A toothless old man stands on the slippery planks of the wooden jetty watching the progress of the ferry towards us. A large spliff droops from the corner of his mouth. We think he might be the ferry *responsável*. Two huge trucks roar up the road and belch to a stop behind us and two dodgy-looking Portuguese swing down from the cabs. Eighteen months of zero-growth Niassa and its exiguous commercial economy render me stupid: who can these drivers be with their great big trucks with Zydeco in yellow letters painted along the sides, just visible through the dirt? The trucks look different—longer, less chunky—from the East German trucks I'm used to. Then I realise: the men are drivers for a private company.

The paddles of the ferry bite into the tangled green mat and move the ferry steadily towards us. It docks, and the toothless old man, spliff still clamped between his lips, whips out a scythe from the waistband of his shorts and helps the pilot cut through the slimy strands of weed that are tightly wrapped around the wheel. Piet drives the Toyota onto the ferry and we follow, accompanied by a small boy with two goats. The two trucks clatter aboard. Huge hyacinth islands hurtle past us as the ferry noses out to the middle of the river. Christopher tells us that water hyacinths are the favourite food of manatees. But can manatees share a river with crocodiles? None of us knows the answer.

We join the truck drivers who, we've noticed, are smoking real Portuguese cigarettes as they lean over the iron railings. I turn from the green hilly landscape north of the river and look south over a flat brown plain. To the east two steel pylons, incongruous in the empty landscape, come into view. What are those for? A bridge, says one of the drivers, part of the new national highway. He speaks with an almost impenetrable southern Portuguese accent. 'But they've stopped work on it. Africa Livre!' He grins, showing two rows of blackened teeth, then draws his finger across his throat and makes a gurgling sound.

'Africa Livre.' That's what I recorded in my diary. We know exactly who the truckers mean: the *bandidos armados*, armed bandits, who come over the Rhodesian border with mines and grenades and knives.

We want to know how far south we can drive on the new road. The truckers shake their heads and go into a rapid, incomprehensible dialogue, then the second one says, slowly: 'Inhaminga-Dondo. But not at night. That's when Africa Livre plant the mines.' More throat-cutting gestures, and the one with blackened teeth winks at me.

We approach the southern bank. Another old man, brother or cousin perhaps to the first one, stands with a pitchfork at the end of the jetty and tries to clear a path for the ferry through the crowding water hyacinths. The truckers leap into their cabs and rev the engines; as soon as the ramp's down they accelerate off, waving goodbye. The second one shouts 'Inhaminga, Dondo,' out of the window as he passes, and gives us a thumbs up.

'I'm not sure it's sensible of Frelimo to be encouraging private transport firms,' says Piet, as we climb into the Toyota.

'If private truckdrivers are prepared to take the risks,' I begin.

'That's so short-termist of you.'

'Short-termist'! Did we really talk like that? Yes, we did. Or some of us did. Piet and I often quarrelled over Frelimo's 'line.' Its twists and turns were a source of anguish for him, while I hotly resented what I thought was his belief that because he was South African, and part of the liberation struggle, he knew better than me.

'Cut it out, can't you?' says Christopher. 'Come on, let's go.'

At first the road is asphalt, and crowded on both sides by dark green leafy bush. Thick swarms of small yellow and white butterflies fly out and smash themselves against the windscreen. We slow down but still they crash into the glass and smear themselves across it. Suddenly the asphalt gives way to a white sandy track, and thick bush gives way to sparse thorn. No more butterflies. The land looks empty; not a village in sight. The Portuguese truckers must have been driving like the wind, for the dust of their passing has already settled.

I'm feeling nervous. Why do Africa Livre or MNR or whatever they call themselves only mine the Inhaminga-Dondo road? I ask after a while. If this is the only road to Inhaminga, why isn't this one mined? I mean, if they're coming over the border from Rhodesia, then they've, um, got to come this way. Haven't they?

We consider this in silence. Then, 'Let's have some music,' says Bernie. He leans across me to put a tape of Kid Creole and the Coconuts into the machine, and turns up the volume.

It's three o'clock when we reach Inhaminga. We're starving hungry, and low on fuel. But we find a garage with diesel, and then find a *pousada* which, incredibly, can offer us something to eat. *Cima* (see ***Cima***) and groundnut stew, and cold black beer. What a feast. The food is cooked and served by the old Indian couple who run the place, both of them small and wizened. They tell us there have been no incidents on the road to Dondo for a couple of weeks. Incidents? 'The mines planted by the bandits. Two weeks ago a goat stepped on a mine and was blown up. Since then, quiet.'

As we leave Inhaminga and set off down the red earth road to Dondo we pass a couple of soldiers who wave beer bottles at us in their left hands and give the clenched fist salute with their right. Bernie's driving. The railway line runs down the east side of the road, on our left. We pass a goods train lying on its side, huge bales of cotton spilling out of the trucks and into the bush.

'Oh my God, that must be Africa Livre,' I say.

'Nah,' says Piet, still annoyed by our earlier disagreement. 'The tracks are bloody awful. It's probably just a derailment.'

'What's this?' says Bernie, looking in the mirror.

'What?'

'Coming up behind us.'

I turn round and see the square squat cab of an East German truck racing up behind us. We pull over as first one truck and empty trailer, then another, then another, six trucks and trailers in all rattle past us and leave us in a thick cloud of dust. 'Any mines ahead, we'll soon know about it,' says Piet. 'They're certainly keen to get to Dondo.' 'Before it gets dark,' says Christopher.

We all look at each other. Somehow we'd forgotten what the lorry drivers had told us that morning. 'Bloody hell,' says Bernie. He puts his foot on the accelerator. To our right the sun's beginning to go down in a peach-coloured haze.

There are about another fifteen minutes of daylight left, and about fifteen miles to go, when we round a corner and in the fading light see a group of small figures ahead of us in the middle of the road. I grab Christopher's arm. 'Fuck me,' says Bernie as he slows down; then he leans forward and flicks on the headlights, presses his foot hard on the accelerator, and the figures ahead scatter, scampering and leaping to the side of the road and then up into the branches of the overhanging trees.

I can't speak. My mouth's dry, my heart thumps, sweat prickles all over my skin. I'm still clutching on to Christopher. 'Ha!' says Bernie. We've shot past where the baboons have vanished into the bush, and he still has his foot hard down. Piet exhales loudly, as if he's been holding his breath. 'That was a bit hairy, wasn't it? But they were too small. It was obvious after the first moment.' It hadn't been obvious to me. 'I thought they were kneeling down,' says Christopher, 'to plant the mines, and that was why they looked so small.' 'Kneeling baboons!' I say. And suddenly we're all shrieking with laughter and we hit the tarmac road and we've made it to Dondo.

By 1979 Samora and some of the ex-guerrilla commanders were beginning to feel very uneasy about the cross-border raids made by the MNR. The uneasiness grew out of their own understanding of guerrilla warfare; they knew from experience how effective small armed groups could be in isolated areas. But they believed that whatever central organisation now propped up the *bandidos* would disintegrate into chaos once white minority rule ended in southern Rhodesia and it became independent Zimbabwe.

What happened was the very opposite of what they hoped. The Mozambique Resistance Movement/MNR moved to South Africa and swapped the Rhodesian secret service for the South African secret service as its master. It was transferred, in the words of Ken Flower, and he should know, 'lock, stock and barrel.' He elaborates: 'In the meantime I had told the British a little of CIO's involvement with the MNR (they were not unaware of it) and had advised the Governor's staff that we had cut all links with the movement. Subsequently, the MNR seemed to go from strength to strength, and I began to wonder whether we had created a monster that was now beyond control.'[10] Indeed.

Throughout the 1980s and until peace was brokered in Rome in 1992, many Western journalists chose to present the carnage inflicted on the people of Mozambique as a civil war; the Mozambican government always called it a war of destabilisation. It was a war of aggression launched by one hostile neighbour, taken up by another hostile neighbour, and then supported for years by hostile special interest groups in places as far away as the Vatican and the USA, and closer to home by the disparate group of anti-Frelimo Mozambicans in Beira (a hotbed of anti-Frelimo sentiment from the early days, see **Frelimo, Mondlane** and **Simango**) headed by the consistently oppositional Catholic Archbishop Jaime Pedro Gonçalves. Rather than a civil war, it was a truly internationalised war, financed by international capital.

In 'The Business of Peace: "Tiny" Rowland, Financial Incentives and the Mozambican Settlement', a 1998 analysis by Alex Vines of foreign commercial interests in Mozambique, and particularly those of the UK-based multinational Lonrho, Vines charts payments made to Renamo to keep them off the Beira oil pipeline in the middle of the country and the Nacala rail line in the north, and out of cotton and tea plantations. Towards the end of the article he asks the question: 'To what extent did the enormous protection payments made to the rebels during the war enable the insurgent group to sustain its activities?'[11]

Other explanations for Renamo's staying power and success jostle each other like the clumps of water hyacinth in the river Zambezi. Some point to perceived failures on Frelimo's, and indeed Samora's, part: their failure to deliver prosperity, their lack of respect for traditional beliefs and customs, their insistence on centralised control over a diverse population, their antagonism towards tribal difference, their disastrously unpopular agricultural policies, their lack of understanding of the history of the very region that they claimed to have liberated, with its traditions of rule by violent domination. And so on.

But no-one is able to deny Renamo's hideous brutality against the civilian population, which was spelled out as early as 1988 in the Gersony Report. Renamo's massacres, mutilations, rapes, the coercion of children into killing their own mothers and fathers, and the creation of armies of brutalised child soldiers, became the very model of warfare in other African countries where land and its mineral wealth have attracted greedy attention.[12]

Literacy levels plummeted as infant and maternal mortality soared. Where Mozambique had once been the darling of the WHO and looked up to by revolutionaries and idealists the world over, within ten years it was on its knees and the cynosure of cynics who for their own multifarious reasons require independent African countries to appear as vortices of chaos.

For all the talk of good neighbourliness (see **Nkomati**), apartheid South Africa could not bear to be flanked by a stable socialist independent Mozambique. On Christmas Eve 1984 a captured Renamo fighter, speaking at a rally in Manhica, described how he had been given military training in South Africa prior to being sent in to Mozambique with Renamo, after the signing of the Nkomati Accord and the consequent Pretoria Declaration. 'Let's make no mistake,' said Samora at the rally, 'South Africa is the key to the problem, and that's why we signed the Nkomati Accord.'[13] Eight months later, in August 1985, Zimbabwean paratroopers, upon whom Mozambique was becoming increasingly reliant, stormed the Renamo HQ, Casa Banana in Gorongosa in the heart of the country, and found piles of documents including diaries kept by one of the Renamo leaders that showed the full extent of South African military, logistic and financial involvement in what they tried to persuade the rest of the world to call a 'civil war.' On 5 September Samora visited Casa Banana and declared: 'We have broken the back of the snake. But,' he went on, 'the tail will still thrash around for a while.'[14]

He was wrong. The back of the snake wasn't broken. A more accurate image would have been a worm cut in two, which goes on to enjoy vigorous life in both its parts. The war would continue for another seven years, gaining a momentum from the very destruction it wreaked, such that it lived on beyond the start of transition from apartheid in South Africa; the monster created by the white Rhodesians and nurtured by the apartheid regime next door acquiring, like Frankenstein's monster, a vital life of its own.

And how was it brought to an end? As attested by the UK-based NGO Conciliation Resources, millions of dollars were poured into Renamo bank accounts by Lonrho and by the Italian government, both of them desperate that the negotiations, hosted by the Sant'Egidio Catholic lay community in Rome, would lead to a peaceful political settlement.[15] The Renamo leaders were kitted out with designer suits and shoes from the most fashionable Italian shops, their families were flown to visit them by private jet, their thousands of dollars worth of telephone bills ($60,000 in the first six months of 1992) were picked up by those anxious to see the papers signed. Gossip still circulating in Mozambique twenty years later has the Renamo representatives drunk as skunks during the final negotiations on the whisky on which they'd squandered their swelling bank accounts.

Would Samora have succeeded in ending the war earlier had he been allowed to live? The general feeling in Mozambique is: no. After laying himself on the line at Nkomati, he would never have swallowed talking to Renamo. And agreeing to share power with men fuelled by greed for the Western baubles that Samora so despised? It's hard to imagine.

Research Trip

2010: Three or four weeks before my research trip to Mozambique I emailed once again all the old comrades whose addresses Paul Fauvet had given me—amongst them Joaquim Chissano, Marcelino dos Santos, President Guebuza, and all their press attachés and secretaries and what-have-yous—asking if I could see them, although by then I'd given up hope of getting a response. Mia Couto, whom I'd met in England on the publication of the English translation of his novel *The Last Flight of the Flamingo* (see ***Pousada***), had joined the growing ranks of those not replying to my emails.

I hoped that when I got to Maputo and rang people, some of them at least, or even one or two, might say, oh yes, I got your email, you're writing a biography of Samora aren't you, please do come and have a chat. Only two people had already said yes: Janet Mondlane, the widow of Eduardo Mondlane, and the writer Nelson Saúte. With Janet it had been such a toing and froing with her already that I wouldn't believe I was talking to her until I was actually sitting in front of her with my recorder switched on. The last flurry of emails we exchanged purported to be about arrangements to speak on Skype, but despite my best efforts I never managed to pin her down to a day or time when we would speak to each other. Tomorrow? I wrote optimistically, then, next week?, then, despairingly, when? And at that our correspondence once more stuttered to a halt. Nelson, who wrote so interestingly in Duarte Tembe's book *O Destino da Memória* about the stories and myths that have sprung up around the freedom fighters, emailed briefly: ring when you get to Maputo. Duarte Tembe was one of the many who didn't reply. The only email address I could find for him placed him at the Police Academy in Maputo, but as that was ten years earlier it was hardly likely he would still be there.

I reminded myself that neither Janet nor Nelson had invited me to do more than ring them: there was still plenty of opportunity left for not meeting them. The same held for Sérgio Vieira, who was the first director of the president's office after Independence, later Agriculture Minister, then Governor of Niassa, and, at the time of Samora's death, Security Minister. He found himself in the terrible position of responsibility for the failure of security that brought about the death of the man who embodied everything for which Vieira himself and all the other loyal comrades had struggled for over twenty years. Whether Samora was assassinated, or whether his death was a ghastly accident, Vieira's ministry was responsible either way. He had failed to look after his President, his comrade, his friend. At the scene of the crash he wept over the broken bodies that lay scattered on the hillside.

Of all the Frelimo cadres I wrote to, to ask for their cooperation, Sérgio Vieira, bearded and intense and characterised some years earlier by Paul Fauvet as an 'abrasive Marxist,' was one of the ones I was least expecting to reply. In fact he replied at once. He would put himself entirely at my disposal, with enormous pleasure. Thus began an exchange of elaborate formal Portuguese-style courtesies that continued for some months without any tangible results, for the questions about his relationship with Samora that I sent by email went unanswered, while he continued to assure me that he was still utterly at my disposal. Could I perhaps meet up with *o exmo senhor*—the most excellent sir—when I visited Maputo? I wondered. Alas, while reaffirming his great desire to help me in any way he could, he would be quite unable to leave the northern province of Tete during the dates of my visit to the capital. Oh how I understood these difficulties, and how I regretted that the chances of my visiting Tete this time were so small, but perhaps we could try Skype? The reply this time was considerably less flowery than customary: *Não uso Skype e não quero usar. Lamento. Ficamos no e-mail.—I don't use Skype and don't want to use it. Sorry. Let's stick to email.—Saudações. SV*

Meanwhile I'd been reading his recently-published memoir, seven hundred plus pages, which Paul Fauvet lugged over to Britain for me from Maputo. *Participei, por isso testemunho*, it's called: I was there, and this is my testament.

He was indeed there, from the age of nineteen. How young they all were. The ones who came from Europe to join Frelimo were students who'd met each other and their peers from the other Portuguese 'overseas provinces'—Angola, Cape Verde and

Guinea-Bissau—at the *Casa Africana* in Lisbon. Sérgio, born and brought up in Tete, of Goan background, had had to flee Portugal and the PIDE before he was able to take his finals. Many of those who fled Mozambique were even younger: secondary school students like Josina. Samora was older: thirty when he reached Dar es Salaam in 1963.

In between the hard graft of building and sustaining a united liberation front, they all larked about. Jacinto Veloso prints a photograph of some of the teachers at the Mozambique Institute climbing a palm tree. There's Aurélio Manave, whom I knew as the grimly authoritarian Governor of Niassa in the late 1970s, crouched halfway up the ridged trunk, hanging on by one arm, turned to the camera and grinning beneath the palm's feathery fronds.

* * *

During the flight to Johannesburg I watch the film of J.M. Coetzee's novel *Disgrace*, which could hardly be better designed to make one feel extremely depressed about South Africa and black/white relations. Then I doze off and on, but nonetheless I feel shattered on arrival. On the hour-long flight from Johannesburg to Maputo I feel my anxiety levels rising. Will anyone agree to see me? Or will it be a wasted journey?

Maputo airport looks less festive and more shabby than when I came in 2008: the flagpoles are bare (then a line of fluttering flags welcomed the arrivals) and the red and blue hoardings exhorting us to explore the world with Visa have been taken down. I wonder about the significance of this. We're stuck in the airport for an hour and a half, as, although my suitcase has arrived and been unloaded, Monica's has not, and we find ourselves at the very end of the queue outside the lost and found office, where one person only is dealing with the many complaining passengers whose luggage has not arrived. I'm desperate for a pee—I wanted to go as we came slowly, oh so slowly through immigration (a Lisbon flight arrived simultaneously with ours) but I couldn't find a ladies', and as soon as we're through immigration I rush to the one I can see only to find the door not only bolted shut and padlocked but screwed tight to the adjacent wall with a hinged metal plate. Desperate as I am I dare not enter the gents'. We wait in the lost and found queue, and then I think I'd better go out into the arrival hall and find Paul Fauvet, who kindly said he would meet us, to tell him we're stuck. On the way I find a lavatory. What a relief. Two Indian women are discussing whether not to use it because there's no paper, and we have a laugh together about waggling instead of wiping.

Back at lost and found we're assured that Monica's suitcase will come in on the 3pm flight from Johannesburg, and at last we emerge and climb into Paul's truck. The road from the airport takes us round the Praça dos Hérois, with a long mural of scenes from the armed struggle flanking one side of it, and a low star-shaped marble structure, in the middle of the central grass island, inside which lie the remains of Samora Machel, Josina Muthemba Machel and Eduardo Mondlane. Paul stood here on Tuesday 28 October 1986, having followed the funeral cortège from the City Hall where the President's body had been lying in state. He was covering the ceremony for the English-language news service. I recently re-read his account of that cold overcast day, with thousands of people gathered in Independence Square outside City Hall, weeping as they listened to Marcelino dos Santos delivering the funeral oration. He wrote:

> ... To the sound of a dead march, top ranking officers of the Mozambican armed forces carried Samora Machel's body onto a waiting gun-carriage, towed by an armoured car. A lone helicopter of the Mozambican air force circled overhead.
>
> The cortege moved slowly off through the streets of the city, arriving at the Square of Mozambican Heroes at 12.36 ... As Samora's body was slowly lifted down from the gun-carriage for the final march to the monument, a 21-gun salute rang out. At the sound of the first shot, every siren in every factory,

every ship's fog-horn, every bell in the city rang out in mournful tribute to the founder of the Mozambican state.

All traffic in the city stopped. All citizens in the street stood stock still for a minute's silence in honour of the man to whom they owed their freedom and independence. In the Square, tears trickled down the cheeks of Graça Machel, Marcelino dos Santos, and many other party and state leaders. The helicopter hovered some 200 metres above the monument—an austere, star-shaped structure, made of slabs of the purest white marble.

The military band then played the national anthem for their President for the last time. Slowly the coffin was carried to the entrance to the monument, accompanied by the members of the Political Bureau and the President's widow.

It was now noticeably colder than earlier in the morning. A biting wind chilled the mourners. The coffin entered the monument, and the rain came—not a downpour but mournful sprays gusting into the faces of all present.

Shortly after 13.00 Graça Machel walked slowly away from the monument, where she had just witnessed her husband being laid in his last resting place.

Samora Machel's coffin now lies fittingly next to that of Eduardo Mondlane. The man who created Frelimo, and the man who led it to victory, are now reunited.[16]

* * *

It seems strange, not exactly dignified, for the heroes of the revolution to be interred in the middle of what is essentially a traffic roundabout: no-one slows down, everyone seems hell-bent on getting as fast as they can to the airport, or to an urgent appointment in town. But when I say this Paul points out the advantages: no special excursion necessary, and is there not something fitting about lying at the centre of such a busy thoroughfare, at the heart of the movement of people?

A lone soldier stands to attention outside the entrance to the mausoleum. According to the guidebook it's open to the public once a year, on 3 February, the anniversary of the murder of Mondlane, but Paul's not sure if that's actually the case.

The road now takes us through an area of concrete shacks with tin roofs, thatched mud huts squeezed into front yards, banana trees bursting over concrete walls—rubbish everywhere on the dirt pavements, which are divided on one side from the road by a wide deep rubbish-filled concrete drainage ditch. In the rainy season, says Paul, it saves the whole area from flooding.

Where once the walls of the roadside shacks and stalls were covered with *Viva Frelimo!* or *Abaixo o imperialismo!* or *Viva o Homem Novo!*, they're now bright squares of colour advertising MCel, Vodacom and Coca-Cola. *Diz ola*: say hello, urges sunshine yellow MCel, or *estamos aquí*: we're here; MCel models grin with enthusiasm. One is a Macua girl in a *misuril*, a white face mask; another is Maria Mutola who won the 800 metres Olympic gold in 2000. Between their hands they hold yellow smiley faces. Blue Vodacom sells itself on cool rather than fun. A white globe of the earth against the blue rather than a yellow smiley face. *Liga já*: connect now. The Vodacom models smile more carefully: this is serious business in a serious world. Coca-Cola adds huge splashes of red to the yellow and blue: flowers burst out from the Coke bottles and dance across the walls.

Paul takes us to the Hotel Moçambicano on the Avenida Samuel Filipe Magaia (commander of the Frelimo army in the early 1960s, engaged to Josina, murdered 1966) in the centre of the upper town. It has all the mod cons—bar, beer, swimming pool (unused throughout our stay)—of the hotels that overlook the sea up at the smart end of town without the drawback of an ill-mannered white clientele who ignore the existence of the black hotel workers (see **Polana**). We have a cold beer while I try to sort out my phone. I've brought my Nokia which I discover won't work even with an MCel SIM card in it, but thank God I've brought a spare phone (just in case), my old cheapo pink Motorola, which functions on MCel once stern-faced but kind-hearted Sra Sonia at reception has gone out into the street and got me some credit for it from a street vendor. We return to the airport at 3.30 in a hotel car and sure enough Monica's suitcase has arrived as predicted, sitting small and lonely outside the empty lost and found in the abandoned airport hall.

Later we dine on cabbage soup and fried chicken and chips in the hotel restaurant and fall into our beds (comfortable mattresses, handkerchief-sized sheets), and I banish from my mind the fear that no-one will speak to me, and drop off to sleep.

The next morning I take a deep breath and ring the artist Malangatana Ngwenya, whose number Polly Gaster (see **CFMAG**) gave me, along with a strict warning about the state of his health. He tells me he's a river run dry, but that he'll see me nonetheless.

Janet Mondlane: I ring her office at the Mondlane Foundation and leave my name and number with a secretary, and Janet rings back on her mobile. She has no idea who I am. I explain, and she agrees to meet me.

Nelson Saúte: I leave a message on answer, and he rings back. He too has no idea who I am. I wonder if I'm pronouncing 'Sarah' in a strange way? He says he'll ring again the next day to arrange a meeting.

After the phone calls we set off down the Avenida Vinte Quatro Julho—24 July, Nationalisation Day—in search of the Museo da Revolução, the Museum of the Revolution, which has never been open any of the times I've been in Maputo. I remember the South African lawyer and ANC activist Albie Sachs, who lived in the flat below us when Christopher and I were in Maputo in 1978 (see **Girassol**), offering to take me round the Museo, but we found it closed. Ten years later Albie would lose his right arm in a car-bomb explosion set up by South African secret agents to kill him; he wrote movingly about his recovery in *The Soft Vengeance of a Freedom Fighter*.

In 2008 the Museo da Revolução was closed for refurbishing. It's still closed, or perhaps it's been open and now is closed again. I've only ever heard of one person finding it open and that was the travel writer Nick Middleton who in the early 1990s described the experience amusingly in *Kalashnikovs and Zombie Cucumbers*. He couldn't tell if the glazed-eyed man taking him round, who smelled faintly of alcohol and responded to everything Middleton said with '*exatamente*' ('exactly'), was an official guide or just a fellow who had happened to wander in off the street. Things were pretty chaotic in the early 1990s. Maybe that was why the Museum was open: they had forgotten to keep it shut.

We walk on down the hill to the Avenida Vinte Cinco Setembro—25 September, launch of the armed struggle. A huge amount of traffic jostles along the main *avenidas*. Lots of the cars are newish-looking 4x4s, but, unlike two years previously, they don't all have names of NGOs stencilled on their sides. Then, all the non-NGO cars had doors hanging off and spider-cracked windscreens.

I remember João Cosmé gloomily telling me that no white person could walk the streets of Maputo without attracting hostile attention (see **Difficulties**). But no-one takes the slightest bit of notice of Monica and me as we pick our way past the vendors on the broken sandy pavements: lads with MCel cards, cooked eggs, barrows of bananas, and women, sitting with their backs against the ropey trunks of the acacias, display on dusty cloths spread out in front of them small pyramids of bright red tomatoes, bowls of oranges, battered paper cups of roasted cashews. Our only anxiety is to avoid tripping on jagged slabs of broken concrete or the iron bars—presumably all that remains once the concrete has crumbled or been hacked away—jutting from the ground, and to avoid the sudden looming large uncovered holes that randomly pockmark what once were pavements.

The tower block facades are faded blues and pinks and yellows, their vertical lines of dividing walls and security grilles crossed with horizontal lines of bright yellows and reds of laundry hanging out to dry on balconies. The travel writer Justin Fox has aptly described these apartment facades lining the *avenidas*, flattened and perspectiveless against the bright blue sky, as 'Mondrianesque.'[17]

Streets are named after leaders of socialist revolutions and liberation struggles. You jump into a taxi: Ho Chi Minh, *faz favor*, you say, or Salvador Allende, or Vladimir Lenin, Karl Marx, Amilcar Cabral. From Julius Nyerere, where the smart hotels are, up Mao Tse Tung, crossing Armando Tivane, Kim Il Sung ... Most are long dead and forgotten, so much old history to a young generation that the tarnish of their reputations is as meaningless as the heroism for which they were first commemorated. Unscathed by the revisions of history, they're just streets now, where people live, trade and hustle. Except where at Independence they were named after living heroes. Fortunate perhaps that Robert Mugabe, about whom the current government is tight-lipped and silent, was granted only a small *praça*—a square—in an unfrequented corner far from the main thoroughfares.

I want to show Monica the elegant green and white painted Edwardian railway terminus with its verandahs and wrought-iron latticework and dome designed by a friend of Monsieur Eiffel. On one of the platforms we see tables and chairs set up outside a bistro, so we sit down and order a dish of prawns and rice for lunch. Groups of men in suits with electronic notebooks at their elbows are lunching either side of us. The tracks are empty, and no trains arrive. It feels like we're on a stage set, but I'm not sure what kind of play or film we're acting in.

The men pack up their electronic notebooks and return to their offices, and the tables are chairs are taken inside. We move to a wooden bench further down the platform and I make a few phone calls. Mateus Katupha (see **OJM**) switches to English as soon as I say where I'm from—what a relief—and says he'll be delighted to see me, and we arrange an appointment for the next day.

With a shriek and a whistle a train comes into view from round the far end of the platform and pulls in on the track in front of us. Its huge engine shudders and clanks, and passengers spill from the doors of a long line of broken-windowed rusty carriages, women with parcels and bowls and packages on their heads, and men in threadbare brown trousers and flip-flops. A little girl with dusty bare feet and with a large round package tied up in chequered cloth wobbling on her head smiles shyly as she passes us and then turns round, her burden lurching to one side, to stare and smile again.

To the AIM offices, where, Paul Fauvet has told me, I'll find a full run of the weekly magazine *Tempo* from 1975 onwards, with another collection in the Radio Moçambique offices next door. I want to look at Samora's 50th birthday issue, from 1983, which contains much of the biographical material that Iain Christie drew on for his book, and the memorial issue that came out in November 1986, just after Samora died. We walk up the hill through the parched and rubbish-strewn botanical gardens. Inside the giant broken ribcage of what had once been the hot-house, where a tangle of overgrown exotics now hurl their seeds skywards through the broken ribs, we stop for one second by the side of a murky pool where carp must once have coolly glided. A mosquito promptly darts up from the fetid water and bites me twice on the thin skin of my instep—or maybe it was two mosquitoes, one bite each.

The back copies of *Tempo* are ranged in a series of upright cardboard file boxes on a high shelf running the length of an office old-fashionedly cluttered with piles of paper. Senhora someone, whose name I don't catch, isn't best pleased to be asked to get them all down, but she does so and between us we carry them upstairs to where there's an empty conference room with a wide polished wooden table. The cardboard containers are mouldy with damp and age, the magazines dog-eared and sticky, but more or less in date order. First I look through 1983: no birthday issue. Then 1986: no death issue either. So we start riffling through the whole run to check all the dates, sneezing as eddies of green dust puff up our nostrils. 1978, 1979: some of these cover photos look strangely familiar, and I realise that these are the ones we used back then for fashioning lampshades, when the covers of *Tempo*, shiny and coloured, provided the only material to hand (see **Camarada**). An illuminated Samora mucking in with the rice harvest in Chokwe used to hang above our dining table in Lichinga. Here it is. But no sign of the two issues I particularly want.

Paul takes us next door and up the stairs to the Radio Moçambique library—Radio Moçambique, the site of the short-lived Portuguese resistance to Independence in 1974—where the *Tempos*, lined up on shelves in a glass-fronted bookcase, are less mouldy. Grateful for Paul's kindness, I'm nonetheless alarmed by his apparently random search methods: he pulls out three or four copies at a time, peers short-sightedly at the dates, then replaces them elsewhere. I try to organise it so that without appearing to be critical of his methods Monica and I manage to check every single copy and put them all back in order. An almost complete run, save, yet again, the birthday issue and the death issue.

We have some beers in a bar over the road on the edge of the botanical gardens and overlooking some spruce tennis courts which are sponsored by one of the banks. They should get private sponsorship for the botanical gardens, I find myself thinking. That's an idea I certainly wouldn't have had in the revolutionary days of the 1970s.

* * *

Of the two people—kind, generous people—with whom I was in touch from England and who invited me to ring when I arrived in Maputo, only one of them, finally, is available to see me. The writer Nelson Saúte doesn't turn up to the appointment we've made, and, when I ring him after waiting for an hour and a half, says he's ill, and that he'll ring me to make another appointment. But he doesn't. Cold feet? Second thoughts about sharing Samora with someone he doesn't know? With a white woman? A non-Mozambican? Or, simply, something more important to do than meeting me? Or, just possibly, feeling ill?

But Janet Mondlane, widow of Eduardo, agrees to see me, and all I worry about is getting to her before she changes her mind. Her airy light-filled house, with a view through trees (one of which was planted by Samora himself) of the sea on two sides, nestles on the Ponta Vermelha below the presidential palace where the bay curls around the land. Samora gave it to Janet at Independence. 'In my way I loved Samora, although we had differences. He said to my kids: "It's my job to take care of you."' He invited one of them, Nyeleti, now a member of parliament, into the presidential household and brought her up with all his own children (the other two children were at school abroad). Janet found Samora dictatorial in both political and personal matters, but extremely charming and charismatic. When he was talking to you, she recalls, 'he was talking to *you*.' She adds: 'That's characteristic of a good leader.' As I'm leaving she suggests I talk to the historian Amélia de Souto (see ***Destacamento Feminino*** and ***Pós-Independência***), who knew Samora in Nachingwea, and gives me her number, saying she'll tell her to expect a call from me.

During the next few days I begin to notice a reluctance in some people to share with me their access to one or two individuals. Jorge Rebelo is one of those individuals. Margaret Dickinson (see ***Behind the Lines***) described how back in the early days when she worked with him in the press office in Dar es Salaam, he would be enigmatically silent, creating an atmosphere around him as if he was busy processing philosophical ideas; later she wondered if he just didn't feel like saying anything. In his memoirs Sérgio Vieira gives us a scene of Rebelo sitting on the beach with the MPLA leader Agostinho Neto (see ***Soledariedade***), while the other revolutionaries swam or frolicked in the sea, and Neto, famous for his brooding silences, eventually leapt up saying, I can't believe I've met a man who has less small talk than I do.

Rebelo played a central role within Frelimo from the early days, suffered racist attacks alongside Mondlane for being married to a white woman, and during *o tempo de Samora* was the powerful Minister of Information, in which role he deployed his legendary silences to full effect, to the annoyance of the Mozambican press corps. Later he became head of the Ideology Department.

Mateus Katupha (see **OJM**): 'There were only two or three people in Mozambique who would stand up to Samora and say: "Eh, Samora, stop there and listen to me. I want to tell you something." One of those was Jorge Rebelo. Samora would listen to him.'

I'd been given Mrs Rebelo's email by Paul Fauvet, but four carefully worded emails to her produce no response. Only one person admits to possibly having a phone number for him, and that person won't give it to me.

I puzzle over the possible motives for such reluctance. Is it that people want to protect him from my intrusion? That they're scared of him? That he has stuff to say (from within his deep silences) that would be better left unsaid? Or is it something to do with his antagonism towards the present leadership, and his public criticisms of Frelimo's lack of self-criticism?

The more people to whom I speak the easier it becomes to speak to others, as the formula 'when I spoke to X yesterday he/she said …' or, even better 'he/she gave me your number …' gives me both courage and credibility. I begin to name-drop Malangatana, and to even greater effect, Mama Graça. But in order to wield the formula you first have to have the phone number, and I'm not tough enough to squeeze Rebelo's out of anybody.

Matias Mboa (see **Frelimo**) is another person whose phone number no-one appears to have in their address books, and emails to his publishers go unanswered. In his case the denial doesn't come surrounded by a crackling electricity of conflict and anxiety. It's more along the lines of, 'oh, I'm sure I've got it somewhere,' and then not finding it. I'd read a recent interview with Mboa on the subject of his post-independence arrest and seven-year imprisonment, in which he spoke of Samora apologising to him on his release and saying it had all been a big mistake, without explaining to the interviewer what it was that Samora had been mistaken about. But in the end I don't manage to see him so can't ask him myself about the reason for his imprisonment.

I conclude that the reluctance of some people to help me with their own contacts, or indeed to speak to me themselves, is because they think that the story of Samora and Mozambique is not mine to tell. For Graça, the fact that I worked as a *cooperante* post-independence is enough; for others it is not. I reflect on some of the people I have spoken to: Oscar Monteiro, for example, who'd been Justice Minister and Governor of Gaza and later architect of the Constitution, the journalist Paul Fauvet, the historians Amélia de Souto and David Hedges (who arrived in Mozambique in 1978 and 'got revolutionized and stayed'). They've all written widely already about Samora and the revolution. Perhaps, I think, the resistance or indeed resentment that I'm picking up on—if it isn't a fantasy of my own making—comes from people who have not yet told their own version of the Samora story. Knowledge is property; the biographer a potential thief.

On my last day in Maputo I visit Pastor Isaias Funzamo, whom Graça Machel has suggested I speak to. I was expecting an extremely elderly man as I thought that he'd been a pastor when Samora was a boy, but I've obviously grasped the wrong end of the stick. Not for the first time. I discover that Isaias was an exact contemporary of Samora, that during the armed struggle he and all his colleagues in the Swiss Presbyterian Mission in Gaza and Maputo raised funds for Frelimo and channelled them through the World Council of Churches, and that the first time he met Samora was in 1974 when he, Pastor Funzamo, led a delegation to Tanzania to hand over, in person, a sum of money earmarked for education and social development.

We sit together at a heavy mahogany table in an otherwise sparsely-furnished living-room, and he shows me a photograph of the delegation on the steps of a building in Dar es Salaam. He and Samora stand side by side in the middle, two short-statured, smiling men who both look younger than their forty years. The Pastor believes that the aims of Frelimo and the aims of the Presbyterian Church always ran in parallel: the development of a sense of the intrinsic value and dignity of all humankind, and a society based on the interwoven rights and responsibilities of a cohesive community. 'Many people said that Samora was a Marxist,' the Pastor tells me. 'But no. He was not a Marxist. He pretended to be a Marxist so as to get support from the Soviet Union and the socialist bloc. No. He was a Christian.' 'Always?' I ask, surprised. 'Always,' says the Pastor firmly. It's certainly what he believes.

When Samora's father died in May 1984, Samora asked Pastor Funzamo to conduct the funeral service at Xilembene, and, the Pastor tells me, expressed his pleasure at the way he did it. Sometime later Samora spoke to Mrs Funzamo, whose family were related to the Machels:

> He said [here the Pastor, like so many others I spoke to, imitates Samora's voice, speaking very quickly in warm tones]: "Here, cousin, I want to ask you something." [Back to normal voice] He asked my wife: "Who do you think is the better speaker, me or your husband?" And she said: "I can't say that one of you is better than the other." He replied: "You're right. I remember how your husband spoke at my father's funeral. He spoke really well."

Which is surely as revealing of Samora, wishing not to be outdone in oratory by his friend the Pastor, as it is of the tactful Mrs Funzamo.

In the last years of his life—and although we are alone in the room the Pastor now lowers his voice—Samora, beset by troubles on all sides, used to come to him privately, unbeknownst even to his family, for spiritual counselling. Pastor Isaias believes, as so many others have told me they do, that Samora lives on inside him, guiding him, alongside the spirit of Mondlane, in his daily decisions and actions (see ***Orientações***).

'Here, I have something for you to take away,' says the Pastor when our conversation is drawing to an end. 'I had them photocopied this morning, because I thought you might be interested.' He pushes a large brown envelope over the table towards me. I look inside: photocopies of the birthday issue, and the death issue, of *Tempo*.

S

SADCC

The Southern African Development Coordination Conference, a loose alliance of seven southern African countries, was inaugurated in Lusaka, Zambia on 1 April 1980. The countries—Mozambique, Angola, Botswana, Lesotho, Swaziland, Tanzania and Zambia (later joined by Zimbabwe)—already made up the Front Line States. In the SADCC their focus was different: to work together in order to strengthen their own economic development and to decrease their dependence on their giant neighbour. As detailed by Joseph Hanlon in his book *Beggar Your Neighbours*, apartheid South Africa was determined to sabotage the SADCC from its very inception and to reassert its own economic dominance of the region.

Samora

S is for Samora. This, the name of a 19th century soldier fighting in the Portuguese army (see **Baobab**), is the name by which President Samora Machel is most commonly known. Heads of state are not usually on first name terms with common parlance: Nelson Mandela is never 'Nelson,' Robert Mugabe never 'Robert' (although 'Uncle Bob' to the disillusioned Left in an explicit reference to 'Uncle Joe' Stalin), Margaret Thatcher, although sometimes 'Maggie Thatcher' ('Maggie Thatcher/Milk Snatcher' when she put an end to free school milk), was more usually a headmistressly Mrs Thatcher. Samora was 'Samora.' He was also, often, '*o nosso presidente Samora Moisés Machel*': our President Samora Moisés Machel. The phrase is said as a line of rolling anapaests, two unstressed syllables leading into a third, stressed, syllable, starting with an intake of breath for the first, missing out the 'o' at the end of '*nosso*,' and inserting a soft 'e' sound after '*Moisés*.' The 'oi' is pronounced as one syllable rather than as a diphthong. Some would put another soft 'e' at the end of 'Machel.' Thus: (breath) *o nóss' presidénte Samóra Moisés(e) Machél(e)*. The 'o' of the masculine ending is never fully formed as an English 'o' would be: to the English ear it can sound more like 'u,' and here, in this appellation, it barely registers.

In English verse anapaests are ideal for fast-moving narrative. They take you galloping from line to line (*'The Assyrian came down like a wolf on the fold/ And his cohorts were gleaming in purple and gold ...'*). But the anapaests in *o nosso presidente Samora Moisés Machel* roll slowly off the tongue. Mozambican Portuguese relishes the sound of each word and, in sharp distinction to both European and Brazilian Portuguese, in which every word swallows the tail of the one preceding it, Mozambicans give every word its own breath of air to float on.

O nosso presidente Samora Moisés Machel: a line of poetry spoken with pride. Or, in no-nonsense prose, Samora, *homem do povo*. Samora, Man of the People: the title of a collection of biographical essays published in 2001, fifteen years after his death.

The final section of the English-language edition of *Samora: Man of the People* provides a photobiography. We see Samora as a teenager, standing with a schoolfriend in front of the steps leading up to the verandah of the São Paolo de Massano Mission School (see **Baobab**). His shorts and open-necked shirt look freshly pressed. The bright sunlight (the shadows of the two boys are etched dark on the ground behind them) glints off his leather sandals. Samora's photocompanion is barefoot, the edges of his shorts are frayed, and a shapeless jumper covers his shirt. Of the two boys, Samora looks like the conformist, the good boy, the potential seminarian.

Mid-1950s and early 1960s: portrait photographs in suit and tie, handkerchief peeping from breast pocket, an unobtrusive neat moustache, the sideways look, the hint of a repressed smile. Here he is in suit and tie holding a bicycle outside the hut at Xilembene (see **Baobab** and **Xilembene**); all the men in formal dress, sharp suits, ties, hats. Does he show any signs of that ingrained rebelliousness, what Oscar Monteiro neatly calls *uma indocilidade permanente*,[1] which came from being brought up to hold resistance to oppression in high regard? Perhaps only in his expression, which seems to say that he knows more than he's letting on, that he's holding back—for the moment.

1963: in Bechuanaland (Botswana), Samora lounges against a rock somewhere in the countryside (see **Frelimo**): he's resting on one elbow, other hand on hip, one knee drawn up. Limbo. He's wearing a light-coloured suit over a dark shirt. Beneath his fedora he stares intently at the camera—held by Matias Mboa?—with not a hint of a smile.

Then follow years of photos of Samora in army fatigues: Algeria, Tanzania, Niassa, Cabo Delgado, his fedora exchanged for a peaked army cap, his neat cotton shirts for khaki, photos taken with Mondlane, with Chipande, with Chissano and the other comrades. In many of these photographs he's smiling or laughing. He never looked so relaxed, before or after, than in the years of the armed struggle. Not, I think, because he was militaristic by nature, but because during those ten years he was more closely engaged with other people, engaged intensely, day after day, than at any other time. He discovered a talent for analysis and organisation, for working alongside other people rather than under them or over them; he discovered he was good at listening, good at getting people to listen to each other.

The mid-1960s was the period when Helder Martins first met this charming man, *homem fantástico e cativante*. Samora was someone to enjoy a drink with, to discuss books with, to talk to at length and intimately.[2]

The marriage to Josina Muthemba in May 1969: the soldier and man of the people, glowing with delight, and the smiling warm-hearted 'freedom fighter lady' (see **Mbuzini**), a marriage solemnised by a white-suited Reverend Uriah Simango.

These were also the years of funerals: those of Magaia, Khankombe, Muthemba, Mondlane. Josina's funeral, 10 April 1971: Samora, thin and diminished, stands alone at her graveside.

June 1975: the armed struggle is over, Independence has been achieved. Samora on the journey south through Mozambique, from the Rovuma to the Maputo: at all the stopping-off points he leaps up onto a hastily-erected wooden stage and exhorts the people to welcome liberation from colonial rule, but warns them that the struggle is not over. He calls them Mozambicans. He whispers, he shouts, he sings. He inspires them. He arrives in the south and a helicopter carries him to his birthplace. He launches himself from the bottom step, into the air, and seems to float, or fly across the intervening space, his arms outstretched, his eyes alight with love, into the arms of the father he hasn't seen for twelve years or more. This is the photograph that hangs on the sitting-room wall in Samora and Graça's little house in Xilembene (see **Malangatana**).

The second wedding, 7 September 1975: Samora slips the ring onto Graça's finger. Graça in a long white dress with three-quarter sleeves, Samora in a dark suit. Chandeliers branch from the walls, heavy curtains drape the windows. This is the wedding of a Head of State: the Nyereres and Kaundas are best men and women. Graça, slim, elegant, an inch or two taller than her husband, hides any nervousness behind a composed expression.

Samora the speechgiver, the soldier, the President, the diplomat, in combat gear, in full military uniform, in formal suits, grinning his gap-toothed grin. We see him shaking hands with the Swedish Prime Minister Olof Palme (who would be assassinated in February 1986). We see him with King Sobhuza II of Swaziland, with Aristides Pereira of Cape Verde, with Fidel Castro, with Boumedienne of Algeria, with stout Podgorny of the USSR, with Kurt Waldheim, with Jimmy Carter, with Erich Honeker, with Robert Mugabe at the funeral of Josiah Tongogara (see **Tongogara**). A 1976 official portrait (trim beard, dark jacket over crisp white shirt, smart tie, dreamy eyes) will feature on the notes of the new currency, the Metical, in 1980. It's the portrait on the poster on the cover of this book.

We follow him into the 1980s: here he is with Forbes Burnham of Guiana and Daniel Ortega of Nicaragua, with Mobuto Sese Seko in a leopardskin hat, with Mohamed Abdel Aziz of the Polisario Front of the Western Sahara; he stands between Joshua Nkomo and Robert Mugabe, raising their hands into the air with his own, he has a medal pinned on his chest by Brezhnev, he addresses a rally with Oliver Tambo of the ANC, he sits, uncharacteristically awkward, on a sofa with big-haired Colonel Gaddafi of Libya, he steps out from Buckingham Palace beside Margaret Thatcher between two rows of ceremonial guards in towering bearskins; here he is with Chester Crocker in 1983 hoping to stem the tide of US support for Renamo, with Ramalho Eanes and Mario Soares of Portugal, with Mitterrand, in military dress uniform signing the Nkomati agreement with P.W. Botha, with David Rockefeller, President of the Chase Manhattan Bank, posing unsmiling with Kim Il Sung, smiling in the embrace of General Giap, another uncomfortable-looking sofa shot with Hastings Banda of Malawi, with Ronald Reagan, with Pope John Paul II, with Iran's President Sayyed Ali Khamenei, with Mikhail Gorbachev, with the South African Minister of Foreign Affairs Roelof 'Pik' Botha, with Emperor Hirohito, with the Reverend Jesse Jackson, with Yasser Arafat and with Coretta Scott King. All these hugs and smiles: Samora carrying out the edict of his former leader Eduardo Mondlane, to strive to increase the number of your friends, and to decrease the number of your enemies.

Three photographs from 1985 are particularly striking. Two of them are by Kok Nam, who must share with Daniel Maquinasse the title of chronicler of the revolution. One is a close-up head and shoulders of Samora in army fatigues. A frown marks his forehead, his eyes are troubled, smile lines have become lines of worry. Perhaps he sees that all his efforts at friendship and at reconciliation are doomed to fail; perhaps he hears the strong wingbeats of his enemies circling. The second of Kok Nam's photographs shows him from behind walking towards the presidential residence, the Ponta Vermelha, alone across a deserted lawn. His figure, again in army fatigues, is dwarfed by mature trees on either side and by the palace itself, Portuguese colonial style with curving arches and open stonework balustrades, designed to provide cool shade from the bright southern African sun, but looking like pools of darkness towards which he walks. The third photograph shows Samora and Graça celebrating their tenth wedding anniversary on 7 September 1985.[3] Both are dressed in white, Samora in a white suit and shoes with dark tie, Graça in a knee-length skirt suit, with open-toed white high heels and a wide-brimmed white hat. They dance side by side down the street, followed by a laughing, singing crowd. Graça, smiling, lowers her eyes to see where she's stepping; Samora, head up and shoulders back, careless and joyful, could be, for a moment, the Samora of the earlier years.

That was the month that he spoke in public of what he'd found at the army barracks he'd visited in June, and articulated for the first time his growing sense of disquiet with the military. On 3 June he'd visited the large barracks at Boane, about 30 km to the west of Maputo. When his entourage left that evening, Samora, unknown to the soldiers in the barracks, stayed behind. He was deeply shocked by what he saw and heard when the soldiers thought they were no longer under inspection. 'All the soldiers believed I had gone back to Maputo. At about 19.00, music began to play in the camp, and later all kinds of guns, including anti-aircraft cannon, were firing into the air. ... It was like that in the Portuguese army in 69 and 70. Shoot before sleeping. Fear.'[4] Another army unit was brought in, arrests were made, new rules implemented, but Samora found the disorganisation and demoralisation to be endemic.

When Samora spoke out about the dreadful things he had found, Jorge Rebelo declared: 'Sometimes we think that Comrade President is not informed, but we see that he is informed.' Comrade President's reply pointed to a widening split between himself and his closest friends and advisers: 'I wasn't informed. I found out.'

If the army units based in barracks just outside Maputo were falling to pieces, what was happening to the units further away, in Manica and Sofala, in Zambezia and Niassa? Were they, too, demoralised and running scared? Yes, by all accounts, and worse. Rumours of corruption and even of atrocities committed by government soldiers filtered back to the capital; nothing like the scale of the relentless Renamo atrocities, but what does scale matter when you are on the receiving end? If Comrade President was not informed of these, doubtless he found out. Samora's army, the cradle of the revolution, the crucible in which was formed the New Man and Woman, the new Mozambique, was out of control.

With the army in such a state of collapse the government was helpless in the face of Renamo. For Samora it was personal. He was unable to defend the ordinary people he had once—and not that long ago—promised so much to.

He determined to stop the slow creeping tide of corruption and weakness by getting rid of the whole of the *Estado Maior Geral*, the General Staff, and putting in their place a group of young officers recently trained in the Soviet Union. According to

Carlos Cardoso—but not mentioned by other commentators—Machel informed the General Staff themselves and the Party leadership of the date he proposed to make these sweeping changes: 20 October 1986.[5]

But there were some things he felt powerless to change: the hearts and minds of Party members themselves. A Central Committee meeting a few months before Samora's death passed new regulations that allowed Party members for the first time to own private property and to hire peasant labour to work on their land. Samora looked around him and saw that, for the first time in twenty-five years, ambition for wealth and for the accumulation of wealth was driving the decisions of some of the comrades.

In the last twelve months of his life Samora called the journalist Carlos Cardoso to the presidential palace a number of times for off-the-record meetings. 'I have no strategy,' said the President on one of these occasions, and, 'I am lost,' thus indicating to Cardoso that 'behind the staged unity of the Frelimo leadership, Samora Machel was almost completely isolated at the top.'[6]

José Luís Cabaço (Minister for Transport at Independence, before taking over Information from Jorge Rebelo) wrote: 'Samora's dream was evaporating in the communal villages destroyed, plantations burned down ... death, dehumanisation, desolation which had taken hold of his beloved Mozambique.'[7]

After the crash that killed Samora Machel on 19 October (see **Aircraft**, **Difficulties**, **Mbuzini** and **Tupolev**), his body was brought back to Mozambique where it lay in state in Maputo City Hall from 24 to 27 October. Julius Nyerere, President of Tanzania, in whose country Frelimo had been born and had grown up, was the first to lay a wreath, to observe a minute's silence, to sign the book of condolences. Nineteen of the other thirty-four victims of the crash lay in state in the Fourth Congress Hall.

On 28 October Samora Machel's body was laid to rest, alongside those of Josina Machel and Eduardo Mondlane, in the

Praça dos Heróis (see **Research Trip**). Presidents and Prime Ministers of over fifteen African countries attended the funeral, along with the leaders of liberation movements, including Oliver Tambo of the ANC and Sam Nujoma of SWAPO, from countries still fighting for independence and majority rule. The history of each country was entwined with that of Samora Machel and of independent Mozambique.

From his prison cell on Robben Island, Nelson Mandela had written to his captors to beg leave to attend the funeral of the man he called 'a true African revolutionary.' During all his years of imprisonment it was the only occasion on which he asked to leave South Africa. Permission was refused.[8]

Marcelino dos Santos in his funeral oration gave a solemn pledge: 'That we shall continue your work, that we shall remain faithful to your example as a man and as a fighter. We swear to defend with our very lives, every inch of land in our sacred country. We swear that we shall build the Mozambique of your dreams, a developed and prosperous country, the socialist Mozambican motherland. *Viva Samora! A Luta Continua!*'[9]

In a commemorative article published in the daily paper *Notícias* one year later, the writer Lina Magaia remembered the occasion that Samora had comforted her on the loss of her first child. He had said to her: 'My daughter, don't cry. It's hard to lose the ones we love, I know what it means, but we must have the courage to go on living and fighting. As individuals we may die, but together we stay alive, we live on in those who are alive.'[10]

Simango

People keep on trying to wipe Uria Simango from the visual record, but he just keeps on reappearing. In the first edition of Eduardo Mondlane's *The Struggle for Mozambique*, which came out just a month or two after Mondlane was assassinated in 1969, the photosection includes a close-up, taken by Basil

Davidson at Frelimo's Second Congress (see **Matchedje**), of Simango and Mondlane, Vice-President and President. Tall broad-shouldered Mondlane smiles down benignly at his Vice-President; Simango, short-statured, chirpy and chipper, with a big smile and big spectacles, looks out under Mondlane's gaze past the camera. In the second edition, published a year later, by which time Simango had been expelled from Frelimo and had left Tanzania, that double portrait has vanished from the book, to be replaced by a photograph of a school in one of the liberated areas: a small group of men, women and children seated on the ground while a soldier writes on a board nailed to the trunk of a palm tree. But Simango's ghost remains. In the photo of Mondlane giving the opening speech, you can see behind him, deep in the shade of a thatched shelter, a flash or glint of light reflected off a pair of spectacles; unidentified in the caption, you nonetheless recognise the small seated figure of Uria Simango.

The Reverend Uria Timotei Simango came from Sofala province, moved to Rhodesia and was preaching in the Congregationalist Church in Salisbury when he met Eduardo Mondlane in 1961. He arrived in Tanzania in April 1962 and joined Udenamo, which a few months later merged with other groups, under Mondlane's leadership, to form a united liberation front (see **Frelimo**). From the beginning Simango was unsympathetic both to Frelimo's privileging of anti-racism over (black) nationalism and to the elaboration of the links between the political and the military sides of the struggle (see ***Político-Militar***), both of which positions were confirmed and elaborated at the Second Congress in July 1968. By then he was out on a limb, alienated not only from the young military commanders whose roots were firmly inside Mozambique but also from the Lisbon- and Paris-educated intellectuals who wanted a people's war and were willing to participate in it. Simango wanted rid of the Portuguese, but was not too keen on a socialist revolution. According to Helder Martins, who saw a great deal of Simango in Tanzania in the years 1965–

68, both Simango and his friend Silvério Nhungu (see **Mondlane**) always saw themselves primarily—and contrary to Frelimo principles—as tribal representatives of their home province of Sofala. Whenever Mondlane was away travelling, frequently accompanied by the Secretary for Foreign Affairs Marcelino dos Santos, Simango would foment trouble, or intrigues, back in Dar es Salaam. As Helder Martins describes it: 'These intrigues always had a tribal base and always snatched the chance to criticise Mondlane himself directly or indirectly, exploiting the fact that Janet was a white American and that the couple had a number of American friends, even in Dar es Salaam.'[11]

Simango was already associated with the Makonde 'chairman' Lazarus N'Kavandame (see ***Behind the Lines*** and **Matchedje**) who sought independence for Cabo Delgado alone and a special deal with the Portuguese, and was responsible for the murder of Paolo Kankhombe.

When the troublesome Catholic priest Mateus Gwenjere stirred up anti-white feeling in the Mozambique Institute in early 1968, which led to the Tanzanian authorities expelling from the country a number of white teachers and health workers, Uria Simango was lurking in the shadows. Simango's *lágrimas de crocodilo*—the crocodile tears he shed at the teachers' leaving party—did not fool Martins, who, together with his wife, was one of those expelled.[12] Samora later gave an analysis of the crisis that explored the deeper issues behind the immediate crude racism: 'Racism led to disunity,' he said:

> Claiming to be very revolutionary, students who had yet to show proof of true revolutionary commitment fought against teachers who had already given ample proof of their dedication to the people's cause, solely because the teachers were white. Combining selfishness and ambition, the students rejected a programme of studies planned to meet the immediate and urgent needs of the struggle and demanded programmes that would give them diplomas and privileges so that they could exploit the people in the future. They wanted to become an elite

of parasites, acquiring wealth and social prominence at the expense of the people's suffering.[13]

Only two months after this crisis Lazaro N'kavandame's supporters attacked the Frelimo offices in Dar (see **Matchedje**). Mateus Sansão Muthemba—Josina's uncle—happened to be there and was hit by someone wielding an elephant's tusk. His skull was fractured and he died soon after. Opinions differ as to the extent of Simango's involvement.

When Eduardo Mondlane was assassinated at the beginning of the following year, in February 1969, Uria Simango, as Vice-President, at once assumed the role of President; but his hopes for power on his own were soon dashed. The forty-strong body of the Central Committee decided Frelimo should be led by a triumvirate made up of Simango, Marcelino dos Santos and Samora Machel.

Samora recalled the period of the triumvirate presidency, in the aftermath of the death of Mondlane, in which Simango was implicated by association only, as hugely stressful. Samora was an astute judge of character, with *uma intuição natural*, a natural intuition;[14] in this he differed from Mondlane, who was over-generous, or some might say credulous, especially when it came to men of the cloth (as with Gwenjere, see **Nachingwea**). Mondlane was 'more easily deceived by opportunists and also more inclined to make excuses for people.'[15]

Gregarious, outward-looking and enamoured of the whole talky process of dialectical debate, during these months Samora was obliged to keep his own counsel and to remain silent.[16] But this period did not last long.

In November 1969 Uria Simango published 'Gloomy Situation in FRELIMO,' an incoherent but nasty document that accused the recently murdered Eduardo Mondlane, Samora Machel and others in the leadership of forming a southern-based tribal conspiracy, and of planning to assassinate their rivals. He complained that Frelimo had been infiltrated by 'vipers,' agents of American imperialism and, in parallel, taken over by the Portuguese. He called for Samora Machel, Marcelino dos Santos and Joaquim Chissano to stand trial for their criminal activity, and he demanded that Mondlane's widow Janet return forthwith to the USA.[17]

Simango ended by threatening to resign if his demands were not met. He hoped to win the support of the Tanzanian government, but it was not forthcoming, and he was asked to leave the country. He first went into exile in Cairo, where he told anybody who would listen that Machel and the Frelimo leadership were double agents. In 1971 he resurfaced in Zambia as foreign secretary of an organisation of Mozambican exiles called Coremo, which had links with Jonas Savimbi's UNITA in Angola, and, like that organisation, was keen to win support from China, an unpredictable player on the African gaming-board. At Machel's request he was expelled from Zambia.

After the Armed Forces Movement coup in Portugal in 1974 he returned to Mozambique and holed up in Beira where he joined forces with the PIDE agent Joana Simeão to set up an anti-Frelimo front called the National Coalition Party. When, in September, in response to the signing of the Lusaka Accord, a group of Portuguese seized control of the radio station in Maputo, Simango flew there and broadcast a speech in their support. This was, in Paul Fauvet's words, 'the biggest mistake of his life.'[18] The revolt quickly collapsed and Simango fled abroad once more, to Nairobi and then to Malawi. But the Malawians handed him back to Frelimo, and he was taken to Nachingwea, where he was one of the counter-revolutionaries displayed to Kaunda and Nyerere when they visited in mid-1975 (see **Nachingwea**). After Independence Simango and the others were moved to a camp in Niassa. Later they were executed. Renamo claims they were shot early on, in 1977, but others believe it was much later, in 1983, when Renamo was making incursions into southern Niassa. 1983: that bad year (see ***Operação***

Produção). The decision to execute them was probably taken by Samora and a small group of military commanders. Whoever took it, it was apparently taken without the knowledge of the rest of the politburo, let alone the central committee. The story remains murky. Frelimo, as Paul Fauvet says, 'will still not come clean about this.'[19]

How awkward it must have been: ordering the execution of the man who conducted your wedding ceremony. And those wedding photos (see **Josina** and **Mbuzini**): how Simango returns and returns. There's no repressing him.

I find Simango again in *Samora: Man of the People* (published in 2001): Samora, Josina, and a third person who can't be removed because he's standing directly in front of the two main players. He's wearing a white suit and his spectacles glint at the camera as he turns his head towards us. All three of them are smiling broadly. He's not identified in the caption. But by now I recognize him instantly.

New photographs keep surfacing, such as the one on the cover of Pachinuapa's 2009 memoir of the Second Congress. Simango is back, forty years after he was removed from the Second Congress photographs in *The Struggle for Mozambique*. The cover is a collage: Simango sits next to President Mondlane, his head cocked to one side as together they listen to one of the speeches. And inside the same book I find the best photograph I have yet seen of the wedding day at Tunduru: bride, groom, sponsors and witnesses all lined up and orchestrated by that familiar white-suited figure.

An interesting common aspect to all the resurrected wedding photographs, cropped or not, is that in none of them do we see Samora looking directly at Simango. When he's not looking into Josina's eyes, his own eyes are downcast, or he's looking to the left or right of Simango. It's as if he's listening to his 'natural intuition.' Already, perhaps, he recognises Simango as his enemy.

2010: On the way back from our visit to Mbuzini (see **Mbuzini**) we stop to get something to eat at a dinky red check-tableclothed diner in the South African border town of Komatipoort, close to where Samora and P.W. Botha signed the—as it turned out valueless—Nkomati Accord in 1984. It feels very different from a Mozambican café. Apartheid is a thing of the past, the very idea of it an abhorrence in South Africa, but we're very aware that Hernani, our guide and driver, is the diner's only black customer. People stare at us. As we wait for our omelettes and *flet broeds* we chat about the current press coverage of Renamo: apparently its leader Afonso Dhlakama has been holed up out of sight in Nampula for weeks; the people of the city of Beira, for years a Renamo stronghold, are fed up to the back teeth with Renamo's flakiness and have come out in support of the recently-formed MDM (Movement for Mozambican Democracy) instead. Oh yes, I say knowledgeably, it's led by an ex-Renamo called Simão or something, isn't it?

Hernani: Not Simão. Simango, Daviz Simango.
Me: What? Simango? No relation of ...?
Hernani: Yes. Yes indeed. One of the sons of Uria Simango.

Soledariedade

Soledariedade: solidarity. Solidarity with the African National Congress (ANC) in South Africa. When Samora boarded an ANC plane in Francistown in 1963 (see **Aircraft**) to take him to Dar es Salaam and Frelimo, Nelson Mandela was about to start a prison sentence that would last beyond Samora's death.

After the 1976 Soweto uprising many ANC members fleeing for their lives found refuge, warmth and friendship in newly-independent Mozambique. Maputo became, as Nadja Manghezi vividly describes in *The Maputo Connection*, a home from home.

The warmth between the South Africans and their Mozambican hosts was mirrored in the close personal friendship between Samora Machel and Oliver Tambo, President of the ANC; it survived the rocky post-Nkomati months when most of the ANC community were asked to pack their bags and given only a few days to leave. The ANC may have had their military training camps in Angola, but it was Mozambique they gave their hearts to.

Solidarity with those fighting white minority rule in Rhodesia. Samora, May 1970, at a meeting with a ZANU delegation led by Herbert Chitepo (later assassinated) (see **Quelimane**) and including Josiah Tongogara (see **Tongogara**) and four other ZANU/ZANLA leaders, explained that Frelimo did not support ZANU as opposed to ZAPU, but would work with whoever was capable of conducting a successful liberation war in Zimbabwe: 'Some of us, when we look at the situation in Mozambique, realize if we liberate Mozambique tomorrow that will not be the end. The liberation of Mozambique without the liberation of Zimbabwe is meaningless.'[20]

Solidarity: built on a shared ideology, a common enemy, and the knowledge that Mozambique's survival depended on the survival, and the success, of the other liberation groups in southern Africa.

For a long time it wasn't clear which group of Zimbabwean nationalists Mozambique should support. Frelimo's natural ally had seemed to be Joshua Nkomo's ZAPU, but when in 1970 Frelimo offered them a base in the liberated zone of Tete province, bordering Rhodesia's north-east, ZAPU was unwilling and unable to accept.

The ZANLA militants (of ZANU) accepted the offer. For the next decade it was with ZANLA that Frelimo worked, while increasingly trying to broker unity between the two organisations.

What did the ZANLA guerrillas get from Frelimo? Not just a rear base from which they could enter Rhodesia, but a political education. They learned that a guerrilla war without the support of the people was doomed to failure. They learned a more general politics. An early ZANLA recruit, George Rutanhire, described taking some of the Frelimo guerrillas to observe the workings of a local court in the north-east of Rhodesia. 'They watched people paying money to have their cases heard and noted that if a person could not pay, even if he might be innocent, the finding was almost always in favour of the party who had paid. Did Rutanhire know what that was, the Frelimo guerrillas asked? He did not. "That," the guerrillas said, "is oppression."'[21]

Solidarity with the liberation movements of the other Lusophone African countries: Angola, Guinea-Bissau and Cape Verde. Solidarity with the MPLA, first under Agostinho Neto and then under his successor, José Eduardo dos Santos, and with the PAIGC, whose leader Amílcar Cabral was assassinated in 1973 on the orders of General Spinola (see **Lusaka Agreement**).

An example of the demands of solidarity: in the first six months of 1979 Samora Machel attended a summit of the heads of the Front Line States in Luanda, met President Julius Nyerere of Tanzania twice on his own, and once with Kenneth Kaunda of Zambia, welcomed Luís Cabral of Guiné-Bissau and Aristides Pereira of Cape Verde to Maputo, returned to Luanda for a summit of all the Lusophone African countries, before leading a Mozambican delegation to a meeting of the OAU (Organisation of African Unity) in Monrovia.

Samora talking, persuading, encouraging, and urging unity. Reminding his counterparts in the other liberation movements that if they did not have the support of their own people, they were nothing.

On one of his visits to Tanzania Samora recalled the beginnings of Frelimo in the newly independent country of 1962, and the words of his constant and steady supporter Julius Nyerere. 'At that time Tanzania still hadn't consolidated its political and economic power, and was lacking in skilled workers. At that time of newly-won independence, President Nyerere made a historic declaration: "Tanzania can never consider itself independent while there are still parts of Africa under the colonial yoke."'[22]

T

Tantalum

A shiny dark grey rare earth or transition metal, number 73 in the Periodic Table, symbol Ta, with a melting point second only to tungsten and rhenium. Tantalum's density, ductility and resistance to heat and corrosion make it highly valued in the electronics industry, where it's used for capacitors and high power resistors; its non-reactivity, like that of gold, makes it ideal for use in the body. Your new hip might be made of tantalum.

In the 1970s tantalum was used to make the nose cones of rockets, as the South African geologist Piet informs us as we crash from trough to ridge of a grey dirt track towards a white-topped hill shining like Trebizond in the unvarying distance. We're on our trip south, from the Rovuma to the Maputo, four of us in a Land Cruiser (see **Renamo**), and have turned east just after Nampula to visit one of the world's few tantalite mines at a village called Moiane. Tantalite is the mineral in which tantalum is found, usually alongside pegmatites: semi-precious stones such as beryl, emerald, rose quartz, aquamarine and tourmaline. The mine is managed by a friend and colleague of Piet and Bernie's, an ex-Portuguese called Filipe Santos Garcia. He doesn't know we're coming to visit him.

Amongst the straggly grey thorn bushes on either side of the track cashew trees begin to appear, the smooth pendulous shape of their red and yellow apples contrasting with the twisted knotty branches from which they hang. If there are cashew trees then we must be approaching a village.

At last the track smooths out and soon we're driving through a cluster of mud and wattle huts. The blazing midday sun beats down on the brown earth of fields of maize and cassava and cabbages that stretch up the slope of the hill beyond the village. We come to more huts and a series of wood-framed open-walled structures containing long wooden tables and benches. Beyond them we see a large whitewashed concrete house with an attractively shady deep verandah, which shouts out across the brown huts and brown fields and brown dusty paths: this is the European house. There's no-one in sight. We all get out and I lean against the side of the Land Cruiser while my stomach slowly settles back into its usual place. My legs feel weak and shaky. 'Pedro! Bernardo!'

As he strides down the steps from the verandah, Santos Garcia manages to sound delighted to see us. Over a long-sleeved black t-shirt he wears a scarlet boiler suit. With black boots and his dark beard and handsome brown face, he looks like a sturdy peasant hero from a Russian folk-tale.

We shake hands and he urges us up the steps and into the house, where his wife, too, acts as if we're exactly the people she's been longing to see. Sturdy and good-looking like her husband, she's smart and tidy in a dark linen skirt and crisp white cotton blouse, with fair hair brushed neatly into a ponytail tied with a black velvet band. Later someone tells me that a few years earlier she was voted 'Miss Mozambique.' We all shake hands again. Scruffy in our dusty t-shirts and jeans, I notice that all of us, me and the three boys, stand a little straighter and take special care with our Portuguese.

'You'll stay tonight, of course,' she says. 'Excuse me a moment while I tell the cooks we have extra guests for lunch.'

Not cook, but cooks! I stare round the dim booklined room, taking in the Turkish rugs scattered on the floor and the silver tinsel Christmas tree on a table in one corner, its needles sparkling in the down-draught from a large slow-moving ceiling fan. Yellow and red angelfish flash and flicker in an illuminated aquarium, and against the opposite wall some tiny yellow birds flutter in a fine-meshed cage. I step up to take a closer look and see that in the bottom of a glass box next to the birds, a python lies coiled.

The European phenomenon of keeping animals as pets or companions, rather than as food or livelihood, was rarely manifest in Mozambique. I knew no *cooperantes*, of any nationality, who kept even a domestic cat. Unlike in colonialist Uganda when I was small, where leathery-skinned old Africa hands would let semi-tame serval cats, with their dark stripes and pointed fluffy ears, sleep on their guests' beds as if they were tabby kittens, and the woman who ran the white children's primary school in Fort Portal taught us our reading and writing and geography of the British Isles with a pet monkey perched on her shoulder.

Sra Santos Garcia returns from her unknown number of cooks in the kitchen and gives orders to two white-aproned servants to lay the table in the dining room. She invites us to take a quick tour of the smallholding while lunch is prepared and shows us out of the back door. We step into a menagerie. Rabbits loll panting in the shade of the outhouse walls while chickens and ducks peck at the dusty ground. Two sad monkeys watch us from behind the bars of their cage. A group of dainty gazelles moves slowly through some trees on the other side of a fence. Suddenly from round the side of one of the outhouses lurches a large baboon. It stops and looks at us. Oh God, I say, stepping smartly behind Christopher. But its eyes are fixed on Piet, who is in the lead. It bounds over the hardpacked earth, scattering the chickens and ducks, and crouches directly in front of him, drawing back its lips to show enormous teeth. Then with a sideways leap it flings itself into the air and up on to the roof of the building next to us, where it clatters up and down on the corrugated iron roof, shrieking at us and throwing sticks and stones, of which it seems to have a ready-prepared cache. Men with sticks come running, and we witness an exchange of missiles.

Sra Santos Garcia materialises behind me. 'It's usually quite friendly, she says. Come, let's go in. The men will catch it.'

Lunch is asparagus soup, goat meat hamburgers and fruit salad. 'We try to be self-sufficient,' says Sra Santos Garcia.

Later, as Santos Garcia walks us round the system of wooden slatted channels at the base of the hill, he explains that Moiane is an inside-out kind of mine. No digging is involved. The tantalite and the tourmalines lie quite close to the surface of the slopes of the shining white hill above us. Water is pumped to the top of the hill and let out to run down the sides into the wooden channels at the bottom. Basically, we're just constantly washing the hill, he says, and extracting the stones and the tantalite. We go into one of the open-air workshops where a dozen men sit on benches at a long table picking over piles of dirty stones. Santos Garcia scoops up a handful. 'Here,' he says, taking my hand and pressing a deep green stone into my palm. 'An emerald for you. He picks out another stone and brushes the dirt off. It's pale blue like the sky.

'For me? These are beautiful.'

'These are nothing. It's the tantalite that's precious. At 120,000 US dollars per barrel.' He pauses: 'If we can get it down to Maputo, that is.'

We follow him into another hut, where two middle-aged white men with patchy beards are shaking dirt through fine-meshed wooden trays onto a metal plate below.

'Our friends from East Germany,' says Santos Garcia with, possibly, a trace of irony. 'They have a big belief in using magnets to extricate the mineral. But we haven't seen it working yet.'

There are about a dozen of us at supper that night: three or four Mozambicans, the two East Germans, and a French geologist. We sit at three tables arranged in an open-sided square beneath a roof of vines, and are served juicy gazelle steaks with crisp cassava chips. Suddenly something explodes above my head, and a small body thuds to the ground behind my chair. I turn to see one of the waiters picking up a large rat by its tail. He drops it in a wooden box against the wall.

'We run electric wires through the vine,' says Santos Garcia in explanation. He holds up a hand.—'Listen.' We hear a scuffling overhead. Another bang, and another rat falls to the ground. This time Santos Garcia picks it up and drops it in the box. 'They're only stunned. The python won't eat them if they're dead.' He sees me looking anxious. 'Don't worry. The wires don't run directly above the tables.'

We wake next morning to the sound of raised voices. The baboon, escaped from its cage once more, spotted Piet crossing the compound. Now it's back on the roof, keeping Piet and a support army of Moiane workers at bay with a selection of mango stones and wizened cassava roots. Inside the house we find Sra Santos Garcia shouting at a small cowering boy in khaki shorts, who, we hear, failed in his duty to keep the caged birds' waterbowl filled up. Five tiny yellow corpses lie on the floor of the cage. Sra Santos Garcia's eyes glisten with tears. Only the coiled python seems immune to accident and distress. It looks as if it hasn't moved, but when I peer into the wooden rat box outside I find it empty.

The admirable order of the previous day suddenly seems fragile. Perhaps the whole endeavour of extracting and exporting viable amounts of tantalite is nothing but a pipe dream. How unlikely this whole project seems, I think to myself, and try not to imagine the dead birds as a symbol of anything wider.

As we breakfast on tea and bread and mango jam Santos Garcia walks up from the workshops. 'For good luck', he says, 'and to remind you in future years of the little mine of Moiane, in the middle of Mozambique.' He gives us each a stone. Mine's a flat smooth round slice of dark frosty pink with a thin rind of glittery green. 'We call it a slice of watermelon,' he says. 'You should be fine as far as Quelimane,' he goes on. 'South of Quelimane, I don't know. We're hearing bad things about *bandidos*.'

During the long years of war the mine at Moiane was abandoned and deserted. With peace and stability came people from all over, from Angola, the Congo, and even further north, crooks and chancers and desperadoes, attracted by the glittering reds and greens of the beryls and tourmalines rather than by the tricky recondite tantalum. But tantalum is where the money is, and from the early 2000s the Jersey-based company Noventa has been exploring the concessions it bought from the government of Mozambique in a cluster of five sites in the area of Moiane. In 2010 it began mining tantalite, and also the rare pink beryl morganite, at Marropino, one of the sites. Moiane remains deserted. The workers' huts have crumbled, the fields have vanished, the baboon was doubtless eaten during the starvation years of the war against Renamo, and wild scrub grows on slopes that used to run with water. I don't know what became of handsome Santos Garcia and his hospitable ex-beauty queen wife, who'd built a fragile haven of hope for the future on the slopes of the shining white hill.

Tongogara

Multifarious and divided were the groups fighting for an end to colonialism and white minority rule in Southern Rhodesia; on top of the crippling effects on the Mozambican economy of implementing sanctions against Ian Smith's illegal regime, the Mozambican government suffered a permanent headache from the infighting of the freedom fighters and their resistance to the unity that Mozambique insisted on.

Amongst the wheelers and dealers between whom Samora had been carefully picking his way in order to help bring about an agreement at Lancaster House that would ensure a peaceful transition to majority rule in Zimbabwe, Josiah Tongogara stood out as the one man who most closely shared Samora's vision of independent African countries built on the principles of social justice; the one man who, like Samora himself, believed in a new form of nationalism that cut across colour, race and tribe. Samora recognised in Tongogara a revolutionary like himself: a man of strong moral principles, a skilful military commander who was also a shrewd judge of character, and a strategist.

Tongogara was the high commander of ZANLA, the military wing of ZANU. By the time the different parties had been brought to the conference table at Lancaster House, he saw and understood that there was no longer any reason to continue the war; Smith wanted and needed the war to end. Samora was not alone in recognising Tongogara's qualities: during the course of the talks he came to be generally regarded as the key figure in reaching the agreement.[1]

The formal agreements were signed on 21 December 1979; a ceasefire would come into effect on 28 December, leading to political campaigning and multi-party elections based on one person, one vote. When asked about his plans for the future, Tongogara replied that there was still a great deal to do: 'I would like to see myself completing this, creating a new Zimbabwe army which has the interests of the people at heart. Probably after that one can ask me what I want to do. I may decide to go back to the countryside and do some ploughing.'[2]

Once the Lancaster House Agreement was signed Tongogara flew to Maputo and swiftly headed north to the ZANLA camp at Chimoio to brief his commanders on the ceasefire arrangements. On the main road, before they reached the turn-off to Chimoio, the jeep he was travelling in had a head-on collision with a Frelimo truck. Josiah Tongogara, sitting in front next to his driver, was killed instantly.

On New Year's Day 1980, a week after the crash, we passed the twisted remains of the new jeep by the side of the road just south of Massinga, on the last leg of our journey from the Rovuma to the Maputo. At that stage I didn't know Tongogara's name, just that 'the commander of the ZANU forces' had been killed. I noted in my diary that it looked like there had been a head-on collision, 'although South Africa is trying to make out he was murdered by dissenters.'

Samora was in the presidential palace when the news was brought to him. He wept. He hadn't wept openly for nearly ten years, not since the death of Josina.[3]

Tongogara joined the growing list of African revolutionaries of whom it would be said, what if ...?, a list that already contained Lumumba and Mondlane, and would soon include Samora himself. Perhaps Samora was weeping not just for his own loss, the loss of a comrade and friend, but for the loss to the people of southern Africa, whose fight for freedom was far from over.

At the funeral ceremony on 3 January, Samora said 'All of us are born, grow and die. But not all deaths are equal. There are light deaths, and others so heavy it is difficult to bear their weight.'[4]

Tupolev

The transcript of the cockpit voice recorder of the Tupolev 134 (see **Appendix 1**) shows the Russian crew relaxed and unconcerned about their flight from Mbala to Maputo on the evening of 19 October 1986. Plans had changed and they were returning to Maputo earlier than expected, but the flight itself was routine. As soon as they left the Zambian airport the radio operator made contact with Maputo airport control to exchange information on estimated arrival time (19.25 GMT), weather, traffic, visibility etc. The radio operator alerted Maputo that they were carrying 'Number One,' the President, on board.[5]

The crew chatted about this and that. The captain started a rambling tale about flying some tiresome Soviet officials and being obliged to land, or not to land, in Warsaw. At 19.01 the radio operator told Maputo they were ready to start their descent, and that he would report again when they saw the airport landing lights. The captain broke off his shaggy dog tale to comment on an apparent malfunction of the low fuel warning light (not the only malfunctioning instrument, as the transcript would reveal). At 19.10 the navigator reported that they were 100km from their destination, and at 19.11 the captain queried why they were turning. The navigator replied: 'VOR indicates that way'.

No-one sounds worried. They look around for a pen so they can write down orders for the drinks they'll have as soon as they've landed. None of these men sound like kamikaze pilots (see **Difficulties**). None of them sound as if they know they're heading towards sudden and certain death. They sound like aircraft crew who expect to be groundside within the half hour, job over, rest and relaxation ahead.

At 19.12 the co-pilot asked why two of the VOR panel lights were lit and two were not. Sixty kilometers, said the navigator. Five minutes to landing, and the captain instructed the flight engineer to report on the non-functioning radio altimeter; the radio operator chipped in to tell the engineer to say it's not the first time that it hasn't been in working order.

So, not everything's working perfectly in this cockpit. But no-one's in a panic.

At 19.17, believing that they were only three minutes away from landing, the captain asked why there was no visible sign of Maputo, and repeated: 'There is no Maputo.' Then: 'Electrical power is off, chaps!' (The transcript is a translation from the Russian by the inquiry officials; the slang sounds old-fashioned; swearing is indicated by '(strong expression).')

The captain assumed Maputo was suffering a power cut, a frequent occurrence at that time as a result of Renamo attacking the power lines. A power cut would have explained why none of the other airport navigational systems seemed to be working either.

During the next minute and a half some references were made to other lights. Some of these comments are marked in the transcript with a question mark, indicating either that they were not completely audible, or that it was not clear who was speaking. At 19.17 the co-pilot said: 'There to the right, it is lit (?).' Navigator: 'There's something I don't understand, aah ...' Captain: 'No there is something ...(?)' Co-pilot at 19.18: 'And there to the left ... what kind of light is there?' The captain at 19.19: 'There to the right lights are seen,' to which the co-pilot repeated that the runway was not lit up.

It is clear the captain and crew were puzzled by the lack of airport lights. 'No, there's nothing, there's neither city nor runway,' said the co-pilot at 19.20. As the radio operator once again asked Maputo to check the runway lights, the ground proximity warning alarm went off. No-one commented on it. Did they think, because they had only just started their descent from 3,000 feet, that it was malfunctioning, like the altimeter and the fuel gauge? The radio operator continued talking to Maputo about the runway lights and concluded, incorrectly, that the lights were indeed out of service. The captain can be heard: 'No, it's cloudy, cloudy, cloudy.' The skies were clear over Maputo that night; he must have mistaken the hillside for cloud.

Twenty seconds later the Tupolev, travelling at 411 kph, ploughed into the hillside at Mbuzini, and in an instant most people on board, including President Samora Machel, were dead.

* * *

In his article 'Samora Machel: The Last Ten Minutes' (see **Appendix 2**) the journalist Carlos Cardoso, who worked closely with the Mozambican members of the tripartite inquiry (Mozambique, Soviet Union, South Africa), went through the transcript of the cockpit voice recorder and of the Maputo air traffic control tapes in careful detail. He pulled out the significance of the exchange about the plane turning. 'VOR indicates that way,' says the navigator. This is the 'stray' VOR that according to the South African story (see **Mbuzini**) the pilot 'inadvertently' locked onto.

Some of those final moments must always now remain impenetrable, most especially the failure of the captain to respond to the ground proximity warning alarm, and to take the plane up. But what seems incontrovertible is that the crew believed until the last split second that they were approaching Maputo airport from the northwest over the wide flat plain of Gaza province. They had been led off course.

'So what VOR was this?' asked Carlos Cardoso. 'If it was a decoy, where had it been placed? These are questions that demand answers before a verdict on the causes of the crash can be given.'[6]

Inadvertently? If indeed the navigator locked onto a stray VOR beacon that drew the Tupolev into South African air space, why didn't South African air control, who'd been following the plane on radar since it crossed Zimbabwe, and who knew perfectly well where it was coming from and who was on board, warn them of their error? Foreign Minister Roelof 'Pik' Botha appeared on South African television ten days after the crash to suggest that the Tupolev had just 'disappeared from the screen;' further, that the radar operatives would not have taken much notice of such a disappearance. As Paul Fauvet described in his article 'Samora Machel's death and South African radar,' Botha cultivated two stories: first, that the Tupolev was just one of many planes cruising along the Mozambique/South Africa border and blipping on South African radar screens that Sunday night in October, and therefore it was not particularly noteworthy when it vanished; and second, that South African radar was some kind of do-it-yourself kit operating out of a backyard and not really sophisticated enough to keep proper track of flying machines. Both stories were ludicrous. In fact, wrote Paul Fauvet, 'South Africa possesses a highly sophisticated integrated military and civilian computer-assisted radar system, whose two prime purposes are to assist in South African Air Force strikes into neighbouring countries, and to detect any plane entering South African air space.' He went on to give details.

Fauvet concluded that the South Africans continued to monitor the Tupolev up until the moment of its crash. 'The radio operators knew it was off course, knew it was entering South African airspace, knew the Pequenos Libombos mountains presented a serious threat to the aircraft, and yet no warning was given, no preventive action was taken.'[7]

As all readers of police procedurals know, any unexplained death prompts three immediate questions: what was the motive, what the opportunity, and what the means?

Motive: The forces of apartheid hoped that with the removal of the intransigently revolutionary Samora Machel they would fatally weaken Frelimo and be able to install a Renamo puppet government.

Opportunity: Were the flight carrying President Machel from Zambia to Mozambique to pass through South African air space, then the opportunity would arise. Since the beginning of the month the South African Defence Minister, Magnus Malan, and his Deputy had been openingly threatening Samora Machel, and orchestrating a media campaign within South Africa for an invasion of its uppity, socialist neighbour, while amassing armed forces in the east of the country close to the Mozambican border. Mozambique was expecting a military attack. On 18 October an order was given for the South African forces to be on full alert in the northern and eastern Transvaal, that is, in the area of the Lebombo Hills where the plane came down.

Means: A decoy VOR beacon, deployed from the back of a flatbed truck, to lure the Tupolev off its normal flight path and into South African air space. Which is not to say that the South Africans wanted or planned for the President's plane to crash on their territory. Perhaps they were hoping for a slightly different outcome.

On the other side of the border just inside Mozambique was a Renamo camp well-equipped with arms provided by South African security forces. If the plane could be shot down, Renamo could claim a victory and South Africa could pretend it was innocent of the whole affair. But the plane crashed before it could be shot.

Although the South Africans agreed to the setting up of an international commission of inquiry the wily Foreign Minister immediately started to be obstructive, particularly over the question of the black boxes, which he had agreed should be looked at in Moscow, but which remained in the hands of the South Africans.

Motive, opportunity, means. And then cover-up.

The commission of inquiry, led by Cecil Margo (see **Aircraft**), concluded that the crash was attributable to pilot error. The South Africans closed their inquiry. They didn't want to ask what it was that caused the pilot to err.

In 1998 South Africa's Truth and Reconciliation Committee's investigation raised a number of unanswered questions (see **Mbuzini**). With documents missing or perhaps destroyed, and many of the main players of the apartheid regime now dead, perhaps it's unlikely that the truth of what happened that night will ever come out. As the years pass, however, some accounts of the circumstances surrounding the mystery emerge piecemeal. Although outside a commission or court of inquiry it's difficult to gauge the reliability of personal accounts, nonetheless it's surely worth hearing what they tell us.

In 2007 the Special Assignment team on SABC News broadcast a programme called 'The Death of Samora Machel,' which included an interview, the transcript of which has been published online, with a former South African Special Forces and CCB (Civil Cooperation Bureau: an organisation every bit as sinister as its name suggests) operative called Hans Louw. Louw had recently been released early from Pretoria prison after serving part of a twenty-eight year sentence for murder. He had been first interviewed in prison in 2003 by Mpikeleni Duma, a freelance journalist who'd been worrying away at the story of the plane crash since 1987. During the course of the television interview Louw told of his unit—5 Recce—having been briefed in October 1986 on an impending attack on a plane carrying the President of Mozambique. Offering a story that contradicted the story that the plane was to be brought down by Renamo, Louw claimed to be a member of a back-up group tasked with bringing the plane down with ground-to-air missiles.

The television crew took him to Mbuzini, where he indicated the positions of the two teams into which his unit was divided, one each side of the border. 'Our job is to make sure that the President is dead ... We withdrew first light the next morning ... back to Komatipoort.'[8]

The programme makers also tracked down another member of Hans Louw's unit, who agreed to speak to them on condition his identity was kept secret. He confirmed that they had been at Mbuzini the night of the crash. Why were they there? 'There was a mission as we all know, taking out of the aircraft which was transporting the President of Mozambique from Zambia to Maputo.' This man was asked if he knew of a false beacon, and replied: 'Ja well, there was a false beacon which was put there. Which distracted the pilot to think he was in Mozambique, whereas he wasn't in Mozambique and he was in Mbuzini and he descended.'[9]

The writer Albino Magaia, imprisoned and tortured by the PIDE during the armed struggle (and uncle of Filipe Samuel Magaia, who was assassinated by a PIDE agent), wrote of the death of Samora Machel: 'The blood of Samora sealed the knot of union between the Mozambican people and the South African people.'[10] But the truth of it is still not known.

Twenty-five years after the Tupolev crashed into the Lebombo hillside, killing Samora Machel and thirty-four others, the Mozambican inquiry remains open.

V

Viva!

Viva! Interj., S/C:

Saudacão revolucionária utilizada em comícios, e não só, no Moçambique pós-Independente, tendo-se também internacionalizado no seio de estados da Linha da Frente como o Zimbabwe e Namíbia e, mais tarde, na África do Sul. Usado frequentemente no contexto do binómio Viva! Abaixo! Viva o Frelimo! Abaixo o apartheid! Formal e informal. N.

Interjection, social/cultural: Revolutionary greeting used in meetings, and not only in meetings, in post-independence Mozambique. Also internationalised and used in the Front Line states such as Zimbabwe and Namibia, and later in South Africa. Often used as part of the binomial *Viva! Abaixo!* Long live! Down with! Long live Frelimo! Down with apartheid! Formal and informal. Nation-wide.

Viva Samora! In the jam-packed *chapas* that rattle and bounce along the pot-holed *avenidas* of twenty-first century Maputo, from Julius Nyerere running parallel to the sea, along Eduardo Mondlane, the backbone of the upper town, crossing Karl Marx, Vladimir Lenin, Amilcar Cabral, Sekou Touré, Guerra Popular, Samuel Magaia and inland to the densely populated *bairros* where concrete and cane houses stand cheek by jowl and the tarmac gives way to dust, the driver slots into his cassette machine one of the many Samora tapes in circulation. Once again the women and men on the bus hear that warm and intimate growl speaking directly to them.

In the ten to fifteen years following Samora's death the Mozambican people had little leisure to meditate on their dead leader; their priority was survival. But now he lives on in the informal cultural economy, in crackly tapes and on grainy DVDs, assumed into the community—not pantheon, for Mozambicans aren't given to hero- or god-worship—of ancestors as a man who came from the people, and occupies a place still in their hearts. *Viva!*

X

Xiconhoca

Xiconhoca: n., Ln, S/C: Termo frequente no período pós-Independência para designar um indivíduo com comportamentos considerados negativos (faltar ao serviço, não participar em reuniões políticas, embebedar-se etc); contra-revolucionário. Caiu em desuso. Palavra formada por composição: Xico (Francisco) da PIDE + nhoca (nyoka, cobra). Formação mista ou hibrida (um elemento da lg portuguesa e um elemento da lg bantu); processo de corte silábico (clipping) e fusão (blend). Inf. N.

A term in common use in the post-independence period to describe someone whose behaviour was considered bad (not turning up for work, not playing their part in political meetings, getting drunk etc); a counter-revolutionary. The term has fallen into disuse. Composite word: Xico (Francisco) of PIDE + snake. Mixed or hybrid (one element from Portuguese and one from Bantu); shortened and fused. Informal. Nation-wide.

Xiconhoca strolled and sauntered across the pages of the daily paper *Notícias* in many guises. He was the bureaucrat, the jobsworth, the bully. Xiconhoca the health worker, in a nurse's smock, admits a patient to hospital. The patient's on a stretcher, dripping blood, almost unconscious. 'Identity card?' asks Xiconhoca with clipboard in hand. 'Date of birth? Place of birth?' The patient is silently expiring below him. 'Father's name? Mother's maiden name?'

Xixconhoca had a whole book of cartoons to himself. He wore a skinny t-shirt with 'Kiss Me' curling across his chest, low-slung hip-hugging bell-bottom trousers, monstrously high platform shoes, overlarge shades and a baseball cap crammed over wild hair. He swaggered rather than walked, and held a ghetto-blaster clamped to his ear. He symbolised everything that was counter-revolutionary. He was the personification of the evils of capitalism. We were meant to hate him for his selfishness, his materialism and his corruption.

I used to tell my students that not many people in the West really looked like *Xiconhoca*, that he was a caricature. But they didn't believe me. Or they didn't want to believe me. Everyone loved to hate *Xiconhoca*.

Xilembene

Village where Samora Moisés Machel was born (see **Baobab**). His ancestral home.

APPENDIX 1

The following pages are a facsimile of the Appendix to the 'Aircraft Accident Factual Report' (see Tupolev, p 274) produced by the tripartite Commission (Mozambican-South African-Soviet) set up to carry out the initial investigation into the crash on 19 October 1986 that killed President Samora Machel and thirty-four others. The Report and Appendix were published on 16 January 1987.

APPENDIX : CVR AND ATC TRANSCRIPT

Explanation of Terms :

CAPT	: Pilot C9-CAA
NAV	: Navigator C9-CAA
COPILOT	: Co-pilot C9-CAA
R/OP	: Radio Operator C9-CAA
ENG	: Flight Engineer C9-CAA
AFIS	: Aerodrome Flight Information Service
MOC 103	: Mocambique TM103, the Boeing 737 from Beira to Maputo:
COMMENT	: Explanation by team to explain terminology or situation to the reader.
INTERJECTION	: Where a member of the aircrew speaks at the same time as somebody else, this is indicated as an interjection.
----	: Where only the carrier wave is received it is indicated by a series of dots or dashes.
STRONG EXPRESSION	: The use of foul language is indicated by the term "strong expression".
VOVA, VOLODYA	: First names of the flight engineer.
TOLIK	: First name of the radio operator.
ATC	: Maputo ATC tapes.
CVR	: Cockpit voice recorder.
?	: Question mark inserted where identity of person or word spoken is uncertain.

COCKPIT VOICE RECORDER

AIR TRAFFIC CONTROL MAPUTO

TIME	SOURCE : CVR	TRANSCRIPTION	TIME	SOURCE : ATC TAPES	TRANSCRIPTION
			1846:19	R/OP	GOOD EVENING MAPUTO, CHARLIE NINE ALFA ALFA
				AFIS	-----
			1847:55	R/OP	MAPUTO CHARLIE NINE CHARLIE ALFA ALFA, GOOD AFTERNOON.
			1848:03	AFIS	CHARLIE NINE CHARLIE ALFA ALFA, GOOD EVENING, GO AHEAD.
			1848:06	R/OP	CHARLIE NINE CHARLIE ALFA ALFA, JUST PASSED POINT KURLA LEVEL THREE FIVE ZERO ESTIMATED ABEAM LIMPOPO AT ZERO FIVE NEXT HOUR, ECHO TANGO ALFA MAPUTO ONE NINE TWO FIVE, TOTAL ON BOARD FOUR EIGHT, ENDURANCE AT DEPARTURE ZERO FOUR ZERO ZERO.
			1848:33	AFIS	ROGER IN CHARLIE NINE CHARLIE ALFA ALFA CONFIRM POSITION LIMPOPO AT ONE NINE, ONE NINE ZERO FIVE.
			1848:41	R/OP	LIMPOPO AT ONE NINE ZERO FIVE.
			1848:46	AFIS	CHARLIE NINE CHARLIE ALFA ALFA NO REPORTED TRAFFIC FLIGHT LEVEL THREE FIVE ZERO, NO DELAY EXPECTED FOR ILS APPROACH RUNWAY TWO THREE.
			1848:58	R/OP	ROGER IN CHARLIE ALFA ALFA MAINTAINING THREE FIVE ZERO TO VICTOR MIKE ALFA, NO DELAY EXPECTED RUNWAY ILS CORRECTION RUNWAY TWO THREE.
			1849:08	AFIS	AFFIRMATIVE AND COPY THE WEATHER, MAPUTO METEO REPORT ONE EIGHT ZERO ZERO, SURFACE WIND ZERO NINE ZERO, ONE ZERO KNOTS, VISIBILITY MORE THAN TEN KILOMETERS, THREE OCTAS AT ONE, ... ONE EIGHT ZERO ZERO FEET, FOUR OCTAS NOT DETERMINATED HEIGHT, TEMPERATURE TWO THREE, DEW POINT TWO ZERO, QNH ONE ZERO ONE SIX.
			1849:42	R/OP	THAT COPIED OK CHARLIE ALFA ALFA QNH ONE ZERO ONE SIX, THANK YOU.
			1849:47	AFIS	AFFIRMATIVE AND REPORT POSITION LIMPOPO OR LEAVING FLIGHT LEVEL THREE FIVE ZERO.
			1849:53	R/OP	YES CHARLIE ALFA ALFA, NEXT REPORT LEAVING THREE FIVE ZERO, PLEASE RELAY, NUMBER ONE ON BOARD.
			1849:59	AFIS	ROGER.
1849:40		....			
1849:55		....			
1850:00	R/OP	BEIRA INFORMATION CONTINUE WITH MAPUTO.			

COCKPIT VOICE RECORDER

	R/OP	BEIRA C9-CAA AFFIRMATIVE.
1850:20		ASK OLEG
1851:12		....
		....
		YES
1851:32	NAV	758.5, 759, 1016, +23, 90° 5-10 KNOTS.
	CAPT	AH?
	NAV	10 KNOTS, LANDING RWY 23. IN 10 MINUTES, 758,5 LANDING AT 20 MINUTES? AT 20 MINUTES? THAT'LL BE OK?
1856:25	ENG	CHECK TIME......
		HERE YOU ARE ....?
1856:37		IT WILL BE SUITABLE?
1858:02		(REMARK ABOUT AIRHOSTESS)
1859:32	NAV	((DME) IT WILL NOT BE THERE)
	CAPT	WHY?
	NAV	ITS STILL EARLY, ITS STILL 8 MORE MINUTES.
	NAV	121 (??)
		WHAT'S THIS
1900:39		AH?
1900:51	CAPT	RECENTLY I SPOKE TO THE "ANGOLIANS" (COMMENT: SOVIET CREW WORKING IN ANGOLA). ON THE 12TH OUR PEOPLE FLEW TO LENINGRAD AND THEN, HE SAYS, TO MINSK. I SAY "45 DAYS?" "NO", HE SAYS "TWO MONTHS", THAT IS CORRECT - TWO MONTHS.

AIR TRAFFIC CONTROL MAPUTO

1852:42	AFIS	CHARLIE NINER CHARLIE ALFA ALFA, MAPUTO INFORMATION.
1852:46	R/OP	GO.
	AFIS	------
1852:51	R/OP	GO AHEAD MAPUTO.
1852:53	AFIS	AH CONFIRM YOUR POINT OF DEPARTURE IS LUSAKA.
1852:57	R/OP	NEGATIVE. POINT OF DEPARTURE IS MBALA. MIKE BRAVO ALFA LIMA ALFA.
1853:11	AFIS	------

COCKPIT VOICE RECORDER		
	CAPT	ON THE 12TH.
1901:49	CAPT?	GO ON.
1903:12	NAV	FLIGHT LEVEL ONE HUNDRED.
1903:17		YES
1903:32	COPILOT	CUT HERE THE BANDAGE.
1905:02	ENG	NO. NO. ILL NOT FORGET. ILL PUT ... AND TAKE STRAIGHT AGAIN.
1905:26	CAPT	YOU UNDERSTAND, AND COULD FLY, BUT IT WOULD BE MUCH COMPLAINING DURING THE FLIGHT, EXACTLY (STRONG EXPRESSION) AND THERE WOULD BE COMPLAINING AFTERWARDS AND HE WOULD REPORT TO (STRONG EXPRESSION), TO MODESTOV (STRONG EXPRESSION), THEN YOU REMEMBER WHEN WE FLEW TO

3

AIR TRAFFIC CONTROL MAPUTO		
1901:07	AFIS	CHARLIE NINE CHARLIE ALFA ALFA, MAPUTO.
1901:09	R/OP	GO AHEAD
1901:12	AFIS	------
1901:15	R/OP	GO AHEAD MAPUTO.
1901:17	AFIS	AH CONFIRM AH CAN YOU SPELL THIS NAME OF AH AIRPORT OF DEPARTURE MBALA AND ICAO INDICATOR.
1901:29	R/OP	POINT OF DEPARTURE MBALA. DEPARTURE IS ONE SIX THREE SEVEN.
1901:38	AFIS	AFFIRMATIVE AND AH YOUR ICAO INDICATOR, ICAO INDICATOR IS FOXTROT LIMA SOMETHING.
1901:50	R/OP	FOXTROT LIMA BRAVO ALFA
1901:54	AFIS	ROGER THANK YOU.
1901:58	R/OP	CHARLIE NINE CHARLIE ALFA ALFA, NOW TOP OF DESCENT.
1902:02	AFIS	CHARLIE NINE CHARLIE ALFA ALFA NO REPORTED TRAFFIC FOR DESCENT, REPORT RUNWAY LIGHTS IN SIGHT OR .... OR REACHING THREE THOUSAND FEET QNH ONE ZERO ONE SEVEN.
1902:16	R/OP	ROGER CHARLIE NINE CHARLIE ALFA ALFA NOW LEAVING THREE FIVE ZERO FOR THREE THOUSAND FEET, NEXT REPORT RUNWAY LIGHTS IN SIGHT. LEAVING THREE FIVE ZERO NOW.
1902:28	AFIS	ROGER

COCKPIT VOICE RECORDER			AIR TRAFFIC CONTROL MAPUTO
		LUSAKA FOR THE FIRST TIME, WE DID NOT REFUEL AND HE	
1905:27	COPILOT	AND NOW SIGN IT PLEASE. ITS NOT YOURS?	
1906:08	CAPT	BUT THAT SALNIKOV OF OURS WAS SO THAT IT WAS DIFFICULT (STRONG EXPRESSION) TO FLY ABROAD WITH HIM, WE FLY FROM MILAN WITH NOCKOLAI EFIMOVICH, DETACHMENT COMMANDER, 76 PASSENGERS 11 FUEL, "WHAT ARE YOU DOING?!!!!" NICKOLAI EFIMOVICH KEEPS QUIET (STRONG EXPRESSION). ON THE FOLLOWING DAY NICKOLAI EFIMOVICH COMES UP TO ME IN ADP (COMMENT: AERODROME DISPATCH POINT), I WENT THERE FOR THE DEPARTURE, KAZBEK REFUSED TO SIGN OUR DOCUMENTS, "I", SAYS HE, "AM NOT A CRIMINAL", "I", SAYS HE, "WILL NOT GO TO PRISON BECAUSE OF YOU", WE ARRIVED WITH THE REMAINING SOME 2700, 2600. HE SAYS, "HE IS NOW IN THE FLIGHT PLANNING ROOM, GO THERE, ONLY", SAYS HE "DON'T SHOUT AT HIM". I'M COMING AND I SAY : "KAZBEK! WHAT IS THE MATTER.... WHAT IS THE MATTER !!" HE BEGINS, BUT CALMLY, HE KNOWS THAT I (STRONG EXPRESSION) IF HE GOES FOR ME I WOULD ALSO STRAIGHT AWAY, HE IS CALM AND I SAY "KAZBEK! STOP TALKING RUBBISH, HE IS A DETACHMENT COMMANDER, ISN'T HE, AREN'T YOU ASHAMED?" "NO, NO, NO, NO, NO! AND LET ORESNIYI SIGN IT FOR YOU". I SAY "OK! NO PROBLEM". I AM COMING TO SERGEEVICH AND SAY: "WHAT! (STRONG EXPRESSION)! A FOOL!" (STRONG EXPRESSION)! I HAD TO TAKE THE FLIGHT FOLDER MYSELF IN THE FLIGHT PLANNING ROOM AND SIGN IT AT ZNA (COMMENT: DEPUTY CHIEF OF THE DEPARTMENT).	
1907:28	CAPT	HE THINKS THAT IT IS NOT ENOUGH?	
1907:36	CAPT	AND HE SAT ALL THE TIME WORRYING "AND SO .... WE SHALL SEE OVER WARSAW! IF THE REMAINING IS LESS THAN SEVEN! IT WILL BE NECESSARY TO LAND IN WARSAW". WE ARE APPROACHING WARSAW! SOME 6400, INDEED IT IS NECESSARY TO LAND. HE IS WORRYING AGAIN. I SAY: "SO KAZBEK! CALM DOWN, STOP IT, STILL ONE HOUR TWENTY OF FLYING, AND HERE WE HAVE NOW MORE, ONE HOUR FORTY FIVE EVEN". BUT THAT MODESTOV ALSO (STRONG EXPRESSION), WHEN, DO YOU REMBER, WHEN IN PEMBA, (STRONG EXPRESSION), IN THAT (STRONG EXPRESSION), AND THE SITUATION IS SO.... YOU FLY FOR SURE, (STRONG EXPRESSION), WEATHER, YOU KNOW, IS BECOMING, (STRONG EXPRESSION) HERE, OR WE CRIMINALS OR WHAT? OR ARE WE WHISKEY (STRONG EXPRESSION) BOOSERS?!	
1909:12	CAPT	LOOK! IT DOES NOT LIGHT UP FOR THE DESCENT (COMMENT: REFERENCE TO LOW FUEL WARNING LIGHT BEING INACCURATE DURING THE DESCENT) (STRONG EXPRESSION), WHAT?	
1909:16	NAV	DISTANCE 120.	

COCKPIT VOICE RECORDER			AIR TRAFFIC CONTROL MAPUTO
1909:38		THIS (?) CAN BE SOLD. TRANSMITTED TOO, (STRON EXPRESSION).	
1910:48	NAV	100KM.	
	ENG	... (EXCLAMATION)	
1911:03	CAPT	I WILL REDUCE THE RIGHT ONE (REFERENCE TO THE RIGHT ENGINE).	
1911:28	CAPT	(STRONG EXPRESSION)(STRONG EXPRESSION) MAKING SOME TURNS (COMMENT: REFERENCE TO THE AIRCRAFT TURNING) COULDN'T IT BE STRAIGHT?	
1911:32	NAV	....VOR INDICATES THAT WAY.	
1911:48	CAPT	HAVE YOU TAKEN AWAY THE PEN, TOLIK?	
	R/OP	HAVE YOU TAKEN AWAY?	
1912:08	CAPT	VOVA, HAVE YOU GOT A PEN HANDY? I HAVE TAKEN AWAY EVERYTHING.	
1912:23	CAPT	THANK YOU (IN PORTUGUESE)	
1912:25	ENG	OK	
NOTE: A SENTENCE WAS PROBABLY LOST HERE DURING REWINDING OF THE TAPE.			
	NAV	UP TO THE APPROACH THEY SHOULD BE WORKING	
		THE PERSON ON THE RIGHT IS DRIVING.	
1912:48	ENG	THREE BEERS AND ONE COKE, HERE	
	CAPT	THREE BEER YES, VOVA?	
	ENG	YES AND ONE COKE EACH	
	CAPT	ALL RIGHT	
1912:51	COPILOT	AND WHY THOSE TWO ARE LIT AND THESE TWO ARE NOT (COMMENT: REFERENCE TO THE VOR LIGHTS O! CENTRE PANEL).	
1912:58	NAV	DISTANCE IS 80.	
	COPILOT	THEY SHOULD BE LIT, IS THAT NOT SO?	
1913:05	CAPT	DO WE ALWAYS HAVE IT LIKE THAT?	
		.... THE REASON .... (?)	
1914:08	CAPT	WILL YOU TAKE IT OR NOT?	
1914:16		BASICALLY ON THE FEET.	
1914:57	NAV	60 KM	

COCKPIT VOICE RECORDER			AIR TRAFFIC CONTROL MAPUTO
1915:01	CAPT	WHAT? WON'T WE LAND AT 20?	
		MAYBE (?)	
1915:05	CAPT	Y-E-E-S!!	
1915:10	ENG	EARLIER WE WERE SORT OF ONE MINUTE AHEAD(?)	
1915:12	CAPT	YES, NOW IS 1443.	
1915:21	NAV	MINE IS 14 NOW .... (?)	
1915:24	CAPT	1445, WELL, 15 MINUTES, LET IT BE ... (?)	
	CAPT	HOW MANY IS IT LEFT?	
1915:30	NAV	60 KM	
	CAPT	5 MINUTES	
	CAPT	WILL YOU TAKE IT, NO VOVA, LATER?	
	ENG	TWO FOR EACH, OR WHAT?	
	CAPT	NO, THREE BEERS AND ONE COKE EACH, THEY BROUGHT EQUALLY FOR EACH (?)	
1916:37	ENG	THREE BEERS AND ONE COKE EACH.	
1916:43	CAPT	WELL	
1916:58	CAPT	VOLODYA, IT IS NECESSARY TO TELL THEM ABOUT RV (COMMENT: REFERENCE TO RADIO ALTIMETER UNSERVICEABILITY)	
1917:02	R/OP	SAY IT, SAY, IT IS NOT FOR THE FIRST TIME	
	CAPT	BECAUSE THEY WRITE, (STRONG EXPRESSION), ANY (STRONG EXPRESSION), (STRONG EXPRESSION).	
1917:21	CAPT	(STRONG EXPRESSION), THERE IS NO MAPUTO?	
	COPILOT	WHAT?	
1917:27	CAPT	THERE IS NO MAPUTO	
1917:31	CAPT	ELECTRICAL POWER IS OFF, CHAPS!	
1917:36	COPILOT	THERE TO THE RIGHT, IT IS LIT (?)	
1917:42	NAV	THERE IS SOMETHING I DON'T UNDERSTAND AHH ...	
1917:45	CAPT	NO THERE IS SOMETHING .... (?)	
1917:49	NAV	ILS SWITCHED OFF AND DME!	
1917:51	CAPT	EVERYTHING SWITCHED OFF, LOOK, CHAPS!	
1917:57	NAV	AND NDBs DO NOT WORK!	

COCKPIT VOICE RECORDER			AIR TRAFFIC CONTROL MAPUTO		
	CAPT	CHAPS!			
1918:04	NAV	YES, YES, EVERYTHING SWITCHED OFF - ILS, DME			
1918:09	COPILOT	AND THEY DO NOT HAVE ELECTRICAL POWER			
	NAV	NDBs?			
	COPILOT	AND THERE TO THE LEFT .... WHAT KIND OF LIGHT IS THERE.			
	CAPT	THIS IS CORRECT .... SOMETHING STRANGE?			
	CAPT	WELL, MAKE CONTACT.			
1918:11	COPILOT	3000 FEET.			
	CAPT	TOLYA, 3000 FEET!			
	R/OP	WHAT?			
	CAPT	3000 FEET			
	CAPT	(STRONG EXPRESSION)			
			1918:24	R/OP	MAPUTO CHARLIE NINE CHARLIE ALFA ALFA
	CAPT	...(INTERJECTION BY CAPTAIN) (STRONG EXPRESSION), KEEP QUIET, CHAPS.			
				R/OP	...MAINTAINING THREE THOUSAND FEET
			1918:31	AFIS	CHARLIE NINER CHARLIE ALFA ALFA ROGER AND CONFIRM YOU HAVE AH FIELD IN SIGHT?
1918:36	CAPT	NO!			
			1918:37	R/OP	NOT YET
			1918:39	AFIS	AND.... RUNWAY LIGHTS NEGATIVE YET?
			1918:43	R/OP	NOT, NEGATIVE.
1918:44	CAPT	(INTERJECTS) NEGATIVE!			
1918:46	CAPT	(INTERJECTS) ILS NEGATIVE!			
			1918:46	AFIS	ROGER... CHARLIE NINE CHARLIE ALFA ALFA CLEARED ILS APROACH RUNWAY TWO THREE....
1918:54	CAPT	(INTERJECTS) NOT WORKING.			
				AFIS	.....TRANSITION LEVEL IS FOUR ZERO, QNH ONE ZERO ONE SEVEN, REPORT ESTABLISHED ON RADIAL ZERO FOUR FIVE.
			1918:59	R/OP	ROGER CHARLIE NINE ALFA ALFA CONTINUE APPROACH AND ILS OUT OF SERVICE?

COCKPIT VOICE RECORDER			AIR TRAFFIC CONTROL MAPUTO		
1919:06	CAPT	AND NDB			
			1919:07	AFIS	AFFIRMATIVE AND AH CLEARED AH ... ... FOR VISUAL APPROACH RUNWAY ZERO FIVE, SURFACE WIND ZERO NINE ZERO, ONE ZERO KNOTS, QNH ONE ZERO ONE SEVEN.
			1919:22	R/OP	ROGER CHARLIE NINE CHARLIE ALFA ALFA CONTINUE APPROACH.
			1919:26	AFIS	-----
1919:30	COPILOT	AND HOW MANY APPROXIMATELY?			
1919:32	NAV	25–30 KM			
	COPILOT	25–30?			
	CAPT	YES			
	CAPT	SOMETHING IS WRONG, CHAPS			
	R/OP	HERE THEY GAVE CLOUD BASE 1800 FEET, AND SO TAKE IT INTO CONSIDERATION			
	CAPT	IS THIS ALTITUDE, ISN'T IT?			
	NAV	EIGHT OCTAS? (10/10)			
1919:38	R/OP	NO, TWO OCTAS (3/10)			
	NAV	AND SO THIS IS ...			
	CAPT	IT SHOULD BE LIT...			
1919:40	CAPT	THERE TO THE RIGHT LIGHTS ARE SEEN			
	COPILOT	RWY IS NOT LIT ... (?)			
	CAPT	RWY IS NOT LIT?			
	CAPT	.... THERE'S A PROBLEM.... (?)			
			1919:50	R/OP	MAPUTO CHARLIE NINE CHARLIE ALFA ALFA, CHECK YOUR RUNWAY LIGHTS.
			1919:56	AFIS	CHARLIE NINE CHARLIE ALFA ALFA ROGER, CLEARED VISUAL APPROACH RUNWAY ZERO FIVE, JOIN POSITION LEFT DOWN WIND, SURFACE WIND ZERO NINE ZERO, ONE ZERO KNOTS.
1920:01	CAPT	I CAN SEE! (INTERJECTION)			
			1920:06	R/OP	ROGER CHARLIE NINE CHARLIE ALFA ALFA, AND WE REQUEST TO JOIN RIGHT DOWN WIND.
			1920:13	AFIS	CHARLIE NINE CHARLIE ALFA ALFA ROGER, RIGHT DOWN WIND IS APPROVED AND REPORT POSITION RIGHT BASE FOR RUNWAY ZERO FIVE.

COCKPIT VOICE RECORDER			AIR TRAFFIC CONTROL MAPUTO		
1920:12	CAPT	WHAT RIGHT?, WAIT, HEADING... 24			
			1920:22	R/OP	ROGER. CHARLIE ALFA ALFA.
1920:22	CAPT	I UNDERSTOOD NOTHING			
	R/OP	DON'T YOU SEE THE RWY YET?			
1920:28	CAPT	..AND WHAT RWY, WHAT ARE YOU TALKING ABOUT?			
1920:32	NAV	WE ARE GOING TO DO STRAIGHT-IN APPROACH?			
1920:35	CAPT	WE ARE DOING STRAIGHT-IN APPROACH			
1920:38	R/OP	NO, WELL, CAN YOU SEE THE RWY?			
	COPILOT	NO, THERE'S NOTHING, THERE'S NEITHER CITY NOR RWY			
	R/OP	AND SO HE SAYS THAT ...			
	CAPT	.... HE SAYS			
	COPILOT	WHAT DOES HE SAY?			
	R/OP	I ASKED TO CHECK THE RWY			
	CAPT	I DON'T UNDERSTAND WHAT HE'S SAYING...?			
	CAPT	NOTHING CAN BE SEEN, CHAPS...			
	COPILOT	TELL HIM ONCE MORE TO CHECK THE LIGHTS.			
	CAPT	SO NO, SURELY IT IS INDEED CLOUDY TO DESCEND.			
1920:54	NAV	SOME 18-20 KILOMETERS LEFT			
			1920:57	R/OP	MAPUTO CHARLIE NINE CHARLIE ALFA ALFA, CHECK AGAIN RUNWAY LIGHTS
1921:02		(COMMENT: DURING THE TRANSMITION OF THE RADIO OPERATOR'S INFORMATION AN ALARM SYSTEM SOUNDED:NAMELY THE SSOS - TERRAIN PROXIMITY WARNING SYSTEM)			
			1921:05	AFIS	ROGER, YOU ARE CLEARED TO VISUAL APPROACH RUNWAY ZERO FIVE JOIN RIGHT DOWN WIND AND REPORT POSITION RIGHT BASE.
1921:12	CAPT	DAMN IT!			
			1921:17	R/OP	CHARLIE NINE CHARLIE ALFA ALFA RUNWAY LIGHTS OUT OF SERVICE?
1921:17	CAPT	NO, IT'S CLOUDY, CLOUDY, CLOUDY			
			1921:18	AFIS	...FIRM, RUNWAY LIGHT OUT OF SERVICE?
			1921:22	R/OP	AFFIRMATIVE, LIGHTS NOT IN SIGHT.
			1921:27	AFIS	AFFIRMATIVE AND JOIN RIGHT DOWN WIND RUNWAY ZERO FIVE, SURFACE WIND ZERO NINE ZERO, ONE ZERO KNOTS.

10

COCKPIT VOICE RECORDER			AIR TRAFFIC CONTROL MAPUTO		
	CAPT	(INTERJECTION) NO! NORMAL!			
1921:32		ALARM STOPS			
			1921:34	R/OP	ROGER ROGER
1921:36	NAV	NO, NO, THERE'S NOWHERE TO GO, NO NDBs, THERE'S NOTHING			
	CAPT	NEITHER NDBs NOR ILS			
1921:39		IMPACT IS REGISTERED BY ONE HALF SECOND OF SILENCE.			
			1924:10	AFIS	CHARLIE NINE CHARLIE ALPHA ALPHA REQUEST YOUR POSITION

NOTE: TRANSMISSIONS BY AFIS CONTINUE PERIODICALLY UNTIL MOCAMBIQUE FLIGHT TM103, A BOEING 737 FROM BEIRA, MAKES CONTACT.

1937:17	TM103	MAPUTO APPROACH MOCAMBIQUE 103 127,3
1937:20	AFIS	103 MAPUTO, GO AHEAD
1937:37	AFIS	MOCAMBIQUE 103, GO AHEAD
1937:49	AFIS	MOCAMBIQUE 103, MAPUTO APPROACH, GO AHEAD
1938:02	AFIS	MOCAMBIQUE 103, MAPUTO APPROACH, GO AHEAD
1938:07	TM 103	.... FINE MOCAMBIQUE 103 AAH MAINTAINING FL310 ESTIMATING LIMPOPO POINT 54 ARRIVAL SHOULD BE AT 2010 WE AH PLEASE REQUEST YOUR LAST WEATHER BREAK AAH WILL YOU PLEASE CONFIRM IF THE AIRPORT IS ABOUT TO CLOSE OR ARE YOU OPEN?
1938:38	AFIS	MOCAMBIQUE 103 AAH THE FIRST THING YOU ARE GOING TO DO IS TO CONTACT C9-CAA, I LOST CONTACT WITH HIM
1938:49	TM 103	ROGER. WE ARE ABOUT AH ARRIVAL C9-CAA WILL BE ABOUT 1925 ... CONFIRM YOU ARE NOT YET CONTACTED?
1939:03	AFIS	AFFIRMATIVE. I HAD CONTACT WITH HIM AND I LOST AH WHEN AH ... WHEN I CLEARED HIM TO .. TO VISUAL APPROACH RIGHT DOWNWIND AND I LOST CONTACT WITH HIM.
1939:18	TM 103	AH ROGER. STANDBY ONE PLEASE.
1939:37	TM 103	AH ROGER WE HAVE COPIED THE WEATHER AH. WE ... FLIGHT LEVEL AND SO ON.
1939:45	AFIS	AFFIRMATIVE AND CONTACT ... AH YOU MUST FIRST CALL C9-CAA, C9-CAA. IF YOU HAVE CONTACT WITH HIM
1939:55	TM 103	BREAK C9-BAA FROM MOC 103 ON 127.3

APPENDIX 1

COCKPIT VOICE RECORDER

AIR TRAFFIC CONTROL MAPUTO

1940:05	AFIS	NEGATIVE! NEGATIVE! IT IS C9-CAA. C9-CAA
1940:12	TM 103	AH ROGER. BREAK C9-A
40:22	TM 103	C9-CAA FROM MOCAMBIQUE 103, 127.3
1940:32	TM 103	C9-CAA THIS IS MOCAMBIQUE 103 DO YOU READ ME? (ON SECOND FREQUENCY)
1940:46	TM 103	APPROACH 103 WE CALLED THAT AIRCRAFT TWICE WITHOUT REPLY
1940:54	AFIS	ROGER
1940:58	TM 103	C9-CAA THIS IS MOCAMBIQUE 103 ON 118 DECIMAL 1.
1941:22	AFIS	C9-CAA MAPUTO DO YOU READ?
1945:05	TM 103	MAPUTO, 103
1945:11	AFIS	SOMEBODY SAY AGAIN YOUR CALLSIGN
1945:14	TM 103	MOCAMBIQUE 103, DO YOU HAVE CONTACT WITH CAA?
1945:18	AFIS	NEGATIVE AH UNTIL ... AT THIS MOMENT NEGATIVE SIR, I DONT KNOW AH WHAT'S WRONG WITH HIM
1945:25	TM 103	ROGER
1945:44	AFIS	MOCAMBIQUE 103, AIRCRAFT WAS A TUPOLEV 34, WAS DESCENDING 3000 FEET AND EH I LOST CONTACT ...WHAT'S YOUR APPROACH? REPORT POSITION LIMPOPO.
1946:03	TM 103	ROGER WE'RE AT FL310 AT THIS MOMENT 1949 FOR LIMPOPO
1946:11	AFIS	ROGER REPORT FOR DESCENT
1946:13	TM 103	ROGER
1946:18	AFIS	C9-CAA MAPUTO
1946:56	TM 103	MAPUTO APPROACH MOCAMBIQUE 103
1947:00	AFIS	MOCAMBIQUE 103 GO AHEAD
1947:04	TM 103	A - THIS HERE OO
1947:11	AFIS	MOCAMBIQUE 103 AH AIRCRAFT IS A TUPOLEV I DONT KNOW ... YOU MAKE VISUAL CONTACT AND REPORT THAT VISUAL ... STANDBY ONE (VOICES IN BACKGROUND GIVING INSTRUCTIONS)
1947:29	TM 103	AH STANDBY ONE COPIED OUT

COCKPIT VOICE RECORDER	AIR TRAFFIC CONTROL MAPUTO		
	1947:42	AFIS	MOCAMBIQUE 103, MAINTAIN FLIGHT LEVEL ... DESCEND FL40 OVERHEAD VMA
	1947:53	TM 103	ROGER DESCEND FL40 OVER VMA, 103
	1952:41	TM 103	MAPUTO APPROACH MOCAMBIQUE 103
	1952:44	AFIS	MOCAMBIQUE 103, GO AHEAD
	1952:48	TM 103	WE ARE 100S FROM MAPUTO WE ARE MAINTAINING 310 FROM ABOUT THE 4 O'CLOCK POSITION AND EH YOUR FURTHER INFORMATION ABOUT THE AIRCRAFT
	1953:02	AFIS	MOCAMBIQUE 103 UNTIL NOW I HAVE NO FURTHER NEWS ABOUT THE AIRCRAFT. I AM NOT SURE WHAT COULD HAVE HAPPENED. I LOST CONTACT WITH HIM WHEN HE WAS DOING AN APPROACH TO RUNWAY 05, FROM THE RIGHT HAND SIDE
	1953:20	TM 103	YOU HAD CONTACT WITH HIM UNTIL 3000 FEET?
	1953:25	AFIS	AFFIRMATIVE
	1953:29	TM 103	OK UUH. MAINTAINING 310 WE ARE REDUCING SPEED NOW, WE ARE (95) MILES FROM MAPUTO. STANDING BY FOR FURTHER INSTRUCTIONS OR DIRECTIVES, MAINTAINING THIS FREQUENCY
	1953:49	AFIS	OK OK
	1956:52	TM 103	MAPUTO APPROACH
	1957:49	TM 103	MAPUTO APPROACH, MOCAMBIQUE 103
	1957:54	AFIS	MOCAMBIQUE 103, GO AHEAD
	1957:57	TM 103	AH ... WE HAVE RECEIVED INFORMATION FROM OUR OPERATIONS, AND WE ARE IN CONTACT WITH YOUR DIRECTOR, TO RETURN BEIRA AIRPORT. WE ARE FLIGHT LEVEL 310, REQUEST 330, AND STAND BY FOR THE ESTIMATES.
	1958:23	AFIS	.....
	1959:..	AFIS	MOCAMBIQUE 103
	2000:34	AFIS	MOCAMBIQUE 103
	2020:42	AFIS	MOMCAMBIQUE 103, MAPUTO CALLING
	2020:54	TM 103	GO AHEAD MAPUTO
	20:01:13	AFIS	WHAT IS YOUR POSITION NOW?
	2001:16	TM 103	80 MILES FROM MAPUTO, PRACTICALLY OVERHEAD LIMPOPO, REQUEST 330, WE ARE 310.
	2001:23	AFIS	CONFIRM YOU CONTACTED OPERATIONS?

12

COCKPIT VOICE RECORDER	AIR TRAFFIC CONTROL MAPUTO		
	2001:27	TM 103	AFFIRMATIVE, WE SPOKE TO OPERATIONS, AND IT WAS OPERATIONS THAT ORDERED US TO PROCEED TO BEIRA.
	2001:42	AFIS	OK, COPIED. WHAT IS YOUR ETA TO BEIRA?
	2001:49	TM 103	OK, STAND BY.....ETA BEIRA 040, AND STAND BY FOR FURTHER...
	2002:29	AFIS	MOCAMBIQUE 103, MAPUTO
	2002:32	TM 103	GO AHEAD
	2002:38	AFIS	CAN YOU TRY AND CALL C9-CAA?
	2004:15	TM 103	C9-CAA, C9-CAA, THIS IS MOCAMBIQUE 103, MAPUTO IS CALLING YOU, DO YOU READ?
	2004:20	TM 103	IF YOU CONTACT 127.3 AND 118.1
	2004:41	TM 103	MAPUTO APPROACH, MOCAMBIQUE 103, ESTIMATING DAVOR POSITION AT 24, AND BEIRA AT 49.
	2004:43	AFIS	REPORT 330
		TM 103	WE ARE NOW 330, MAINTAINING
		AFIS	REPORT WHEN YOU CONTACT
		TM 103	AH ... WILL DO
		TM 103	MAPUTO, MOCAMBIQUE 103
		AFIS	MOCAMBIQUE 103, GO AHEAD
	2009:12	TM 103	WE ARE IN CONTACT WITH BEIRA
	2009:15	AFIS	INFORM WHEN YOU ARRIVE. SEE YOU
	2009:18	TM 103	SEE YOU. THANK YOU.

13

APPENDIX 2

A Mozambique News Agency Feature, February 1987

Samora Machel: the last ten minutes

Carlos Cardoso

From the transcripts of the conversations between members of the crew of President Samora Machel's Tupolev 134, and between the plane and the Maputo airport control tower, it is clear that the crew believed the plane was flying towards Maputo.

Indications that might have sown doubts as to the route were apparently not strong enough for the crew to react so as to save the plane and the lives of its passengers.

According to the CVR (cockpit voice recorder) transcript, at 19.11 and 28 seconds (all times are gmt) the pilot commented on the plane making a turn, and asked if it should not be going straight ahead.

"VOR indicates that way", replied the navigator (VOR stands for very high frequency omnidirectional radio—a powerful radio signal used as a navigation aid for aircraft). At this point the plane was 100 kilometres northwest of Maputo between the town of Magude and the South African border.

In principle, the VOR signal is sufficient grounds for a turn—but the fact that the plane was so far north of Maputo could have led to further doubts as to the correctness of this manoeuvre. However, VORs are normally the most conclusive sign that the plane is on the right course.

The conversation then turned to trivial matters such as the whereabouts of a pen and orders for drinks. This discussion indicates that the crew was not worried, and that the pilot had overcome his initial surprise at the turn. He was psychologically prepared to go home: which is incorrect from the point of view of work discipline.

As for the drinks, these were from the plane's bar and were to be taken home. Airmen are forbidden to drink alcohol during and twelve hours before a flight. The autopsy results on the dead men disprove South African Foreign Minister Roelof Botha's claim that the crew had been drinking.

At 19.12 and 51 seconds the co-pilot noticed something strange. "Why these two are lit and these two are not?", he asked, referring to the VOR lights on the central instrument panel.

The navigator informed the pilot that Maputo was 80 kilometres away, but the co-pilot was still worried about the lights. "They should be lit. Is that not so?", he asked.

"Do we always have it like that?", asked the pilot.

There seems to be no further reference to these lights, and at 19.14 and 57 seconds, the navigator said that Maputo was 60 kilometres away—a further sign that the dominant belief in the cockpit was that the Tupolev was heading for Maputo.

The captain thought something was odd. "What? Won't we land at 20?", he asked. The next word is unclear, as is the identity of the speaker, but the commission of inquiry thought it was "maybe".

"Y-e-e-s", said the captain apparently still doubtful. The flight engineer, in another phrase that was not well heard, remarked "earlier we were sort of one minute ahead"—referring to the estimated time of arrival.

After a further unclear reference to arrival time, the pilot asked how far there was still to travel, and the navigator replied "60 kms". The pilot then estimated they would land in five minutes. The drinks to be taken home had now been brought to the cockpit and further reference to them follows.

At 19.16 and 58 seconds the captain remarked to the flight engineer "Volodya, it is necessary to tell them about RV".

"Say it, say it. It is not for the first time", chipped in the radio operator. The reference is to a radio altimeter that was not functioning (a point of importance for understanding what happened later).

At 19.17 and 21 seconds the pilot swore and asked "there is no Maputo?" (it should be pointed out that the translation from Russian to English in the transcript is somewhat stilted). "What?", replied the co-pilot. "There is no Maputo", insisted the captain.

"Electrical power is off, chaps", he added. Evidently the captain believed that the reason he could not see Maputo was that there had been a major power cut. He still did not consider the possibility that they were off course.

"There is something I don't understand", muttered the navigator, and five seconds later he exclaimed "ILS switched off and DME".

"Everything switched off, look chaps", added the captain. "And NDBs do not work", exclaimed the navigator.

The references are to the instrument landing system (ILS), the distance measuring equipment (DME), and the non-directional beacons (NDBs)—all navigation aids at Maputo airport. The crew clearly thought that none of these systems was working.

But none of the crew mentioned the VOR—leading one to suppose that the VOR which had misled them was still functioning.

Once more, at 19.18 and nine seconds, the pilot remarked "They do not have electrical power". The crew had been in Maputo for 18 months, and knew that the city was occasionally plunged into darkness, particularly when South African backed MNR bandits blew up the transmission lines. Given the rising tension between Mozambique and South Africa in the fortnight preceding the crash, such an incident would not have been altogether surprising.

The pilot then ordered contact with the Maputo control tower and gave the plane's altitude (twice) as 3,000 feet. The radio operator informed the tower that the plane was maintaining 3,000 feet (but the digital flight data recorder showed that in fact the plane did not stop losing height).

The air traffic controller asked if the plane had the airport in sight. "Not yet", replied the radio operator, adding to a further question that they could not see the runway lights.

The controller then authorised an ILS approach to runway 23. The surprised captain interjected "not working". The radio operator asked "ILS out of service?"

The controller's response "affirmative" confused the matter: the controller thought he had told the plane the ILS was functioning, but the crew probably interpreted him as meaning "you are right, it is not working".

The controller then authorised a visual approach to runway 05, and gave the necessary wind information.

The radio operator said the plane was continuing its approach. Thus the crew still believed they were somewhere in the Maputo area.

At 19.19 and 32 seconds the navigator said the plane was 25 to 30 kilometres from Maputo, and the captain remarked "something is wrong, chaps".

The radio operator referred to the meteorological information given by the controller. "It should be lit", said the pilot (presumably referring to the runway), adding immediately "there to the right lights are seen".

"Runway is not lit?", asked both the co-pilot and the navigator. The radio operator therefore asked the controller to "check your runway lights". The controller again authorised a visual approach.

According to sources AIM has spoken to, a controller should not authorise a visual approach unless the crew tells him they can see the runway (by day), or its lights (by night). But the controller evidently also thought the plane was heading towards the city, and that it had the lights in view, merely requiring confirmation that these were indeed the runway lights. He reduced and then increased the intensity of the lights—a normal procedure.

At 19.20 and 22 seconds the radio operator asked the captain "Don't you see the runway yet?" "What runway? What are you talking about?", came the reply. 15 seconds later the co-pilot confirmed "No, there's nothing. There's neither city nor runway".

There had, however, been a lack of coordination between the radio operator and the pilot. The latter still believed he should be making an approach for runway 23, whereas the controller had changed this to 05, implying a different approach manoeuvre.

"Tell him (the controller) once more to check the lights", suggested the co-pilot. As the radio operator contacted the tower, the ground proximity warning system (GPWS) sounded, indicating that the Tupolev was perilously near ground level.

"Damn it", exclaimed the captain, while once again the radio operator asked the controller "runway lights out of service?". The controller, puzzled, asked the radio operator to confirm the question—which he did, replying "affirmative, lights not in sight". Once again, at 19.21 and 27 seconds, the controller authorised a visual approach (but ten seconds earlier the captain had exclaimed "No, it's cloudy, cloudy, cloudy". He seemed to believe that the reason they could see no lights was that a bank of cloud was in the way).

At 19.21 and 21 seconds the ground proximity alert stopped sounding.

Four seconds later the navigator said "no, no, there's nowhere to go. No NDBs. There's nothing". "Neither NDBs nor ILS", added the captain—the last words on the transcript.

At 19.21 and 39 seconds the Tupolev, travelling at 411 kilometres per hour, ploughed into an Mbuzini hillside, and within instants President Samora and most of the other passengers were dead.

From a strictly technical point of view there was only one thing the pilot should have done on hearing the ground proximity warning—gain height. This is a lesson drummed into the heads of all pilots. There is nothing to think about. The pilot has about 30 seconds to lift the plane to a comfortable height, from which he can then re-examine the situation.

So why did the pilot break this sacred aviation rule? First, his belief that he was flying towards Maputo at the safe altitude of 3,000 feet above flat terrain may have led him to believe that something was wrong with the GPWS.

Secondly, the pilot had already referred to a malfunction of the radio-altimeter. Since the radio-altimeter is linked to the GPWS, the pilot may have thought that this too was malfunctioning, thus leading him to make the extremely serious mistake of ignoring the warning.

A further factor is that the crew had been working for 17 hours (close to the maximum permitted), with a rest of a few hours at Mbala, but under uncomfortable circumstances (inside the aircraft), so their concentration may have been affected. A further subjective factor is that highly experienced pilots such as Yuri Novodran sometimes tend to overestimate their own skills and downplay the instruments.

But it is certainly strange that none of the five crew members so much as mentioned the apparently loud noise from the GPWS. On the tape nobody says "What's that noise?" There is no indication from the CVR that they noticed or even heard the warning. So did something else happen on board to stop the crew from reacting and taking the plane up—something that has left no record?

The last words of the captain indicate that he realised he was lost—so why ignore the alarm?

But it would be a mistake to examine only the last few tragic seconds. For the origin of the disaster was ten minutes earlier—it lay in the turn to the south-west provoked by the mystery VOR.

Up until Magude the plane was flying with a deviation of only four to six kilometres from its flight path—which is quite normal. Had that VOR not interfered, the plane would have continued its trajectory north to south-east, to the right of Maputo, and would have been able to see the city perfectly. The weather over Maputo was good, with the sky virtually free of cloud.

So what VOR was this? If it was a decoy, where had it been placed? These are questions that demand answers before a verdict on the causes of the crash can be given.

From South Africa's point of view, it is important to persuade public opinion that, even if there were a phoney VOR, the crew could technically have avoided the crash. It is not in their interest to make a detailed examination of the reason for any human error.

From Mozambique's point of view, it is important to clarify whether the technical failings have technical explanations or if they arise from a criminal action exterior to the plane. If there was a crime intended, even if we suppose that it was technically possible for the crew to have avoided disaster, then this has drastic implications for the immediate future of the country.

Apart from anything else, the Mozambican people have the right to know everything about what caused the death of their president.

NOTES

A

1. Joe Slovo, quoted in Iain Christie, *Machel of Mozambique*, p. 23.
2. Jacinto Veloso, *Memórias em Voo Rasante*, p. 21.
3. Matias Mboa, *Memórias da Luta Clandestina*, p. 87.
4. Paul Fauvet, email to author 23/7/11, reporting conversation with Joe Slovo after Samora's funeral.
5. Susan Williams, *Who Killed Hammarskjöld?: The UN, the Cold War and White Supremacy in Africa*, pp. 97–110.
6. 'Make Beira the Starting-Point for an Organisational Offensive,' 11 January 1980, translated by Michael Wolfers, in *Samora Machel: An African Revolutionary*, Barry Munslow (ed.), p. 77.
7. See biographical essays by Fernando Ganhão and Gerhard Liesegang in *Samora: Man of the People*, ed. António Sopa. In some of the following quotations from *Samora: Homem do Povo/ Samora: Man of the People*, I have preferred to use my own translations.
8. Orlando Machel, in Duarte Tembe, *Samora: O Destino da Memória*, p. 32.
9. See chapter 3, 'Education and Submission,' in Eduardo Mondlane, *The Struggle for Mozambique*, pp. 58–75.
10. Eduardo Mondlane, *The Struggle for Mozambique*, p. 75.
11. Josina Machel, quoted in Eduardo Mondlane, op. cit., p. 66.
12. See the numerous letters and internal memos on the subject of the Azores quoted by José Manuel Duarte de Jesus in *Eduardo Mondlane: Um Homem a Abater*.

B

1. Much of the biographical material in this section is drawn from Fernando Ganhão's 'Samora Machel: Lightning in the Sky,' Gerhard Liesegang's

'Samora Moises Machel: The Formative Years,' in António Sopa (ed.) *Samora: Man of the People*, and from Iain Christie's *Machel of Mozambique*.
2. Conversation with author, September 2010.
3. Samora Machel, in discussion with John Saul, Dar es Salaam 1974, quoted by Iain Christie, *Machel of Mozambique*, p. 6.
4. *Tempo*, 2/10/83, 50th birthday issue, p. 45.
5. Samora Machel, in an interview with Jean Ziegler, quoted by Oscar Monteiro, 'Samora que Conheci' ('The Samora that I Knew'), speech delivered 29/9/06 at Xilembene, 73rd anniversary of Samora Machel's birth; an abridged version of this speech was published in *Savana*, 13/10/06.
6. Iain Christie, *Machel of Mozambique*, p. 3.
7. *O Pais*, 3/10/08, p. 11.
8. Samora Machel to John Saul, quoted by Iain Christie, *Machel of Mozambique*, p. 6.
9. Ibid.
10. Gerhard Liesegang, 'Samora Moises Machel: The Formative Years,' in *Samora: Man of the People*, p. 23.
11. Samora Machel, quoted by Iain Christie, *Machel of Mozambique*, p. 7.
12. Ibid.
13. Fernando Ganhão, 'Samora Machel: Lightning in the Sky' in *Samora: Man of the People*, p. 12.
14. Samora Machel, quoted by Iain Christie, *Machel of Mozambique*, p. 9.
15. Iain Christie, *Machel of Mozambique*, p. 166.
16. Raimundo Domingos Pachinuapa, back cover, *II Congresso: Memórias*.

C

1. Samora Machel, 'The People's Democratic Revolutionary Process in Mozambique,' in *Samora Machel: An African Revolutionary*, Barry Munslow (ed.), p. 49.
2. Samora Machel, 'Make Beira the Starting-Point for an Organisational Offensive,' in *Samora Machel: An African Revolutionary*, op. cit., p. 78.
3. Samora Machel, 3 February 1971, Mozambique Institute publication, CFMAG/Bishopsgate 21.
4. 'The Role of Cooperantes,' *People's Power* no. 13, Spring 1979, p. 51.
5. Samora Machel, 'Establishing People's Power to Serve the Masses,' in *Samora Machel: An African Revolutionary*, p. 21.
6. Joseph Hanlon, *Mozambique: Who Calls the Shots?* p. 224.

D

1. Amélia de Souto, interview with author, September 2010.
2. Jacinto Veloso, *Memórias em Voo Rasante*, p. 205.

E

1. Samora Machel, 'Establishing People's Power to Serve the Masses,' in *Samora Machel: An African Revolutionary*, p. 25.

F

1. Matias Mboa, *Memórias da Luta Clandestina*, pp. 85–6.
2. Oscar Monteiro, 'Samora e o Mundo,' in *Samora: Man of the People*, p. 53.
3. Ibid.
4. Helder Martins, email to author, 4/6/11.
5. Aquino de Bragança, 'O Marxismo de Samora,' speech given in Upsala, Sweden to the Conference of Sociology, reprinted in *Três Continentes*, no. 3, September 1980; my thanks to David Hedges for sending me a copy of this article.
6. Oscar Monteiro, 'Samora e o Mundo,' in *Samora: Man of the People*, p. 51.
7. Matias Mboa, *Memórias da Luta Clandestina*, p. 87.
8. Helder Martins, *Porque Sakrani?*, p. 301.
9. Matias Mboa, op. cit., p. 88.
10. See Frelimo's 1965 statement on all possibilities for a peaceful solution having been exhausted, quoted by Oscar Monteiro, 'Samora e o Mundo,' in *Samora: Man of the People*, p. 52.
11. Oscar Monteiro, 'Samora que Conheci' ('The Samora that I Knew'), speech delivered 29/9/06 at Xilembene, 73rd anniversary of Samora Machel's birth.
12. Sérgio Vieira, *Participei, Por Isso Testemunho*, p. 163.

H

1. Samora Machel, 'Desalojemos o Inimigo Interno do Nosso Aparelho do Estado' ('Let us Expel the Internal Enemy from our State Apparatus'), *Palavras de Ordem* No. 19, 1980, quoted by José Luís Cabaço in '*O Homem Novo*,' in *Samora: Man of the People*, p. 106.
2. José Luís Cabaço, '*O Homem Novo*,' in *Samora: Man of the People*, p. 107.

3. Iain Christie, *Machel of Mozambique*, pp. 9–10.
4. Gerhard Liesegang, 'Samora Moisés Machel: The Formative Years,' in *Samora: Man of the People*, p. 24.
5. Gerhard Liesegang, op. cit., see note 34, p. 29.
6. Fernando Ganhão, 'Samora Machel: Lightning in the Sky' in *Samora: Man of the People*, p. 12.
7. Gerhard Liesegang, 'Samora Moisés Machel: The Formative Years,' in *Samora: Man of the People*, see note 44, p. 29.
8. Gerhard Liesegang, op. cit., p. 25.
9. Not all accounts make a link between Samora Machel and the Commercial School students.
10. *Mozambique Revolution*, no. 58 (1974), quoted by Iain Christie, *Machel of Mozambique*, p. 11.
11. Samora Machel, quoted by Iain Christie, op. cit., p. 16.

J

1. An extract is printed in Barry Munslow's introduction to *Samora Machel: An African Revolutionary*, p. xvii. The complete poem, along with two others by Samora Machel, can be read under 'Josina' on Colin Darch's Mozambique website, www.mozambiquehistory.net, along with two poems by Josina herself, all from *Tempo*, 6 April 1975.
2. Helder Martins, *Porque Sakrani?*, pp. 319–20.
3. Janet Mondlane, in interview with author, September 2010.
4. Quoted in Wikipedia entry on Josina, from *Josina Machel: Icone da Emancipação da Mulher Moçambicana* by Renato Matusse and Josina Malique (Colecção Embondeiro 29, Maputo, 2008). No page references given.
5. Oscar Monteiro, 'Também o vi chorar,' ('I also saw him cry'), speech given on the 15th anniversary of the death of Samora Machel, Maputo, October 2001. Copy kindly provided by Oscar Monteiro.
6. Henri Alexandre Junod, *The Life of a South African Tribe*, Vol. I, p. 15.

L

1. My thanks to Paul Fauvet for reminding me of the second stanza.
2. Paul Fauvet, email to author, 7/9/11.
3. Samora Machel, quoted by Oscar Monteiro, 'Samora e o Mundo,' in *Samora: Man of the People*, p. 56.
4. Oscar Monteiro, op. cit., p. 57.
5. Quoted by Oscar Monteiro, op cit., p 58.

6. José Mateus Katupha, interview with author, September 2010.
7. Mozambican Revolution no. 11, October 1964, item 53, CFMAG/Bishopsgate archives.
8. Samora Machel, 'The People's Democratic Revolutionary Process in Mozambique, *Samora Machel: An African Revolutionary*, in Barry Munslow (ed.), p. 55.
9. Samora Machel, 'The People's Democratic Revolutionary Process in Mozambique,' in *Samora Machel*, op. cit., p. 46.

M

1. Hastings Banda, quoted in Iain Christie, *Machel of Mozambique*, p. 51.
2. Samora Machel, quoted in *Machel of Mozambique*, p. 119.
3. Quoted by Raimundo Domingos Pachinuapa, *II Congresso*, p. 59.
4. Ibid., p. 44.
5. José Manuel Duarte de Jesus, *Eduardo Mondlane: Um Homem a Abater*, p. 373.
6. Matias Mboa, *Memórias da Luta Clandestina*, p. 48.
7. Sérgio Vieira, *Participei, Por Isso Testemunho*, p. 258.
8. Iain Christie, *Machel of Mozambique*, p. 149.
9. *Eu, o povo: poemas da revolução*, Frelimo, Lourenço Marques, 1975. In 2008 a new edition was published by Livros Cotovia in Lisbon. My thanks to Gustavo Infante for bringing the 2008 edition to my attention.
10. Nelson Saúte, in *Samora: O Destino da Memória*, ed. Duarte Tembe, p. 35.
11. See: http://newritings.wordpress.com/2007/08/23/in-our-land-bullets-are-beginning-to-flower-poem-by-jorge-rebelo; or *New Poetry Works*, ed. Robin Malan, p. 166.
12. George Steiner, review of *The Book of Disquiet* by Fernando Pessoa, tr. Richard Zenith, *Observer* 3/6/01.
13. disquiet.com/thirteen.html; pessoa's trunk, 13+ ways of looking at a poem; according to this website there are at least 16 English translations of this poem.
14. Nelson Saúte, in *Samora: O Destino da Memória*, ed. Duarte Tembe, p. 36.

N

1. Fernando Ganhão, 'Samora Machel: Lightning in the Sky,' in *Samora: Man of the People*, p. 14.
2. Iain Christie, *Machel of Mozambique*, p. 26.
3. Ibid., p. 27.

4. Oscar Monteiro, 'Samora e o Mundo' in António Sopa (ed.) *Samora: Man of the People*, p. 49.
5. Quoted by Oscar Monteiro in 'The Samora that I Knew.'
6. Samora Machel, 'We Must Remove the Enemy Within the Defence and Security Forces,' in *Samora Machel: An African Revolutionary*, p. 196.
7. Oscar Monteiro in 'The Samora that I Knew.'
8. N. Valdez dos Santos, *O Desconhecido Niassa*, p. 156.
9. Iain Christie, *Machel of Mozambique*, p. 39.
10. John Paul, *Mozambique: Memoirs of a Revolution*, p. 11.
11. Quoted in Paul Fauvet, *Carlos Cardoso: Telling the Truth in Mozambique*, p. 122.
12. Fauvet, op. cit., p. 125.
13. Fauvet, op. cit., p. 124.
14. Oliver Tambo quoted in Paul Fauvet, op. cit., p. 129.
15. reported by José Luís Cabaço, Minister of Information, quoted by Nadja Manghezi, *The Maputo Connection*, p. 175.
16. Jacinto Veloso, *Memórias em Voo Rasante*, p. 180.
17. Joseph Hanlon, *Beggar Your Neighbours*, p. 145.

O

1. Samora Machel, 'We Must Strengthen People's Power in our Hospitals,' in *Samora Machel: An African Revolutionary*, pp. 156–68.
2. Samora Machel, 'Make Beira the Starting-Point for an Organisational Offensive,' in *Samora Machel: An African Revolutionary*, pp. 73–80.
3. Samora Machel, 'We are Declaring War on the Enemy Within,' in *Samora Machel: An African Revolutionary*, pp. 86–103.
4. Ibid.
5. Ibid.
6. Joseph Hanlon, *Mozambique: Who Calls the Shots?*, p. 16.
7. Jacinto Veloso, *Memórias em Voo Rasante*, p. 191.
8. Joseph Hanlon, *Who Calls the Shots?*, p. 166.
9. *O País*, 9 Feb. 2011.
10. Samora Machel, 'We are Declaring War on the Enemy Within,' in *Samora Machel: An African Revolutionary*, pp. 86–103.
11. Paul Fauvet, email to author, 13/9/11.
12. Joseph Hanlon, 'Mozambique: Under New Management,' *Soundings*, Issue 7, autumn 1997.
13. Paul Fauvet, email to author, 13/9/11.
14. Samora Machel, 'We Must Remove the Enemy within the Defence and Security Forces,' in *Samora Machel: An African Revolutionary*, pp. 185–99.

15. Paul Fauvet, *Carlos Cardoso*, p. 81.
16. Samora Machel, *Mozambique: Sowing the Seeds of Revolution*, pp. 21–36.
17. Malyn Newitt, *A History of Mozambique*, p. 548.
18. Amélia de Souto, interview, September 2010.
19. José Mateus Katupha, interview, September 2010.
20. Paul Fauvet, *Carlos Cardoso*, p. 112.
21. Samora Machel, quoted in Paul Fauvet, op. cit., pp. 112–13.
22. Samora Machel, quoted in *Tempo*, 50th birthday issue, September 1983, p. 36.
23. Samora Machel, quoted by Paul Fauvet, *Carlos Cardoso*, p. 117.
24. Paul Fauvet, ibid., p. 117.
25. Samora Machel, 'Production is an Act of Militancy, in *Samora Machel: An African Revolutionary*, p. 121.
26. Valente Malangatana Ngwenya, interview, September 2010.

P

1. Helder Martins, 'Samora and Health' in *Samora: Man of the People*, pp. 89–94.
2. Isaias Funzamo, interview, September 2010.
3. Albino Magaia, *Yô Mabalane!*, p. 45.
4. Jacinto Veloso, *Memórias em Voo Rasante*, p. 161.
5. Samora Machel, 'We Must Remove the Enemy Within the Defence and Security Forces,' in *Samora Machel: An African Revolutionary*, p. 196.
6. Fernando Ganhão, 'Lightning in the Sky,' in *Samora: Man of the People*, p. 16.
7. UNE&SC report, E/5812, 30/4/76, quoted by David Martin and Phyllis Johnson, *The Struggle for Zimbabwe*, p. 226.
8. Note no. 28, 17/3/76, British Embassy in Maputo to Moz Government, Martin & Johnson, op. cit., endnote 32 to Chapter 11, p. 355.
9. Amélia de Souto, interview, September 2010.
10. Helder Martins, 'Samora and Health' in *Samora: Man of the People*, p. 90.
11. Helder Martins, 'Samora and Health' in *Samora: Man of the People*, p. 94.
12. Helder Martins, ibid., p. 91.
13. Amélia de Souto, interview, September 2010.
14. Mia Couto, *The Last Flight of the Flamingo*, p. 23, translated by David Brookshaw.
15. Samora Machel, in Barry Munslow (ed.), *Samora Machel: An African Revolutionary*, pp. 124–9.

R

1. Summary of World Broadcasts, 6/10/81, in the section on re-education on Colin Darch's website, www.mozambiquehistory.net
2. *The Review* [International Commission of Jurists], December 1981, www.mozambiquehistory.net, re-education.
3. Lina Magaia, *Notícias*, 15/10/87, www.mozambiquehistory.net, literature section.
4. Valente Malangatana Ngwenya, interview, September 2010.
5. See press clippings under Homoíne Massacre, www.mozambiquehistory.net
6. Quoted by Paul Fauvet, *Carlos Cardoso*, p. 115.
7. Paul Fauvet, 'Malawi on the Wrong Side,' Mozambique News Agency, Sept. 1986.
8. Ken Flower, *Serving Secretly*, pp. 300–302.
9. Joseph Hanlon, *Mozambique: Who Calls the Shots?*, p. 36.
10. Ken Flower, *Serving Secretly*, p. 262.
11. Alex Vines, *Accord*, 1998; see www.c-r.org/our-work/accord/mozambique/business-peace.php) . See also Alex Vines' detailed discussion of the international dimension of support for Renamo in *Renamo: From Terrorism to Democracy in Mozambique*.
12. Robert Gersony, The Gersony Report: Summary of Mozambican Refugee Accounts of Principally Conflict-Related Experience in Mozambique, submitted April 1988 to the US State Department.
13. Samora Machel, quoted by Paul Fauvet, *Carlos Cardoso*, p. 136.
14. Samora Machel, quoted by Paul Fauvet, ibid., p. 138.
15. www.c-r.org/our-work/accord/mozambique/key-actors.php
16. Paul Fauvet, AIM, News Review, nos. 89/90, 31/10/86.
17. Justin Fox, *Under the Sway*, p. 36.

S

1. Oscar Monteiro, 'Samora que Conheci' ('The Samora that I Knew').
2. Helder Martins, *Porque Sakrani?* p. 299.
3. Telecine collection.
4. Quoted in Carlos Cardoso, 'The Loneliness of the President,' in *Samora: Man of the People*, p. 148.
5. Carlos Cardoso, ibid., p. 148.
6. Cardoso, ibid., p. 145.
7. José Luís Cabaço, 'O Homem Novo' in *Samora: Man of the People*, p. 109.
8. Mozambique Information Office News Review, Nos. 89/90, 31/10/86.
9. Ibid.

10. *Notícias* 15/10/87, reproduced in the literature section of Colin Darch's website, www.mozambiquehistory.net
11. Helder Martins, *Porque Sakrani?* p. 258.
12. Helder Martins, *Porque Sakrani?* p. 357.
13. Samora Machel, quoted by Iain Christie, *Machel of Mozambique*, p. 151.
14. Helder Martins, *Porque Sakrani?* p. 310.
15. Helder Martins, *Porque Sakrani?* p. 311.
16. Fernando Ganhão, 'Samora Machel: Lightning in the Sky,' in *Samora: Man of the People*, p. 15.
17. 3/11/69, CFMAG/Bishopsgate33 and website macua.blogs.com/files/uria-simango-gloomy-situation-in-frelimo.doc
18. Paul Fauvet, email to author, 6/2/11.
19. Ibid.
20. Quoted in David Martin and Phyllis Johnson, *The Struggle for Zimbabwe*, p. 17.
21. Quoted in Martin and Johnson, ibid., p. 80.
22. Quoted in *Tempo* 50th birthday issue, p. 45.

T

1. David Martin and Phyllis Johnson, *The Struggle for Zimbabwe*, p. 319.
2. Ibid.
3. Oscar Monteiro, '*Também o vi chorar*,' 'I also saw him cry,' speech given on the 15th anniversary of the death of Samora Machel.
4. *Notícias* 4/1/79; quoted as an epilogue, *Samora: Man of the People*, p. 325.
5. All quotes are from transcript of the cockpit voice recorder. For full transcript see Appendix 1, and for Carlos Cardoso's interpretation, 'Samora Machel: The Last Ten Minutes,' see Appendix 2, which is reprinted with the kind permission of the English service of AIM.
6. Carlos Cardoso, 'Samora Machel: The Last Ten Minutes,' Mozambique News Agency, February 1987.
7. Paul Fauvet, 'Samora Machel's Death and South African Radar,' Mozambique News Agency, November 1986.
8. Transcript of interview, their ellipses.
9. The_death_of_Samora_Machel.doc which can be found on www.macua.blogs.com
10. Albino Magaia, quoted by Lina Magaia, *Notícias* 15/10/87, reproduced in the literature section of Colin Darch's website, www.mozambiquehistory.net

10. Notícias 15/10/87, reproduced in the literature section of Colin Darch's website, www.mozambiquehistory.net
11. Helder Martins, *Porque Sakrani?*, p. 258.
12. Helder Martins, *Porque Sakrani?*, p. [illegible]
13. Samora Machel, quoted by Iain Christie, *Machel of Mozambique*, p. [illegible]
14. Helder Martins, *Porque Sakrani?*, p. 310.
15. Helder Martins, *Porque Sakrani?*, p. 311.
16. Fernando Ganhão, 'Samora Machel: Lightning in the Sky' in *Samora: Man of the People*, p. 15.
17. [illegible]
18. Paul Fauvet, [illegible]
19. *Ibid.*
20. Quoted in David Martin and Phyllis Johnson, *The Struggle for Zimbabwe*, p. [illegible]
21. Quoted in Martin and Johnson, *ibid.*, p. [illegible]
22. [illegible] p. 18.

1. David Martin and Phyllis Johnson, *The Struggle for Zimbabwe*, p. 327.
2. *Ibid.*
3. [illegible] the death of Samora Machel.
4. [illegible]
5. [illegible]
6. [illegible]
7. [illegible]
8. [illegible]
9. [illegible]
10. [illegible] website, [illegible]

BOOKS CITED

Agualusa, José Eduardo, *My Father's Wives (As Mulheres do Meu Pai)* (translated by Daniel Hahn) (Arcadia, London, 2008)

Avery, Catherine B. *et al.* (eds), *Mirador Dictionary of the Portuguese and English Languages* (Mirador Internacional, Chicago, 1972)

Christie, Iain, *Machel of Mozambique* (Zimbabwe Publishing House, Harare, 1988)

Couto, Mia, *The Last Flight of the Flamingo (O último voo do flamingo)* (translated by David Brookshaw) (Serpent's Tail, London, 2004)

Darch, Colin (website) www.mozambiquehistory.net

Duarte de Jesus, José Manuel, *Eduardo Mondlane: Um Homem a Abater* (Edições Almedina, Coimbra, 2010)

Fauvet, Paul and Marcelo Mosse, *Carlos Cardoso: Telling the Truth in Mozambique* (Double Storey, Cape Town, 2003)

Flower, Ken, *Serving Secretly: An Intelligence Chief on Record* (John Murray, London, 1987)

Fox, Justin, *Under the Sway* (Umuzi, Cape Town, 2007)

——— *With Both Hands Waving: A Journey through Mozambique* (Kwela, Cape Town, 2002)

Grabato Dias, João Pedro, *O povo é nos* (Edições Pouco, 1991))

Greene, Graham, *The Human Factor* (The Bodley Head, London, 1978)

Hanlon, Joseph, *Mozambique: The Revolution Under Fire* (Zed Books, London, 1984)

——— *Beggar Your Neighbours: Apartheid Power in Southern Africa* (James Currey, London, 1986)

——— *Mozambique: Who Calls the Shots?* (James Currey, London, 1991)

Honwana, Luís Bernardo, *We Killed Mangy-Dog & other Mozambique Stories (Nós Matámos o Cão-Tinhoso)* (translated by Dorothy Guedes) (Heinemann African Writers Series, Oxford, 1969)

Junod, Henri Alexandre, *The Life of a South African Tribe, Vols I and II*

Imprimerie Attinger Frères, Neuchatel, 1912 & 1913; Macmillan, London, 1913 (Vol II)

Lopes, Armando Jorge *et al.* (eds), *Moçambicanismos: Para um Léxico de Usos do Português Moçambicano* (Livraria Universitária UEM, Maputo, 2002)

Machel, Samora, *Mozambique: Sowing the Seeds of Revolution* (CFMAG, London, 1974)

Magaia, Albino, *Yô Mabalane! A Mozambican Political Prisoner's Diary Penned in Blood* (translated by Renato Matusse) (Imprensa Universitária UEM, Maputo, 2005)

Magaia, Lina, *Dumba Nengue: Run for Your Life: Peasant Tales of Genocide in Mozambique* (translated by Michael Wolfers) (Karnak House, London, 1989)

Manghezi, Nadja, *The Maputo Connection: The ANC in the World of Frelimo* (Jacana, Johannesburg, 2009)

Mankell, Henning, *Chronicler of the Winds* (translated by Tiina Nunnally) (Harvill Secker, London, 2006)

Martin, David and Johnson, Phyllis, *The Struggle for Zimbabwe: The Chimurenga War* (Faber and Faber, London, 1981)

Martins, Helder, *Porquê Sakrani? Memórias dum Médico duma Guerrilha Esquecida* (Terceiro Milénio, Maputo, 2001)

Mboa, Matias, *Memórias da Luta Clandestina* (Marimbique, Maputo, 2009)

Middleton, Nick, *Kalashnikovs and Zombie Cucumbers: Travels in Mozambique* (Sinclair Stevenson, London, 1994)

Mondlane, Eduardo, *The Struggle for Mozambique* (Penguin, Harmondsworth, 1969)

Munslow, Barry (ed.), *Samora Machel: An African Revolutionary: Selected Speeches and Writings* (translated by Michael Wolfers) (Zed Books, London, 1985)

Mutimati, Barnabé João, *Eu, o povo: poemas da revolução*, Frelimo, Lourenço Marques, 1975. In 2008 a new edition was published by Livros Cotovia in Lisbon.

Newitt, Malyn, *A History of Mozambique* (Hurst, London, 1995)

Nordstrom, Carolyn, *A Different Kind of War Story* (University of Pennsylvania, Philadelphia, 1997)

Pachinuapa, Raimundo Domingos, *II Congresso da Frente de Libertação de Moçambique (FRELIMO): Memórias* (privately printed, Maputo 2009)

Paul, John, *Mozambique: Memoirs of a Revolution* (Penguin, Harmondsworth, 1975)

Sachs, Albie, *The Soft Vengeance of a Freedom Fighter* (Grafton, London, 1990)

Scuccato, Rino, *La Deviazione di rotta: Memorie dal Mozambico* (L'Harmattan Italia, Turin, 2006)
Sopa, António (ed.), *Samora: Man of the People* (*Samora: Homem do Povo*) (translated by Paul Fauvet and Mugama Matolo) (Maguezo Editores, Maputo, 2001)
Tembe, Duarte, *Samora: O Destino da Memória* (Ndjira, Maputo, 2000)
Valdez dos Santos, N., *O Desconhecido Niassa* (Junta das Investigações do Ultramar, Lisbon, 1964)
Veloso, Jacinto, *Memórias em Voo Rasante* (JVCI Lda, Maputo, 2006)
Vieira, Sérgio, *Participei, Por Isso Testemunho* (Ndjira, Maputo, 2010)
Vines, Alex, *Renamo: From Terrorism to Democracy in Mozambique* (James Currey, London, 1991/1996)
Williams, Susan, *Who Killed Hammarskjöld?: The UN, the Cold War and White Supremacy in Africa* (Hurst, London, 2011)